fundamentals
of forecasting

william g. sullivan
w. wayne claycombe

UNIVERSITY OF TENNESSEE
KNOXVILLE, TENNESSEE

Reston Publishing Company, Inc.
Reston, Virginia
A Prentice-Hall Company

Library of Congress Cataloging in Publication Data

Sullivan, William G
    Fundamentals of forecasting

    Includes bibliographies and index.
    1. Business forecasting. 2. Forecasting.
I. Claycombe, W. Wayne,   joint author.
II. Title.
HB3730.S785   338.5'44   76-50053
ISBN 0-87909-300-5

© 1977 by
Reston Publishing Company, Inc.
A Prentice-Hall Company
Reston, Virginia 22090

10 9 8 7 6

Printed in the United States of America.

This book is dedicated to

**Janet, Tracy, William,
and Ann**

contents

preface   *ix*

chapter 1 . . . an introduction to forecasting   *1*

   what is forecasting?   *1*
   characteristics of forecasts   *2*
   how to make forecasting successful   *4*
   purpose and overview of the book   *6*

chapter 2 . . . the essential materials of forecasting   *9*

   introduction   *9*
   a forecasting program   *9*
   sources of information for forecasting   *11*
   data bases for forecasting   *16*
   product group forecasts and item forecasts   *16*
   questions   *18*

chapter 3 . . . the choice of appropriate techniques for
   implementing a forecasting strategy   *19*

   introduction   *19*
   formulating a forecasting strategy   *20*

                                                                            v

underlying patterns in historical data   *22*
evaluating and utilizing forecasting error   *23*
how to choose the right forecasting technique   *30*
questions   57

chapter 4 . . . forecasting based on regression techniques   *59*

introduction   *59*
assumptions of regression   *60*
the correct use of regression for forecasting   *61*
simple linear regression   *65*
multiple linear regression   *72*
nonlinear regression   *79*
questions   79

chapter 5 . . . moving averages and exponential smoothing   *83*

introduction   *83*
simple moving averages   *85*
double moving averages   *88*
fundamental exponential smoothing   *91*
double exponential smoothing   *94*
triple exponential smoothing   *95*
developing initial estimates for moving
    averages and exponential smoothing   *96*
winters' method   *99*
choosing a smoothing constant   *104*
a computer program for making forecasts with
    techniques described in chapters 4 and 5   *108*
questions   137

chapter 6 . . . the use of subjective information in
forecasting   *139*

introduction   *139*
the delphi method   *140*
the use of the delphi procedure in manpower forecasting   *143*
subjective probability methods   *152*
the cross-impact method   *164*
an application of the cross-impact method   *172*
questions   189

chapter 7 . . . technological forecasting   *191*

introduction *191*
applications of technological forecasting   *193*
description of technological forecasting techniques   *194*
technological forecasting in the chemical process industries   *202*
questions   218

chapter 8 . . . advanced forecasting techniques   *221*

introduction   *221*
adaptive filtering   *221*
the box-jenkins method   *223*
econometric models   *226*
input-output tables   *227*
forecasting in the future   *228*
questions   229

appendix a . . . a manager's primer on forecasting   *231*

appendix b . . . tests for serial correlation in regression
analysis   *249*

introduction   *249*
von-neuman ratio test   *250*
durbin-watson test   *251*

appendix c . . . statistical tests for regression methods   *261*

appendix d . . . forecasting high consequence, low
probability events   *269*

introduction   *269*
bayes' law   *270*
a procedure for event forecasting based on bayes' law   *278*

index   *289*

preface

The objective of this book is to enable the reader to apply popular forecasting techniques and to be aware of their strengths and limitations. A manager, an engineer, or a scientist should be able to read this material and use the discussions, equations, examples, and illustrations to develop forecasts in his or her area of specialization.

The only mathematical background assumed of the reader is basic algebra. This material is not intended to be a theoretical or philosophical overview of forecasting. A general discussion of various forecasting techniques and examples of their application will be presented as a means of facilitating the reader's understanding of the mechanics involved. Such an approach has been found highly effective for the reader who must actually develop forecasts. For the manager, engineer, or scientist who utilizes forecasts developed by others, we also believe this to be the best approach to gaining an understanding of each technique. To use someone else's forecasts without some comprehension of how the projection was derived is analogous to piloting an aircraft without understanding how to use information available from gauges on the instrument panel.

Forecasting is like auto safety; it is a very serious problem to the people involved. In both areas, experts are mounting a massive assault on 5 percent of the real problems. We all want and need better, safer automobiles and better, more accurate forecasts. Unfortunately, 95% of disasters in actual practice result from the improper use of both. This does not mean we need less emphasis on safe cars and better forecasts. It does mean that we need more emphasis on the intelligent use of both. Defensive driving is based on the principle of expecting the worst and being prepared to react to it. This is exactly what we need to do to get better use of forecasts.

One of our primary aims in this book is to promote a better use of forecasts by providing a practical, straightforward presentation of forecasting techniques. After reading this book, it will not be possible for the forecaster to predict future events with absolute certainty. No one can expect to do this. However, material in this book will enable the practitioner to use suitable techniques to prepare a forecast and to obtain some notion regarding the confidence that can be placed in the forecast.

The techniques and approaches discussed in this text should be useful to those persons who are attempting to predict the outcome of a future event. The applied nature of our discussion and example problems should appeal to individuals who are currently working in industry or government. Furthermore, we have found this book to be an ideal text for a one-quarter or one-semester course in practical forecasting. Many of the examples are economic or industrial in nature since these areas are dependent on high-quality forecasts for their success. The same techniques could be used, for example, by a chemist or an environmentalist in predicting the CO_2 concentration in the atmosphere of a major urban area at some future time.

Some of the material in Chapters 1 and 2 is excerpted from George W. Plossl's book, *Manufacturing Control—The Last Frontier for Profits* (Reston Publishing Co., Inc., 1973) and from a book by G. W. Plossl and O. W. Wight entitled *Production and Inventory Control: Principles and Techniques* (Prentice-Hall, Inc., 1967). The reader will discover these comments regarding current industrial forecasting practices to be informative and helpful in "seeing" the art of forecasting. Also included in Chapter 1 are several paragraphs from William Copulsky's book, *Practical Sales Forecasting* (American Management Association, 1970).

We wish to thank several of our students—Alec Tsui, Gerald Rimmer, and Seong-Soo Kim—for their contributions to and helpful suggestions on materials contained in this book. To our typists, Mrs. Teresa Gilbert and Mrs. Sylvia Ross, we owe a special note of appreciation for their extra efforts in preparing our manuscript for class use.

William G. Sullivan
W. Wayne Claycombe

A prudent man foresees the difficulties ahead and prepares for them; the simpleton goes blindly on and suffers the consequences.

PROVERBS 22:3
Tynedale Translation

My interest is in the future, because I'm going to spend the rest of my life there.

CHARLES F. KETTERING

chapter 1 . . . an introduction to forecasting

what is forecasting?

Forecasting involves the preparation of a statement concerning uncertain or unknown events. In most cases these events lie in the future. The main purpose of making forecasts is to gain knowledge about uncertain events that are important to our present decisions. A sound understanding of the forecasting problem in addition to the rational study and analysis of available data and/or expert opinion are prerequisite to preparation of a forecast.

The importance of forecasting can be seen in numerous ways. Every year key forecasts of nationwide economic activity are routinely published by the Council of Economic Advisors, the Office of Management and Budget, the Department of Commerce, and many other government agencies. These projections reflect the role that the federal government will play in establishing and executing its policy decisions. Obviously, they are vital to forecasting that occurs in the private sector of the economy.

With regard to the business community, good forecasting is becoming more and more necessary to the survival and prosperity of individual firms. Most large corporations are deeply involved in attempting to forecast opportunities for new products, sales, profit margins, manpower requirements, etc. Because factors affecting business activity are complex in nature, the management of a company needs increasing amounts of information that shed light on the future. Successful forecasting, then, should have its payoff in additional profits.

True forecasting is a blend of science and art that defies precise definition for a successful application. Preparation of a forecast entails more than just using historical data and mathematical formulas to project into the future. The key to realistic forecasting is the inclusion of informed judgment and intuition into the methodological framework being employed in order to minimize uncertainty associated with the future development, or event, in question. Most forecasting techniques, or methodologies, are founded on replicable scientific relationships, and it is this aspect of the overall forecasting effort that is emphasized in this book. The *art* of forecasting is learned by experience rather than by academic study. To improve your understanding of various techniques, several articles regarding actual forecasting experience are included in chapters to follow.

It must be stressed that a forecast is useful if it reduces the uncertainty surrounding an event, and by doing so results in a decision that has increased value (because of the forecast) in excess of the cost required to produce the forecast. This should be kept in mind as forecasting techniques discussed in following chapters are considered.

In short, we must bear in mind the simple truth that forecasts are necessary to give corporate management an *image* of the company that it guides. Companies are often what they want themselves to be. An open-minded, optimistic vision of the future can lead to growth and profit; a narrow, pessimistic view can lead to stagnation or worse. But the main point to remember is that a forecast should have an objective. A forecast done merely to satisfy curiousity is of no value. Forecasts must result in present action to improve the future.

characteristics of forecasts

There are several basic characteristics of practical forecasting that the reader should understand before we begin describing and illustrating some of the more widely used techniques.

FORECASTS ARE USUALLY INCORRECT   Everyone recognizes that this is a fact, but it is surprising how few people ever plan on the forecast being incorrect and get ready to react to the errors that will inevitably result. Apparently history teaches us very little; we keep hoping that accuracy, like peace, will come because we all wish for it.

FORECASTS SHOULD BE TWO NUMBERS   Since forecasts will more than likely be incorrect, it is vital to have some estimate (itself a forecast) of how wrong it can be. Any forecast that does not indicate a range, for example ±15% or 2300-2800, is only half a forecast. There is no excuse for lacking some measure of accuracy in the statement of a forecast.

FORECASTS ARE MORE ACCURATE FOR FAMILIES OF ITEMS   Few companies have errors of more than five percent in their forecasts of total annual sales. Whenever it can be done and still suit the purpose, forecasts should be made for groups of products. This should be possible in equipment and man-power planning, ordering common components, buying capacity from vendors, and many more cases.

FORECASTS ARE LESS ACCURATE FAR IN THE FUTURE   There is fre-quently a belief that long-term forecasts could not be any worse than fore-casts for a closer time period. However, the forecast of average sales next week will probably be more accurate than one for the corresponding week next year. Thus, we should endeavor to minimize forecast lead times to mini-mize forecast error.

Different forecasters define the time horizons differently. In this book, we shall refer to *short-term* forecasts as those that project up to three months into the future, *medium-term* as three months to two years into the future, and *long-term* as over two years into the future. When discussing forecasting problems, it is advisable to reach a common understanding of definitions regarding the different time horizons involved.

In many manufacturing companies the need for short-term, intermediate-term, and/or long-term forecasts of *product demand* are determined by the relationship between the production cycle for a product and the maximum permissible time during which a customer's order can be filled. For example, if a company's competitors can fill customer orders in slightly more than the required shipping time, the company will have to maintain a finished good in-ventory to meet its competition. This in turn means that the company will have to determine raw material requirements, purchase and manufacture parts and schedule production based on its sales forecasts. In general, the longer the production cycle, the longer-term forecasts that will be required. In other cases where products are custom built (e.g., ships, bridges, blast furnaces), the customer expects to wait a longer period of time prior to delivery and the manufacturer needs very few forecasts since most raw materials, subassem-blies, etc. are individually ordered.

FORECASTS ARE NO SUBSTITUTE FOR CALCULATIONS   For example, a company may *know* how many orders it has for a particular product line. This information should be used to calculate directly a material requirements plan for a certain component of the product line rather than attempting to forecast its demand. On the other hand, if orders for independent product lines *are not known*, forecasts of demand for each must be developed. Then after a forecast has been made, it is possible to determine directly a material requirements plan for a product's components and subassemblies. Forecasting a component's demand when it can be simply calculated is an indication of ineffective communication among departments within a company.

how to make forecasting successful

In the practical application of forecasting techniques, there are many ingredients to the successful implementation of forecasts. Just as important are the reasons why forecasts fail. In the paragraphs that follow we present common causes of forecasting failures—by *avoiding* these pitfalls you will have learned several valuable points regarding how to be a successful forecaster. The reader should keep these points in mind as he considers the suitability of specific techniques presented in later chapters.

INDIVIDUAL EFFORT   No individual or small group within a single department can possibly know enough about all the factors affecting the future to be able to develop an adequate forecast. Such a person or group can, of course, analyze historical data and use various techniques to draw a few conclusions about possible future trends, cycles, and sources of random variations. Evaluating how the future will differ from the past, however, is another question.

Forecast *users* must understand fully the thinking behind the forecast. To use a forecast intelligently, you need to know as much as possible about the factors that were evaluated in arriving at the prediction. Such understanding is too limited when the forecast is an individual effort. Effective forecasting must be a group effort.

UNREALISTIC EXPECTATIONS   Hope springs eternal in the human breast for the "perfect forecast." This hope always seems associated with the idea that someone else will have to make the forecast. Failure to realize perfection sometimes results in rejection of the forecast but not the hope for one.

SECOND GUESSING   We know why the other person's figures were wrong as surely as stock market analysts tell us today why yesterday's market went up or down. Faced with this reality, many amateur forecasters suffer from delusions of adequacy. Second guessers are rarely able to communicate their knowledge and beliefs so that those responsible for "official" forecasts can use this information to improve the overall forecasting effort.

CONFLICTING OBJECTIVES   Major groups within a company view forecasts differently. The sales group wants an optimistic figure, a carrot to be held out in front of salesmen to get them to exert themselves to the maximum. Top management and financial groups, of course, never want to overstate projected profits. Those responsible for manufacturing try to strike some happy medium between the optimism of the sales group and the conservatism of the financial group in estimating what they will be called on to produce. Each of these groups believes its objective is valid. Unfortunately, in too many cases, forecasts produced by the various groups are inconsistent. The result is that the battle for company survival is fought by the major forces in terms of different strategies. Chaos among allies in most situations causes the war to be lost.

FORECASTING THE WRONG THINGS   Sales of *independent demand* products must be forecasted; this is the most direct way to develop estimates of future requirements. (By independent demand, we mean that demand for one product line is unrelated to demand for another line.) For subassemblies of these products, however, there is no need to forecast their demand. It can be calculated by using bills of material showing which subassemblies and component parts make up each end-product. Any company making *assembled products* can dramatically reduce the number of forecasts it needs by making them only for the end-products and calculating requirements for all components that feed into these assemblies.

Many companies give their customers a wide variety of options in selecting special features and accessories in their products. Marketing departments will balk at forecasting individual items but will not object to forecasting (1) total sales for each family or products and (2) a percentage of this total for each option.

NO AUDITING   Many of those who work with forecasts produced by others feel as though they are victims of their numbers. This is unnecessary. Anyone with access to data can compare actual experience with the forecasts to see how wrong the predictions have been in the past. The use of past deviations as a forecast of future error is frequently more accurate than resorting to past demand as a forecast of future requirements. This practice holds the key to better use of bad forecasts.

From the above list of "what not to do," some general suggestions can be formulated to assist the individual forecaster:*

1. The analyst should know his field. Statistical analysis of available data is only a tool. The researcher must have an adequate knowledge of the facts of his field, both technical and otherwise. A good forecast involves knowledge of trade channels, historical trends, end-use patterns, market shares, geographical factors, correlation with economic indicators, trade expectations, and political, psychological, and other technical and economic factors.

2. All forecasts are based on assumptions. The forecaster should know and be prepared to state his assumptions. These assumptions should cover both external and internal factors. External factors are those over which his company has no control: the state of the economy, competition, and so on. Internal factors are the result of policies set by the company in re-

---

*William Copulsky, Practical Sales Forecasting *(New York: American Management Association, Inc., 1970), p. 18-20.*

lation to such matters as inventories, product line, and quality. The fore-caster must know his product, his industry, and his company.

3. The objective of the forecast must be clearly stated in terms of the question or questions to be answered. The mere collection of statistics and their analysis are of no use unless they are done with a purpose in mind.

4. Having his data on hand, the forecaster should develop a hypothesis, or tentative solution, to be tested in the course of the study. This hypothesis should arise out of the theoretical and practical training of the analyst, literature searching, interviews, pilot studies, and all other means at his disposal for gathering pertinent facts.

5. Data pertinent to the hypothesis should be gathered, refined, and care-fully checked. A well-defined and complete hypothesis expedites the gathering of pertinent numerical data completely and economically.

6. If possible, apparent relationships between the quantity being forecasted and influencing factors should be tested by simple graphical analysis. The graphic scatterchart is an essential prelude to mathematical manipulation. Actually, a graph contains more information than an equation; an equa-tion is only a shorthand notation of the data. The scatter diagram, on the other hand, simultaneously shows both the individuality of each point and the general trend of all the points, which the equation cannot do. Mathematical equations do, however, emphasize the main movements. The value of the graph as a screening device cannot be overemphasized.

7. A simple hypothesis is both useful and practical. It should explain *most* of the changes in the quantity being forecasted but it cannot explain all the data. It is very important for the forecaster to discover how the small number of data that cannot be "explained" by the hypothesis can be taken into account. Did normally minor factors become of major im-portance or did extraordinary events take place in producing these strange observations (outliers)? In every forecast, the analyst should con-sider not only the effects of the main controlling factors included in his hypothesis but also other possibilities.

8. No forecast should be accepted as final. All forecasts should be constant-ly reviewed in the light of the latest data. Each new datum contributes to the hypothesis and demonstrates the reliability or unreliability of the hy-pothesis used.

purpose and overview of the book

The purpose of this book is to enable the reader to gain a working knowledge of several widely-used forecasting techniques. Therefore, we shall be con-cerned with a variety of tools and techniques that are routinely applied by forecasters in many fields of study such as engineering and business administration. Because the book is intended to be of practical value, we have attempted to keep the level of presentation quite straightforward and to the point. In addition, numerous excellent articles have been included to demonstrate clearly how a certain technique was applied successfully to make forecasts.

Chapter 2 deals with the collection and organization of data useful to forecasting. Numerous sources of data are identified, and their utility in preparing product group and item forecasts is discussed. An article by Robert S. Sobek entitled "A Manager's Primer on Forecasting" is presented as Appendix A to supplement the material in Chapter 2. This article describes many economic indicators found helpful to forecasting and summarizes the important features of each.

In Chapter 3 we turn to a discussion of how to select the most appropriate forecasting technique for a given type of problem. The process of choosing a method focuses on the cost and accuracy of its application as well as the applicability of the method for available data and management know-how. An excellent article from the *Harvard Business Review* is included that describes the applicability of numerous techniques in terms of the stage of the product life cycle at which a forecast is desired. The article is "How to Choose the Right Forecasting Technique," written by J. C. Chambers, S. K. Mullick, and D. D. Smith.

The remaining chapters describe in considerable detail forecasting techniques that can be separated into two broad categories: quantitative techniques and qualitative techniques. In this book the *quantitative* techniques deal with regression analysis (Chapter 4) and time-series analysis (Chapter 5). Example problems are included to illustrate the various techniques covered in each chapter.

On the other hand, *qualitative* techniques discussed in Chapter 6 are based on subjectively derived data and include the Delphi method, forecasting with subjective probabilities, and cross impact analysis. Chapter 7 describes a family of qualitative techniques that has been referred to as *technological forecasting*. As in Chapter 6, example problems and a state-of-the-art article have been included in Chapter 7 to facilitate accomplishing the purpose of our book—enabling the reader to obtain a practical and working understanding of commonly used forecasting techniques.

Finally, in Chapter 8 several techniques suitable for large-scale forecasting problems are briefly described. These techniques are presently being used chiefly by larger companies and government agencies in this country because they are rather expensive to apply. The reader should have some knowledge of forecasting procedures discussed in Chapter 8 so that he or she is generally familiar with the advantages and disadvantages of each.

chapter 2 . . . the essential materials of forecasting

introduction

There are three fundamental steps in forecasting: (1) gathering and evaluating the data, (2) preparing the forecast and (3) monitoring the performance of the forecasting system. Probably the most important aspect of preparing and implementing a forecast in a particular situation is the initial phase in which the purpose of the forecast is established and the necessary data are gathered. In subsequent sections of this chapter the characteristics of a successful forecasting program are outlined, external data sources are summarized and an example of data collection for product forecasts is given. Because many companies encounter formidable problems in obtaining good data, the present chapter deals chiefly with this subject. The following chapter describes the development of a forecasting strategy and how to monitor the performance of the forecasting system.

a forecasting program

Any organization that develops forecasts should have a well-defined forecasting program. Forecasts are necessary—they must be made. Some estimate of future events is vital to almost every endeavor. If a formal, official forecast is not prepared, everyone making decisions about future activities—ordering materials, hiring people, buying equipment, performing research—will be forced to make his own estimates. It seems evident that it would be better if the best informed people were involved in a formal effort to produce an official forecast that would provide a consistent basis for all planning activities. The following general steps are offered as a means of establishing such a program.

define the purpose

The objectives of each forecast should be clearly specified in writing. No future event should be forecasted unless the forecast could result in a change in present action. Forecasting is not an esoteric, academic exercise. It must affect present behavior to prepare you for future events.

Defining the purpose also sets the length of the forecast period. A forecast for capital investment purposes would normally be long-range, two to five years. At the other extreme, forecasts for procuring materials and scheduling production should cover next week or next month. Once the forecast period is established, the frequency of review is also indicated. It is not necessary to revise an annual forecast more than once a month; on the other hand, weekly forecasts should be updated at least weekly.

Setting the purpose of the forecast also establishes the units in which it is expressed. Profit plans and financial data need to be in dollars, while manufacturing data must be expressed in pieces, tons, gallons, or similar units meaningful to people using the forecasts. One company president used a forecast expressed in total sales dollars to reach a decision on the construction of a new plant, without accounting for the fact that his product had increased in price at the rate of 10 percent per year for the previous few years. The units for his forecast should have been dollars adjusted for inflationary effects, or units of product.

collect and analyze historical data

This subject is discussed later in this chapter. The purpose is to determine if anything can be learned from the history of previous demand. Because the intent is to project into the future, the trends and cyclical tendencies exhibited in historical data should be purged of any one-time occurrences that might not reappear in the future. Big government orders, material to fill a new distributor's pipeline, peaks of demand due to preannounced price changes and the like have to be drawn from history. Analyzing and purifying such data takes a thorough knowledge of past activities both in the marketplace and in the company.

develop and refine a forecast model

The objective here is to find one or more usable scientific forecasting techniques. Do not expect any mathematical technique to handle the complexities of forecasting without management being involved. All mathematical techniques make the basic assumption that the patterns of the past will extend into the future.

It must be recognized that forecasts are always subject to error. In any given situation there will be techniques available to improve the art of forecasting, but the amount of time and effort required to apply them quickly reaches a point of diminishing returns. When this point has been reached, it is more advisable to build flexibility in dealing with forecast inaccuracies into the system than it is to try to improve further upon the forecasting technique.

evaluate internal factors

For a sound forecast, specific evaluations must be made of those factors that are likely to make the future different from the past. New product designs, marketing promotions, price changes, quality improvements and lead-time reductions are all aimed at making the future better than the past. Estimates of their influence must be converted into a quantitative adjustment of a mathematical forecast.

evaluate external factors

The evaluation of external factors usually depends on the subjective appraisal by individuals with expertise in the area of the forecast. Some of the most useful subjective techniques are presented in Chapters 6 and 7.

As an example of how external factors are considered in practice, many companies first use a computer to develop forecasts for family groups of individual products. The group totals are next reviewed by marketing and top management people who decide if overrides or alterations are necessary. Any changes are then prorated among individual products in the family to develop each item's forecast. This approach uses the power of the computer to update many individual forecasts frequently. With this approach, management judgment needs to be applied only to a limited number of product families. Management can then take adequate time to review these thoroughly, thinking about internal and external influences that might significantly alter the "objectively" derived data.

sources of information for forecasting

No matter to what degree an organization utilizes forecasting, considerable emphasis must be put on reliable information. Poor or incomplete information can jeopardize the outcome of a forecast or make forecasting a complete impossibility. A great diversity of external information is required by groups involved with forecasting, and several sources of this information are available. External data sources and available information are summarized here.

The United States government is by far the largest source of information. At all levels of government—federal, state, and local—there exist organizations that are dependent on large amounts of information. Since economic statistics are used by virtually all agencies of the government in either raw or compiled forms, a large selection in types and forms of information is available. Most of this information is available to the public.

Among the agencies of the federal government that regularly publish economic statistics for business and public use is the Department of Commerce. The Department of Commerce is perhaps the most frequently consulted source of business data. A large amount of the information that the Commerce Department records for private sector use is contained in the monthly publication, *Survey of Current Business*. Containing statistical information on many measurable indicators of the economy, the *Survey of Current Business* is one of the most comprehensive sources of statistics on national accounting, labor force, business investment, production and trade, commodity prices, and financial data available to business. More details regarding this source of data are given later.

Another government agency that can be relied upon as a source of data is the Department of Labor. Among the statistical and informative publications released by the Department of Labor are: *Monthly Labor Review*, *Handbook of Labor Statistics*, and *Survey of Consumer Expenditures*. The first two contain both statistical data and interpretations of the data on labor productivity, employment, and wage rate. The *Survey of Consumer Expenditures* is a study of consumer patterns.

Financial information is made available to business through the Federal Reserve and the Department of the Treasury. The *Federal Reserve Bank Monthly Reviews* and the *Federal Reserve Bulletin* (also monthly) contain financial information in addition to industrial and commercial statistics. The *Annual Report to the Secretary of the Treasury*, published by the Department of the Treasury, contains information of the status of Government finances for the preceding year.

State and local governments are viable sources of information. By publishing information of the same type as the Federal government, but reduced to a statewide level, the information may be more valuable to a local company than the information from the Federal government. By contacting the local Department of Commerce and other local agencies, a large amount of inexpensive yet concise data can be obtained.

A second major source of statistical information is the economic periodicals and journals published by private companies. These companies will often use government statistics in addition to statistics they have collected themselves, including good interpretations and analysis with the data. Dun and Bradstreet, Inc., Standard and Poor's Corporation, Moody's Investor Services, McGraw-Hill Publishing Company, and Barron's Publishing Company are some of the companies that supply current information. *Dun's Review*, containing information of business failures; *New Business Incorporations* (monthly); *Business Failures* (weekly), and *Wholesale Commodity Prices* (weekly), a listing of price changes in thirty basic commodities, are the major publications of Dun and Bradstreet, Inc.

Standard and Poor's Current Statistics, a monthly publication of stock prices, dividends, and company earnings ratios, and *Standard and Poor's Outlook* (weekly), containing information on bond and stock yields are often important sources of information to the forecaster. Moody's Investor Services' major information sources are *Moody's Stock Survey* and *Moody's Bond Survey*, containing information on stock and bond yields.

McGraw-Hill Publishing Company publishes many informative periodicals helpful in forecasting. Among their periodicals are *Business Week* (weekly), including an interpretive text and the "Business Week Index," a series of weekly statistics; and *Engineering News-Record*, a report on construction and building news that includes important statistics.

Fortune, a monthly publication by Time, Inc., and *Survey of Consumer Finances*, published yearly by Survey Research Center Institute for Social Research, are two other sources of data. *Fortune* magazine includes a weekly survey on business expectations, and the *Survey of Consumer Finance* is an informative list of survey data on consumer finances, attitudes, and inclinations to buy.

Another source of forecasting information that can be included under private sector sources is research organizations. Almost any statistic a forecaster would want can be obtained from these companies, provided he is willing to pay for the information. This source is by far the most expensive method of obtaining data but may be easily justified by the necessity to have data not already available from less expensive sources. Companies such as the Office of Population Research and the Survey of Consumer Finances are capable of supplying the forecaster with information.

A fourth source of statistical information is trade associations and professional societies. Often containing information more specifically related to the company making the forecast, the trade association publications can be invaluable sources of information concerning the industry's production, sales, and other relevant data for accurate forecasting.

Because of the usefulness of the *Survey of Current Business* (published monthly by the U.S. Department of Commerce), a few more details about its contents are provided at this point. To subscribe to this service, one should write to the Superintendent of Documents, U.S. Government Printing Office, Washington, D.C., 20402. The publication includes articles on the current industrial and business situation. Some examples are "The Utilization of Manufacturing Capacity," "Labor Markets," "Collective Bargaining," "Inventory Sales Ratios," "Foreign Investment in the United States," and "Residential Construction."

In addition to the articles, there is a considerable amount of statistical information. Each July issue contains fully revised data for the preceding two years. The Bureau of Economic Analysis (BEA), which is part of the U.S. Department of Commerce, can provide a reprint of fully revised data for the years 1964-1974. National income and production data for 1929-1972 are also available from the BEA.

It is worthwhile to note that in the *Survey of Current Business* there are eight basic categories of statistics. The titles of these categories and examples of data included in each are listed below:

1. "Gross National Product and National Income" includes information on gross national product by major type of product and purchasing, gross corporate product, and national income by type of income and industry.

2. "Personal Income and Outlay" presents data on personal income and its disposition and consumption by type of product.

3. "Government Receipts and Expenditures" reports information on federal, state and local government income and expenditures by type of function.

4. "Foreign Transactions" includes data on receipts from and payments to foreigners.

5. "Saving and Investment" provides statistics on private purchases of durable equipment by type, on sources and uses of gross savings, and on purchases of building structures by types.

6. "Income and Employment by Industry" includes information relative to corporate profits by industry, and number of employees and their average annual earnings.

7. "Supplementary Tables" gives additional information on gross national income and products.

8. "Implicit Price Deflators" provides detailed information on inflationary trends. These factors are used to adjust dollars to a common base (usually 1958 dollars).

"Current Business Statistics," a supplement to the *Survey of Current Business*, contains a large volume of detailed information. A few examples would include furniture price indexes, housing starts and permits, unemployment, interest rates, Dow-Jones averages, plastic production, beer production, coffee imports, petroleum production and imports, textile products, and motor vehicle production.

Three of the statistics that are most frequently used by forecasters are the Consumer Price Index, the Wholesale Price Index and the Gross National Product. These are frequently misunderstood and are described in more detail in Appendix A. Let us first consider the Consumer Price Index (CPI), which is a lagging indicator of national economic behavior. Individuals and companies carefully monitor the CPI as they forecast economic conditions, but generally they have little understanding of how it is derived. To compute the CPI, approximately 400 goods and services are priced in 18,000 stores in 56 cities across the United States. The prices are recorded by personnel of the Bureau of Labor Statistics and sent to Washington where they are compiled.

A computer program is used to weight the prices according to the manner in which urban workers are believed to spend their income: 33% for housing, 25% for food, 19% for health and recreation, 13% for transportation, and 10% for clothing. The goods selected for inclusion in the CPI are representative of the buying habits—as determined more than a decade ago—of city wage earners and clerical workers. Thus, the index reflects the characteristics of a group that makes up less than 55 percent of the population, and it ignores the buying pattern of those who live in rural areas, the elderly, higher income individuals, the poor, the self-employed and the unemployed.

Actually, the CPI was never intended to be representative of the nation as a whole. Yet strangely enough, the incomes of many Americans are affected by the CPI. Payments from the Social Security Administration and benefits paid to retired military personnel and federal civil-service workers are directly related to rises and falls in the CPI. Food stamp eligibility hinges on behavior of the CPI. More than five million union members are covered by contracts that provide extra pay when the index rises. One economist estimated that a one-percent change in the index over a year triggers at least a one billion dollar increase in income because of wage escalator provisions in labor contracts.

Government statisticians believe the CPI is extremely accurate for what it was designed to measure; namely, the cost of living for urban workers as indicated by their past buying patterns. They claim to be 95 percent sure that the monthly error is not more than four-hundredths of one percent. As we have seen, problems can arise in the misuse of this index. It should be noted that work is now in progress to develop an additional index that will measure about 80 percent of price changes experienced by the populace of this country.

Another often-quoted government statistic is the Wholesale Price Index (WPI). The WPI is a coincident indicator of what to expect later at the retail level (see Appendix A). This may be misleading since wholesale prices are gathered from those parties who are doing the selling. Data submitted are usually listed prices that do not reflect discounts or concessions. This may bias the index higher than it should be.

The Gross National Product is another coincident indicator of economic activity. This index does not include income from goods and services produced in the United States if the production facilities are owned by foreign interests. However, it does include income from foreign investments to citizens of the United States. These effects have not been significant in the past but are expected to become more important in the future. For this reason Gross Domestic Product, which measures only production within the United

States regardless of ownership, may become a more meaningful indicator of economic activity.

An excellent article, entitled "A Manager's Primer on Forecasting," is included as Appendix A to supplement this chapter. Its purpose is to describe in more detail many of the economic indicators and external sources of data that are easily obtained and highly useful to companies in preparing a wide variety of forecasts.

data bases for forecasting

Data bases are means of organizing and storing information that should prove useful to the forecaster. Because a data base is not a forecasting tool in itself, it is mentioned only briefly. Data bases originated in the early 1960s when the first operable systems—properly called data base systems rather than file handling systems—were developed. Among the earliest of these was the "Integrated Data Store" system developed by the General Electric Company and the formatted file systems developed for the United States Air Force and other defense agencies.

The data base concept is an effort to retain all relevant forecasting information so that it can be easily and quickly referenced for future use. In such systems there is a tendency to summarize groups of data. For example, annual sales is a summary of daily sales of many individual items through many different channels of distribution. The average salary for a certain job title is another aggregate that may not give a clear picture of the total variation in the underlying data. Such classifying and summarizing to some extent is necessary for effective maintenance of the filing system. However, in the process much information inherent to the basic data is lost.

Modern computer systems enable us to retain vast amounts of raw and summarized data that are possibly of use in the preparation of forecasts. For example, a carpet manufacturer could record the dollar value of blue industrial carpet sold by Mr. Jones in February of 1976. One index in the computer system could be assigned to the color blue, one for industrial carpet, one for February 1976, and one for Mr. Jones. It would then be a simple matter for the company to obtain a listing regarding sales of blue carpet, sales of industrial carpet, total sales over any time period, and/or Mr. Jones' sales. For a large company, these different summaries of data would be exceedingly tedious with a manual data system.

product group forecasts and item forecasts

This section illustrates the collection of external data and its utilization, along with internal data, in the forecasting process. A farm implement manufacturer, for example, might make his overall business forecast in dollars, relating it to the government estimate of disposable farm income. He would then need to break the overall dollar total into dollars for each major product group (such as tractors, combines, or balers). This could be done using a percentage based on past experience, modified by any sales department or marketing department knowledge of trends in demand for a particular product group. He should then search for indicators that relate directly to a particular product, such as the numbers of acres of wheat under cultivation or a change in the subsidy being awarded for soybeans. External data is usually considered at this initial stage of forecasting when product group forecasts are developed. Internal data is more important in refining the overall product group forecasts and developing forecasts for each specific item.

The next step would be to apply known seasonal indexes peculiar to the product groups, particularly in a business such as the manufacture of farm implements. Table 2-1 shows the development of such a seasonal index for each month, stating it as a percent of the year's sales of combines. In this case, five years of history have been analyzed, and the monthly sales are shown as a percentage of the annual total. An overall average for each month is calculated, using the data for the five years. A good forecaster would want to have one or two additional years of data that he could use to test the validity of the seasonal percentage. Using the annual forecast of sales for this product group, he could apply the average percentages of Table 2-1 to each month and thus come up with a monthly forecast.

table 2-1 . . . developing a seasonal index

(monthly sales as a percent of annual total)

Month	Y*-1	Y-2	Y-3	Y-4	Y-5	Average %
January	7.48%	5.46%	6.36%	6.56%	6.54%	6.50
February	8.24	4.70	6.68	7.35	5.78	6.55
March	8.27	7.30	8.84	7.90	8.03	8.05
April	7.95	9.34	9.40	8.79	9.29	8.95
May	9.66	9.65	10.50	11.11	10.44	10.30
June	10.00	11.30	10.60	8.79	9.71	10.10
July	9.06	8.70	7.66	9.01	9.96	8.90
August	9.85	11.10	10.80	10.12	11.00	10.60
September	9.71	9.50	8.15	9.70	7.90	9.00
October	6.65	8.72	8.09	8.78	8.95	8.25
November	7.80	8.08	7.64	7.34	7.72	7.70
December	5.12	6.15	5.13	4.54	4.64	6.10
Total	99.79	100.00	99.85	99.99	99.96	100.00

SOURCE: G. W. Plossl and O. W. Wight, *Production and Inventory Control: Principles and Techniques* (Englewood Cliffs, N.J.: Prentice-Hall, Inc., 1967), p. 34.

Note: Y denotes the current year.

Product group forecasts are used to determine the manpower and machine capacity requirements for each major production facility. The important purpose of product group forecasts is to establish overall production levels. This application makes use of the principle that group forecasts are more accurate than item forecasts.

Item forecasts are needed for determining order points, materials plans, order quantities and schedules of independent product lines. They are best made using simple statistical techniques based on their own demand history. Contrary to opinion in many production control departments, it is not good practice to have the marketing department make all item forecasts. These should be made by production control. Marketing should be asked to provide information needed to adjust the statistical forecasts for items with significant changes expected because of new market trends, promotions, competitive influences and the like. The sum of individual item forecasts for each product group should equal the group forecast prepared by marketing for planning production levels.

A particularly challenging type of item to forecast is the product that is custom-assembled from many standard components. An automobile manufacturer, for example, could hardly hope to forecast the number of green sedans with standard transmission and air conditioning that he might sell. He can, however, forecast the total number of cars reasonably well and then forecast the percent that will be green, the percent to be sedans, and so on.

It should be clear to the reader that data collection, including internal and external information, is fundamental to successful forecasting. The next chapter expands discussion on the forecasting strategy and reemphasizes the importance of sound data collection.

questions

1. Try to list the types of things that can happen in a small- or medium-sized company when departments develop their own forecasts without consulting with other departments.

2. How is the Wholesale Price Index computed and how often? What is the Consumer Price Index designed to measure?

3. Go to the library and find the *Survey of Current Business*. Gather data regarding national manufacturing inventories ($) by quarter for the past ten years.

4. Describe how national or regional data might be used by a medium-sized furniture manufacturing company to prepare group and item forecasts for its products.

5. List and describe four leading indicators of economic activity (see Appendix A).

6. What is a diffusion index and how can it be useful to a forecaster (see Appendix A)?

chapter 3 . . . the choice of appropriate techniques for implementing a forecasting strategy

introduction

Our aim here is to describe several considerations affecting the choice of a forecasting technique(s) to apply in a particular situation. In addition, guidelines for formulating a forecasting strategy are given, basic data patterns are categorized, and criteria for measuring and evaluating forecasting error are presented in this chapter.

As we shall see in subsequent chapters, forecasting techniques in widespread use are highly diverse. The most influential factor in developing a forecasting strategy is the potential economic value of the forecast. Forecasts of major corporations influence their decisions on investment, research expenditures, personnel policies, marketing plans, etc. The importance of such decisions often justifies expenditures for market surveys, research by experts, and sophisticated mathematical analysis. The small business tends to be more limited financially in its approach to making forecasts.

The forecasting strategy also depends on the nature of the organization. For example, public utilities have a relatively stable demand for their products and services, and they have a different view of forecasting from fashion clothing manufacturers that must react very quickly to new concepts with little or no numerical data at hand. An organization's basic technical capability also determines its selection of forecasting tools. A company with a large percentage of scientists and engineers in management should be comfortable with the more mathematically based techniques. In short, an organization must adopt a forecasting strategy that it can afford, that is suitable to the nature of its business, and that its management can understand.

The selection of a particular technique is also determined by its accuracy and patterns in available data. The expense of forecasting techniques, their applicability, and their ease of interpretation are discussed in subsequent chapters. Evaluation of forecast accuracy and basic data patterns are presented later in this chapter.

This chapter is concluded with an article entitled "How To Choose the Right Forecasting Technique" by John Chambers, Satinder Mullick, and Donald Smith, and it illustrates a coordinated forecasting strategy. The stage of the product life cycle where various techniques have been found particularly useful is also considered in the article. We believe the remainder of Chapter 3 will be extremely helpful to the reader as he attempts to place techniques discussed in subsequent chapters in perspective with regard to their practical use.

formulating a forecasting strategy

A conscientious forecaster will follow a logical step-by-step procedure in developing and revising forecasts. As we noted earlier, the first step is to decide what response, or quantity, to forecast. Then pertinent numerical data are gathered and summarized in graphical form, whenever possible. Often the data represent some response as a function of time, such as sales per quarter. Such data are referred to as a *time-series*. The time-series should be examined for an underlying pattern, and the forecaster should attempt to explain this pattern. For instance, a large sudden increase in sales may be explained by increased government spending. A long-term steady rise in sales may be a result of gradual public acceptance of a new product.

An analysis of time-series data merely extends historical patterns into the future and is not capable of predicting turning points in activity levels. In this respect, the forecaster should search for a *causal relationship* between the response variable and other variables. For example, a rise in interest rates is usually followed by a decline in new residential housing construction. This is a causal relationship that is useful in forecasting turning points (upswings and downturns) in the construction industry.

The next step of the forecasting process is to apply expert judgment to forecasts obtained by utilizing causal relationships and/or time-series analysis. All relevant data, mathematical analysis, and other related information should be summarized and made available to the experts. The result of this evaluation, whether it takes the form of a Delphi study or simply a group's or an individual's opinion, should be documented and included in the *forecasting strategy*. Consequently, we shall speak of the forecasting strategy as the coordinated approach to collecting data, identifying and mathematically testing causal realtionships and/or selecting a procedure for projecting time-series data, and choosing a structured approach for eliciting expert opinion concerning the problem under consideration.

Thus, one of the most effective forecasting strategies is to use mathematical techniques to routinely forecast demand for large numbers of different product groupings and then to introduce judgment in attempting to decide where the future will probably differ from the past. Forecasts for individual items are then adjusted accordingly. A prime advantage of this approach to forecasting is that it reduces the number of factors to which human experience must be applied. If our marketing expert were trying to evaluate simultaneously past trends, current sales, seasonal variations, actions of competitors, outside economic indicators, etc. in making forecasts of a large number of products, he would not be able to thoroughly consider and assimilate these factors in the limited time usually available. By wisely combining mathematical techniques and informed judgment, both methods can serve as checks on each other and tend to eliminate gross errors.

In practice, there will be many departures from the general strategy suggested above. In forecasting sales of a new product where there are no historical data, the forecaster may rely on previous sales of a similar product as an analogy, or he may resort to market surveys, expert opinion, or some combination of these methods for generating data. The forecaster should use every bit of information he can locate if it is economically judicious to do so. To illustrate, some manufacturers are able to observe retail sales and adjust to changes in trends before the actual effect reaches them through their channel of product distribution. Thus, formulation of a forecasting strategy is an art that involves the selection, coordination, application, and interpretation of objective and subjective procedures.

Additional examples of how companies formulate their forecasting strategies are given in the following paragraphs.

A small company manufactures over 100 different types of sewn products such as women's handbags and men's shaving kits. Management found it nearly impossible to forecast annual sales for any single product line. After analyzing historical sales data, the decision was made to forecast total product sales by channel of distribution. A fairly accurate forecast could be derived for sales to drug stores, discount houses, etc. by utilizing historical sales data for each of these areas and obtaining salesmen's opinions on changes in the trends. These forecasts were then summarized to obtain a total sales forecast that was useful in decisions regarding such things as production lot sizes, numbers of personnel required, and purchases of materials.

For each of the product lines, a plot was then made of its relative historical contribution (as a percentage) to total sales. These percentages were used to predict the future breakout of total sales to each product line. By resorting to this round-about method, management of the company was able to obtain reasonable forecasts for each product line. Some time later, management concluded that total sales was the forecast it really needed and that forecasts for each product line should not necessarily be made on a routine basis. This was due to the fact that effort spent to obtain detailed forecasts could not be justified relative to benefits derived from them. The company president eventually set a policy that no forecast was to be developed unless a written request was presented that included a specific statement of need for the forecast.

In another situation a major corporation was considering the purchase of highly automated equipment, costing about two million dollars, to produce an electrical component used in the construction industry. The company obtained estimates of their competitor's sales and gathered data on construction trends to forecast national supply and demand for the component. Based on this information, a decision was made to purchase the equipment. Less than one year after the equipment was purchased, a technological improvement in the building trades industry made the component obsolete in 90 percent of its applications. The company had been prudent in mathematical analysis of data, but it had failed to consider any technological changes that might have been identified by applying an appropriate technological forecasting technique.

As a final example of how companies go about choosing a forecasting approach, we shall consider a firm that fabricates bridges and structural steel. Management needed a forecast of labor hours required on specific jobs to prepare competitive bids. The estimators were calculating weight of the steel required on the job from engineering plans and next applying average man-hours per ton of steel (from historical records) to obtain their forecast. In practice, the actual man-hours required ranged from 50 percent to 200 percent of the forecast. Many jobs with large amounts of steel required very little labor and a large proportion of "light" jobs needed many man-hours to complete. The causal relationship being used was not very effective.

An improved system was developed that was based on the number of steel beams of various sizes and the number of special attachments to the beams. When bidding on a job, the number of beams of each size and their attachments were counted, the appropriate manhour conversion factors were applied, and the results were summed to obtain a forecast of labor requirements. The new forecasting system now produces results that are within ±20% of the actual labor requirements.

The reader should not consider any of the techniques presented in subsequent chapters as the final solution to a forecasting problem, but you should consider how each can fit into an overall forecasting strategy. Causal relationships are discussed in Chapter 4, time-series analysis in Chapter 5, and the problem of eliciting and compiling expert opinion is treated in Chapters 6 and 7. The final chapter (Chapter 8) briefly describes several techniques that can be applied to large-scale forecasting problems.

underlying patterns in historical data

In many forecasting situations, historical data are available or can be obtained. Data should first be plotted on graph paper in an effort to determine an underlying pattern that, once identified, may simplify the choice of a fore-casting technique. The graphing of data often reveals a pattern that would not otherwise have been discovered if the data were inspected only in tabular form. We shall soon learn that some techniques are more suitable for a par-ticular data pattern than for other underlying patterns.

A plot of the independent variable and the associated response will quickly reveal the general strength and nature of a causal relationship. For ex-ample, a meat packing company may use the ratio of price of beef to price of corn at the middle of a month as its independent, or observed, variable and number of cattle processed in the following month as the response. These data could be plotted for the previous 20 to 50 months. If the plot resembled that of Figure 3-1A, the forecaster would know that there is no relationship between the variables. If the plot resembled that of Figure 3-1C, the fore-caster could apply linear regression to further define and test this apparent linear relationship. Figure 3-1D indicates that nonlinear regression may be an appropriate tool to consider.

For time-series data, the placement of a single data point is determined by four factors:

1. Trend factors that occur over a period of many years,

2. Cyclical factors that are usually between one and five years in length,

3. Seasonal factors that usually repeat themselves within a year's period, and

4. Random factors that result from one-time occurrences.

In this presentation, the basic underlying pattern of time-series data is viewed as consisting of the *long-term plus the cyclical factors.*

Mathematical methods are seldom used to project trends over two years into the future and almost never over five years. Because most cycles are be-tween one and five years in length, they are considered to be part of the basic pattern. In Figure 3-1, time-series data are illustrated that have general random effects with a horizontal pattern (B), an underlying linear trend (C), an underlying quadratic trend (D), and a linear trend plus a strong seasonal factor (E). A summary of the forecasting procedure most appropriate for each pattern is given in Table 3-1.

evaluating and utilizing forecasting error

To evaluate any quantitative forecasting procedure, the procedure should be first completely defined and then applied to representative data. For ex-ample, if your goal is to forecast sales one month in advance, you could start by applying your proposed forecasting technique to the last two years of monthly data. Begin with the first month and apply the procedure to take each new month's actual sales into account in developing the next month's

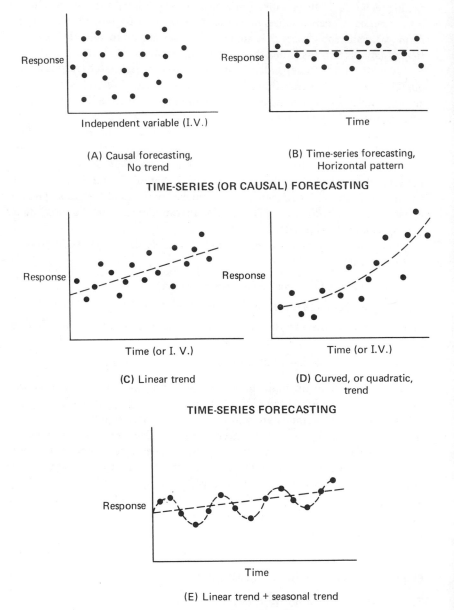

(A) Causal forecasting,
No trend

(B) Time-series forecasting,
Horizontal pattern

TIME-SERIES (OR CAUSAL) FORECASTING

(C) Linear trend

(D) Curved, or quadratic,
trend

TIME-SERIES FORECASTING

(E) Linear trend + seasonal trend

figure 3-1 . . . basic data patterns

table 3-1 . . . appropriate forecasting techniques

an introductory summary

Pattern	Relationship	
	Causal	Time-Series
Horizontal (no trend)	No applicable technique	Simple moving average or exponential smoothing
Linear trend	Linear regression	Double moving averages or exponential smoothing
Quadratic trend	Nonlinear regression	Triple moving averages or triple exponential smoothing
Seasonal and linear trend	Not applicable	Winters' method

forecast. Then for the historical data you can measure the difference between your forecast and actual sales.

An illustrative example of this situation is given in Table 3-2. The sum of the error should be close to zero when the forecasting technique is unbiased. If error (error = forecast – actual) sums to a large positive number, then this indicates that your forecasts are too high; a large negative number indicates they are too low. The *absolute value* of the errors (i.e., all error terms are considered positive) should be summed and averaged to calculate the mean absolute deviation, MAD. The MAD can be misleading in some cases. For example, if sales of a product in thousands of dollars are forecast at 100 a month, and actual sales turn out to be 105 for five months out of the next ten months and 95 for the other five months, then MAD = 50/10 = 5. If sales equal 100 for nine months and 50 for one month, then MAD = 5 also. Most forecasters would believe the second error to be far more serious than the first, and this is not indicated by the MAD.

To provide a more meaningful evaluator for such situations, the mean square error (MSE) can be calculated by squaring the errors, summing, and averaging. In the above example, for the first case MSE = 250/10 = 25, and for the second case MSE = 250. Both of these indicators of forecasting "goodness" (MAD and MSE) are illustrated in the example of Table 3-2. When you are attempting to decide which of several forecasting techniques to use with a given set of data, the format of Table 3-2 can be utilized to compute the above indicators. Usually the technique having the smallest MSE is considered to be the best when several forecasting methods are compared quantitatively.

table 3-2 . . . evaluating forecast error

an example

(1) Period No.	(2) Actual Response	(3) Forecast	(4) Error*	(5) Absolute Deviation	(6) Squared Error
1	96	100	+4.0	4.0	16.0
2	86	98.8	+12.8	12.8	163.8
3	94	95.0	+1.0	1.0	1.0
4	80	94.7	+14.7	14.7	216.1
5	107	90.3	−16.7	16.7	278.9
6	83	95.3	+12.3	12.3	151.3
7	87	91.6	+4.6	4.6	21.2
8	84	90.2	+6.2	6.2	38.4
9	102	88.3	−13.7	13.7	187.7
10	114	92.4	−11.6	11.6	134.6
11	117	98.9	−18.1	18.1	327.6
12	114	103.4	−10.6	10.6	112.4
13	112	104.3	−7.7	7.7	59.3
14	114	107.2	−6.8	6.8	46.2
15	106	106.8	+0.8	0.8	0.6
16	98	104.2	+6.2	6.2	38.4
17	80	96.9	+16.9	16.9	285.6
18	114	102.0	−12.0	12.0	144.0
19	103	102.3	−0.7	0.7	0.5
20	81	95.9	+14.9	14.9	222.0
21	110	100.2	−9.8	9.8	96.0
22	91	97.4	+6.4	6.4	41.0
23	108	100.6	−7.4	7.4	54.8
24	101	100.7	−0.3	0.3	0.0
TOTAL			**−14.6**	**216.2**	**2637.4**

$$\text{MAD} = \frac{216.2}{24} = 9.0 \qquad \text{MSE} = \frac{2637.4}{24} = 109.9$$

Error = forecast − actual

There is a need for continuous evaluation of forecast error. To react wisely to change, it should be recognized that forecasts are highly likely to be incorrect, and error must be measured as actual data are accumulated. The estimate of error is at least as important as the forecast itself. Unfortunately, too few forecasters measure and estimate error—this is necessary for the effective use of forecasts. The error will never be eliminated, so the forecaster should learn to use it intelligently.

One simple means of examining forecast error is to plot the actual response as a percent of the forecast, as illustrated in Figure 3-2. This simple chart will provide some insight into the behavior of forecasting error. If a long string of these percentages is either above or below 100%, the source of this pattern should be determined and corrections made.

A control chart is an interesting tool for measuring forecast error. This method is based on the principle that if the forecast is "perfect" on the average, the cumulative sum of forecast error should approach zero. However, in reality, a cumulative sum of zero is extremely difficult to obtain. A large negative or positive sum of forecast errors can be due to either the choice of an inappropriate model to represent the systematic variations in the variables or the result of shifts in the way certain variables are related to each other. In either case, a persistent large nonzero sum of errors should warn the forecaster that his model is not providing an adequate representation of reality. Such a warning can be quantitatively obtained with the control chart illustrated in Figure 3-3.

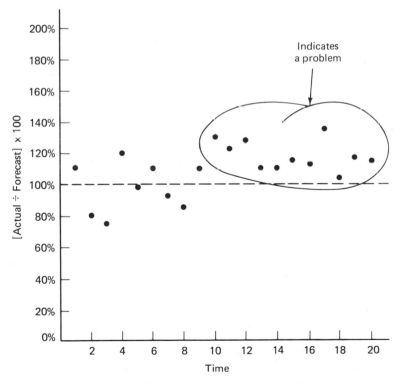

figure 3-2 . . . recording forecast error

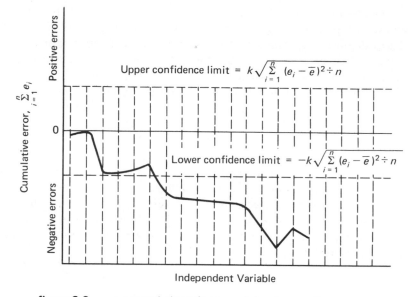

figure 3-3 . . . a control chart for examining forecasting errors

A control chart can be constructed by following these steps:

1. Keep a record of cumulative forecasting error.

2. Plot cumulative error along the y-axis of the control chart (see Figure 3-3) versus the corresponding independent variable.

3. The x-axis is used to represent the independent variable (e.g., time).

4. Determine the location of upper and lower confidence limits as follows. The distance from the upper confidence limit to the zero line = $(k) \times$ (standard error). The distance from the zero line to the lower confidence limit = $- (k) \times$ (standard error), where k = some number determined in advance as being "reasonable." (This number is usually 2 or 3.)

$$\text{Standard error of the forecast} = \sqrt{\frac{\sum\limits_{i=1}^{n} (e_i - \overline{e})^2}{n}}$$

e_i = the forecast error for the ith observation.
$\overline{e}$ = the average forecast error up to the ith observation.

If the cumulative sum of forecast errors is found to be positive or negative but it falls *within* the upper and lower confidence limits, the results can be interpreted as having arisen by chance. In other words, there are probably only random influences present in the data and/or the forecasting system. If, on the other hand, the forecast goes out of control, i.e., the cumulative sum is found to be above or below the confidence limits for two or more successive observations, this should be a signal that something is wrong. Then, the forecaster should attempt to discover the cause of his problem.

Referring to Figure 3-3, it is conceivable, although highly unlikely, that the string of negative errors could have resulted from chance. In this situation, the forecaster should set the sum of cumulative errors back to zero and see if the next few observations also result in negative errors. If this pattern continues and the forecaster is still unable to locate the source of the problem, he might be able to improve his forecasts by making use of the observed and perhaps predictable negative pattern in the forecast errors. For example, this might be done by adjusting future forecasts upwards by the average error calculated from Figure 3-3.

Repeated calculations of the MAD and MSE, a plot of forecast error such as that of Figure 3-2, and a control chart are means of providing up-to-date evaluations of forecast accuracy. In addition, expert opinion and executive judgment cannot be ignored in evaluating the accuracy of forecasts. Once the accuracy of the forecast has been determined, this information becomes an integral part of the decision making process.

In most situations very little thought has been given to applying forecast error to production planning. As an example, a company introduced a new product that was similar to others in its line but it was still sufficiently unique to raise serious questions about the production forecast that had been prepared. A preliminary figure of 40,000 per week was proposed by the marketing group. Pinned down about possible variations from this figure, they said their most optimistic figure was 70% higher and their most pessimistic 70% lower—a range from 12,000 to 68,000 per week. The first reaction was "ridiculous." To this reaction the marketing group replied, "You asked for our best estimate and you got it. What number would you like?" This put things back into perspective and everyone settled down to see if even such a large range of forecasts could be useful in making some critical production decisions.

The number of forging dies to make for the first production runs was determined by the low forecast because extra forging dies can be made in short lead-times and at relatively little extra expense, compared to the time and cost of the first set of dies. On the other hand, the number of required plastic molding dies was based on the high forecast, since it was cheaper to make extra die capacity initially. In the case of both forgings and plastic moldings, parts were produced based on the middle, or most likely, forecast so that adequate supplies would be on hand to get the product off and running, fill the pipeline in the distribution system, and support sales if they should "take off."

Jigs and fixtures to hold parts for turning, boring, milling, and drilling could also be simple and inexpensive until the actual sales rate was high enough to justify additional investment in more specialized, high-rate production tooling. Conversely, large inventories of small, inexpensive materials would be a relatively low price to pay for the insurance against holding up shipments of a successful product. An interesting footnote is that the demand for this product really took off but production stayed with it. This company had hedged its bets smartly and had tracked actual sales closely in planning its production schedules.

how to choose the right forecasting technique*

ABSTRACT   In virtually every decision he makes, the executive today considers some kind of forecast. Sound predictions of demands and trends are no longer luxury items, but a necessity, if the manager is to cope with seasonality, sudden changes in demand levels, price-cutting maneuvers of the competition, strikes, and large swings of the economy. Forecasting can help him deal with these troubles; but it can help him more, the more he knows about the general principles of forecasting, what it can and cannot do for him currently, and which techniques are suited to his need of the moment. Here the authors try to explain the potential of forecasting to the manager, focusing special attention on sales forecasting for products of Corning Glass Works as these have matured through the product life cycle. The authors also include a run-down of the whole range of forecasting techniques.

introduction

To handle the increasing variety and complexity of managerial forecasting problems, many forecasting techniques have been developed in recent years. Each has its special use, and care must be taken to select the correct technique for a particular application. The manager as well as the forecaster has a role to play in technique selection; and the better he understands the range of forecasting possibilities, the more likely it is that a company's forecasting efforts will bear fruit.

The selection of a method depends on many factors—the context of the forecast, the relevance and availability of historical data, the degree of accuracy desirable, the time period to be forecast, the cost/benefit (or value) of the forecast to the company, and the time available for making the analysis.

*By J. C. Chambers, S. K. Mullick, and D. D. Smith, "How to Choose the Right Forecasting Technique," *Harvard Business Review*, July-August 1971, pp. 45-74; Reprinted by permission of the publisher, © 1971 by the President and Fellows of Harvard College; all rights reserved.

These factors must be weighed constantly, and on a variety of levels. In general, for example, the forecaster should choose a technique that makes the best use of available data. If he can readily apply one technique of acceptable accuracy, he should not try to "gold plate" by using a more advanced technique that offers potentially greater accuracy but that requires nonexistent information or information that is costly to obtain. This kind of trade-off is relatively easy to make, but others, as we shall see, require considerably more thought.

Furthermore, where a company wishes to forecast with reference to a particular product, it must consider *the stage of the product's life cycle for which it is making the forecast.* The availability of data and the possibility of establishing relationships between the factors depend directly on the maturity of a product, and hence the life-cycle stage is a prime determinant of the forecasting method to be used.

Our purpose here is to present an overview of this field by discussing the way a company ought to approach a forecasting problem, describing the methods available and explaining how to match method to problem. We shall illustrate the use of the various techniques from our experience with them at Corning, and then close with our own forecast for the future of forecasting.

Although we believe forecasting is still an art, we think that some of the principles which we have learned through experience may be helpful to others.

manager, forecaster and choice of methods

A manager generally assumes that when he asks a forecaster to prepare a specific projection, the request itself provides sufficient information for the forecaster to go to work and do his job. This is almost never true.

Successful forecasting begins with a collaboration between the manager and the forecaster, in which they work out answers to the following questions.

1. What is the purpose of the forecast—how is it to be used?

This determines the accuracy and power required of the techniques, and hence governs selection. Deciding whether to enter a business may require only a rather gross estimate of the size of the market, whereas a forecast made for budgeting purposes should be quite accurate. The appropriate techniques differ accordingly.

Again, if the forecast is to set a "standard" against which to evaluate performance, the forecasting method should not take into account special actions, such as promotions and other marketing devices, since these are meant to change historical patterns and relationships and hence form part of the "performance" to be evaluated.

Forecasts that simply sketch what the future will be like if a company makes no significant changes in tactics and strategy are usually not good enough for planning purposes. On the other hand, if management wants a forecast of the effect that a certain marketing strategy under debate will have on sales growth, then the technique must be sophisticated enough to take explicit account of the special actions and events the strategy entails.

Techniques vary in their costs, as well as in scope and accuracy. The manager must fix the level of inaccuracy he can tolerate—in other words, decide how his decision will vary, depending on the range of accuracy of the forecast. This allows the forecaster to trade off cost against the value of accuracy in choosing a technique.

For example, in production and inventory control, increased accuracy is likely to lead to lower safety stocks. Here the manager and forecaster must weigh the cost of a more sophisticated and more expensive technique against potential savings in inventory costs.

Exhibit I shows how cost and accuracy increase with sophistication and charts this against the corresponding cost of forecasting errors, given some general assumptions. The most sophisticated technique that can be

exhibit I . . . cost of forecasting versus cost of inaccuracy for a medium-range forecast, given data availability

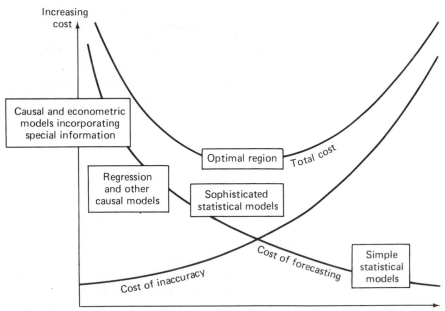

economically justified is one that falls in the region where the sum of the two costs is minimal.

Once the manager has defined the purpose of the forecast, the forecaster can advise him on how often it could usefully be produced. From a strategic point of view, they should discuss whether the decision to be made on the basis of the forecast can be changed later, if they find the forecast was inaccurate. If it *can* be changed, they should then discuss the usefulness of installing a system to track the accuracy of the forecast and the kind of tracking system that is appropriate.

2. What are the dynamics and components of the system for which the forecast will be made?

This clarifies the relationships of interacting variables. Generally, the manager and the forecaster must review a flow chart that shows the relative positions of the different elements of the distribution system, sales system, production system, or whatever is being studied . . . .

In the part of the system where the company has total control, management tends to be tuned in to the various cause-and-effect relationships, and hence can frequently use forecasting techniques that take causal factors explicitly into account.

The flow chart has special value for the forecaster where causal prediction methods are called for because it enables him to conjecture about the possible variations in sales levels caused by inventories and the like, and to determine which factors must be considered by the technique to provide the executive with a forecast of acceptable accuracy.

Once these factors and their relationships have been clarified, the forecaster can build a causal model of the system which captures both the facts and the logic of the situation—which is, after all, the basis of sophisticated forecasting.

3. How important is the past in estimating the future?

Significant changes in the system—new products, new competitive strategies, and so forth—diminish the similarity of past and future. Over the short term, recent changes are unlikely to cause overall patterns to alter, but over the long term their effects are likely to increase. The executive and the forecaster must discuss these fully.

three general types

Once the manager and the forecaster have formulated their problem, the forecaster will be in a position to choose his method.

There are three basic types—*qualitative techniques, time series analysis and projection,* and *causal models*. The first uses qualitative data (expert opinion, for example) and information about special events of the kind already mentioned, and may or may not take the past into consideration.

The second, on the other hand, focuses entirely on patterns and pattern changes, and thus relies entirely on historical data.

The third uses highly refined and specific information about relationships between system elements, and is powerful enough to take special events formally into account. As with time series analysis and projection techniques, the past is important to causal models.

These differences imply (quite correctly) that the same type of forecasting technique is not appropriate to forecast sales, say, at all stages of the life cycle of a product—for example, a technique that relies on historical data would not be useful in forecasting the future of a totally new product that has no history.

The major part of the balance of this article will be concerned with the problem of suiting the technique to the life-cycle stages. We hope to give the executive insight into the potential of forecasting by showing how this problem is to be approached. But before we discuss the life cycle, we need to sketch the general functions of the three basic types of techniques in a bit more detail.

QUALITATIVE TECHNIQUES   Primarily, these are used when data are scarce—for example, when a product is first introduced into a market. They use human judgment and rating schemes to turn qualitative information into quantitative estimates.

The objective here is to bring together in a logical, unbiased, and systematic way all information and judgments which relate to the factors being estimated. Such techniques are frequently used in new-technology areas, where development of a product idea may require several "inventions," so that R&D demands are difficult to estimate, and where market acceptance and penetration rates are highly uncertain.

The [chart on pp. 36-39] presents several examples of this type (see the first section), including market research and the now-familiar Delphi technique.[1] In this chart we have tried to provide a body of basic information about the main kinds of forecasting techniques. Some of the techniques listed are not in reality a single method or model, but a whole family. Thus our statements may not accurately describe all the variations of a technique and should rather be interpreted as descriptive of the basic concept of each.

A disclaimer about estimates in the chart is also in order. Estimates of costs are approximate, as are computation times, accuracy ratings, and ratings for turning-point identification. The costs of some procedures de-

---

[1] See Harper Q. North and Donald L. Pyke, " 'Probes' of the Technological Future," HBR May-June 1969, p. 68. [The Delphi method is discussed later in Chapter 6.]

pend on whether they are being used routinely or are set up for a single forecast; also, if weightings or seasonals have to be determined anew each time a forecast is made, costs increase significantly. Still, the figures we present may serve as general guidelines.

The reader may find frequent reference to this chart [pp. 36-39] helpful for the remainder of the article.

TIME SERIES ANALYSIS   These are statistical techniques used when several years' data for a product or product line are available and when relationships and trends are both clear and relatively stable.

One of the basic principles of statistical forecasting—indeed, of all forecasting when historical data are available—is that the forecaster should use the data on past performance to get a "speedometer reading" of the current rate (of sales, say) and of how fast this rate is increasing or decreasing. The current rate and changes in the rate—"acceleration" and "deceleration"—constitute the basis of forecasting. Once they are known, various mathematical techniques can develop projections from them.

The matter is not so simple as it sounds, however. It is usually difficult to make projections from raw data since the rates and trends are not immediately obvious; they are mixed up with seasonal variations, for example, and perhaps distorted by such factors as the effects of a large sales promotion campaign. The raw data must be massaged before they are usable, and this is frequently done by time series analysis.

Now, a *time series* is a set of chronologically ordered points of raw data—for example, a division's sales of a given product, by month, for several years. Time series *analysis* helps to identify and explain:

•   Any regularity or systematic variation in the series of data which is due to seasonality—the "seasonals."

•   Cyclical patterns that repeat any two or three years or more.

•   Trends in the data.

•   Growth rates of these trends.

(Unfortunately, most existing methods identify only the seasonals, the combined effect of trends and cycles, and the irregular, or chance, component. That is, they do not separate *trends* from *cycles*. We shall return to this point when we discuss time series analysis in the final stages of product maturity.)

Once the analysis is complete, the work of projecting future sales (or whatever) can begin.

We should note that while we have separated analysis from projection here for purposes of explanation, most statistical forecasting techniques actually combine both functions in a single operation.

Basic forecasting techniques

Technique	A. Qualitative methods		
	1. Delphi method	2. Market research	3. Historical analogy
Description	A panel of experts is interrogated by a sequence of questionnaires in which the responses to one questionnaire are used to produce the next questionnaire. Any set of information available to some experts and not others is thus passed on to the others, enabling all the experts to have access to all the information for forecasting. This technique eliminates the bandwagon effect of majority opinion.	The systematic, formal, and conscious procedure for evolving and testing hypotheses about real markets.	This is a comparative analysis of the introduction and growth of similar new products, that bases the forecast on similarity patterns.

Accuracy
  Short term (0-3 months)
  Medium term (3 months-2 years)
  Long term (2 years and up)
	Fair to very good
	Fair to very good
	Fair to very good
		Excellent
		Good
		Fair to good
			Poor
			Good to fair
			Good to fair

Identification of turning points	Fair to good	Fair to very good	Poor to fair
Typical applications	Forecasts of long-range and new-product sales, forecasts of margins.	Forecasts of long-range and new-product sales, forecasts of margins.	Forecasts of long-range and new-product sales, forecasts of margins.
Data required	A coordinator issues the sequence of questionnaires, editing and consolidating the responses.	As a minimum, two sets of reports over time. One needs a considerable collection of market data from questionnaires, surveys, and time series analyses of market variables.	Several years' history of one or more products.

Cost of forecasting in 1971 dollars*
  With a computer
  Is calculation possible
  without a computer?
	$2,000+
	
	Yes
		$5,000+
		
		Yes
			$1,000+
			
			Yes

Time required to develop an application and make a forecast	2 months+	3 months+	1 month+
References	North & Pyke, " 'Probes' of the Technological Future," HBR May-June 1969, p. 68	Bass, King & Pessemeier, *Applications of the Sciences in Marketing Management* (New York, John Wiley & Sons, Inc., 1968).	Spencer, Clark & Hoguet, *Business & Economic Forecasting* (Homewood, Illinois, Richard D. Irwin, Inc., 1961).

*These estimates are based on our own experience, using this machine configuration: an IBM 360-40, 256 K system and a Univac 1108 Time-Sharing System, together with such smaller equipment as G.E. Time-sharing and IBM 360-30's and 1130's.

B. Time series analysis and projection			
1. Moving average	2. Exponential smoothing	3. Box-Jenkins	4. Trend projections
Each point of a moving average of a time series is the arithmetic or weighted average of a number of consecutive points of the series, where the number of data points is chosen so that the effects of seasonals or irregularity or both are eliminated.	This technique is similar to the moving average, except that more recent data points are given more weight. Descriptively, the new forecast is equal to the old one plus some proportion of the past forecasting error. Adaptive forecasting is somewhat the same except that seasonals are also computed. There are many variations of exponential smoothing: some are more versatile than others, some are computationally more complex, some require more computer time.	Exponential smoothing is a special case of the Box-Jenkins technique. The time series is fitted with a mathematical model that is optimal in the sense that it assigns smaller errors to history than any other model. The type of model must be identified and the parameters then estimated. This is apparently the most accurate statistical routine presently available but also one of the most costly and time-consuming ones.	This technique fits a trend line to a mathematical equation and then projects it into the future by means of this equation. There are several variations: the slope-characteristic method, polynomials, logarithms, and so on.
Poor to good Poor Very poor	Fair to very good Poor to good Very poor	Very good to excellent Poor to good Very poor	Very good Good Good
Poor	Poor	Fair	Poor
Inventory control for low volume items.	Production and inventory control, forecasts of margins and other financial data.	Production and inventory control for large-volume items, forecasts of cash balances.	New-product forecasts (particularly intermediate- and long-term).
A minimum of two years of sales history, if seasonals are present. Otherwise, less data. (Of course, the more history the better.) The moving average must be specified.	The same as for a moving average.	The same as for a moving average. However, in this case more history is very advantageous in model identification.	Varies with the technique used. However, a good rule of thumb is to use a minimum of five years' annual data to start. Thereafter, the complete history.
$0.005	$0.005	$10.00	Varies with application
Yes	Yes	Yes	Yes
1 day—	1 day—	1-2 days	1 day—
Hadley, *Introduction to Business Statistics* (San Francisco, Holden-Day, Inc., 1968).	Brown, "Less Risk in Inventory Estimates," HBR July-August 1959, p. 104.	Box-Jenkins, *Time Series Analysis, Forecasting & Control* (San Francisco, Holden-Day, Inc., 1970).	Hadley, *Introduction to Business Statistics* (San Francisco, Holden-Day, Inc., 1968); Oliver & Boyd, "Techniques of Production Control," Imperial Chemical Industries, 1964.

Technique	C. Causal methods		
	1. Regression model	2. Econometric model	3. Intention to buy and anticipation surveys
Description	This functionally relates sales to other economic, competitive, or internal variables and estimates an equation using the least-squares technique. Relationships are primarily analyzed statistically, although any relationship should be selected for testing on a rational ground.	An econometric model is a system of interdependent regression equations that describes some sector of economic sales or profit activity. The parameters of the regression equations are usually estimated simultaneously. As a rule, these models are relatively expensive to develop and can easily cost between $5,000 and $10,000, depending on detail. However, due to the system of equations inherent in such models, they will better express the causalities involved than an ordinary regression equation and hence will predict turning points more accurately.	These surveys of the general public (a) determine intentions to buy certain products or (b) derive an index that measures general feeling about the present and the future and estimates how this feeling will affect buying habits. These approaches to forecasting are more useful for tracking and warning than forecasting. The basic problem in using them is that a turning point may be signaled incorrectly (and hence never occur).
Accuracy Short term (0-3 months) Medium term (3 months 2 years) Long term (2 years and up)	Good to very good Good to very good Poor	Good to very good Very good to excellent Good	Poor to good Poor to good Very poor
Identification of turning points	Very good	Excellent	Good
Typical applications	Forecasts of sales by product classes, forecasts of margins.	Forecasts of sales by product classes, forecasts of margins.	Forecasts of sales by product class.
Data required	Several years' quarterly history to obtain good, meaningful relationships. Mathematically necessary to have two more observations than there are independent variables.	The same as for regression.	Several years' data are usually required to relate such indexes to company sales.
Cost of forecasting in 1971 dollars* With a computer Is calculation possible without a computer?	$100 Yes	$5,000+ Yes	$5,000 Yes
Time required to develop an application and make a forecast	Depends on ability to identify relationships.	2 months+	Several weeks
References	Clelland, de Cani, Brown, Bush & Murray, *Basic Statistics with Business Applications* (New York, John Wiley & Sons, Inc., 1966).	Evans, *Macro-economic Activity: Theory, Forecasting & Control* (New York, Harper & Row Publishers, Inc., 1969).	Publications of Survey Research Center, Institute for Social Research, University of Michigan; and of Bureau of the Census.

*These estimates are based on our own experience, using this machine configuration: an IBM 360-40, 256 K system and a Univac 1108 Time-Sharing System, together with such smaller equipment as G.E. Time-sharing and IBM 360-30's and 1130's.

C. Causal methods		
4. Input-output model	5. Leading indicator	6. Life-cycle analysis
A method of analysis concerned with the interindustry or interdepartmental flow of goods or services in the economy or a company and its markets. It shows what flows of inputs must occur to obtain certain outputs. Considerable effort must be expended to use these models properly, and additional detail, not normally available, must be obtained if they are to be applied to specific businesses. Corporations using input-output models have expended as much as $100,000 and more annually to develop useful applications.	A time series of an economic activity whose movement in a given direction precedes the movement of some other time series in the same direction is a leading indicator.	This is an analysis and forecasting of new-product growth rates based on *S*-curves. The phases of product acceptance by the various groups such as innovators, early adapters, early majority, late majority, and laggards are central to the analysis.
Not applicable Good to very good Good to very good	Poor to good Poor to good Very poor	Poor Poor to good Poor to good
Fair	Good	Poor to good
Forecasts of company sales and division sales for industrial sectors and subsectors.	Forecasts of sales by product class.	Forecasts of new-product sales.
Ten or fifteen years' history. Considerable amounts of information on product and service flows within a corporation (or economy) for each year for which an input-output analysis is desired.	The same as an intention-to-buy survey + 5 to 10 years' history.	As a minimum, the annual sales of the produce being considered or of a similar product. It is often necessary to do market surveys.
$50,000+	$1,000	$1,500
No	Yes	Yes
6 months+	1 month+	1 month+
Leontief, *Input-Output Economics* (New York, Oxford University Press, 1966).	Evans, *Macro-economic Activity: Theory, Forecasting & Control* (New York, Harper & Row Publishers, Inc., 1969).	Bass, "A New Product Growth Model for Consumer Durables," *Management Science*, January 1969.

A future like the past: It is obvious from this description that all statistical techniques are based on the assumption that existing patterns will continue into the future. This assumption is more likely to be correct over the short term than it is over the long term, and for this reason these techniques provide us with reasonably accurate forecasts for the immediate future but do quite poorly further into the future (unless the data patterns are extraordinarily stable).

For this same reason, these techniques ordinarily *cannot* predict when the rate of growth in a trend will change significantly—for example, when a period of slow growth in sales will suddenly change to a period of rapid decay.

Such points are called *turning points.* They are naturally of the greatest consequence to the manager, and, as we shall see, the forecaster must use different tools from pure statistical techniques to predict when they will occur.

CAUSAL MODELS   When historical data are available and enough analysis has been performed to spell out explicitly the relationships between the factor to be forecast and other factors (such as related businesses, economic forces, and socioeconomic factors), the forecaster often constructs a *causal model.*

A causal model is the most sophisticated kind of forecasting tool. It expresses mathematically the relevant causal relationships, and may include pipeline considerations (i.e., inventories) and market survey information. It may also directly incorporate the results of a time series analysis. . . .

If certain kinds of data are lacking, initially it may be necessary to make assumptions about some of the relationships and then track what is happening to determine if the assumptions are true. Typically, a causal model is continually revised as more knowledge about the system becomes available.

Again, see the [chart on pp. 36-39] for a rundown on the most common types of causal techniques. As the chart shows, causal models are by far the best for predicting turning points and preparing long-range forecasts.

methods, products & the life cycle

At each stage of the life of a product, from conception to steady-state sales, the decisions that management must make are characteristically quite different, and they require different kinds of information as a base. The forecasting techniques that provide these sets of information differ analogously. *Exhibit [II]* summarizes the life stages of a product, the typi-

exhibit [II] . . . types of decisions made over a product's life cycle, with related forecasting techniques

Stage of life cycle	Product development	Market testing & early introduction	Rapid growth	Steady state	Phase Out
Typical decisions	Amount of development effort Product design Business strategies	Optimum facility size Marketing strategies, including distribution & pricing	Facilities expansion Marketing strategies Production planning	Promotions, specials Pricing Production planning Inventories	
Forecasting techniques	Delphi method Historical analysis of comparable products . . . Input-output analysis Panel concensus	Consumer surveys . . . Market tests . . .	Statistical techniques for identifying turning points . . . Market surveys Intention-to-buy surveys	Time series analysis & projection Causal & econometric models Market surveys . . . Life-cycle analysis	

Sales

cal decisions made at each, and the main forecasting techniques suitable at each.

Equally, different products may require different kinds of forecasting. Two CGW products that have been handled quite differently are the major glass components for color TV tubes, of which Corning is a prime supplier, and CORNING WARE® cookware, a proprietary consumer product line. We shall trace the forecasting methods used at each of the four different stages of maturity of these products to give some firsthand insight into the choice and application of some of the major techniques available today.

Before we begin, let us note how the situations differ for the two kinds of products:

- For a consumer product like the cookware, the manufacturer's control of the distribution pipeline extends at least through the distributor level. Thus he can affect or control consumer sales quite directly, as well as directly control some of the pipeline elements.

  Many of the changes in shipment rates and in overall profitability are therefore due to actions taken by the manufacturer himself. Tactical decisions on promotions, specials, and pricing are usually at his discretion as well. The technique selected by the forecaster for projecting sales therefore should permit incorporation of such "special information." One may have to start with simple techniques and work up to more sophisticated ones that embrace such possibilities, but the final goal is there.

- Where the manager's company supplies a component to [an original equipment manufacturer], as Corning does for tube manufacturers, the company does not have such direct influence or control over either the pipeline elements or final consumer sales. It may be impossible for the company to obtain good information about what is taking place at points further along the flow system . . . and, in consequence, the forecaster will necessarily be using a different genre of forecasting from that he uses for a consumer product.

Between these two examples, our discussion will embrace nearly the whole range of forecasting techniques. As necessary, however, we shall touch on other products and other forecasting methods.

1. product development

In the early stages of product development, the manager wants answers to questions such as these:

- What are the alternative growth opportunities to pursuing product X?

- How have established products similar to X fared?
- Should *we* enter this business; and if so, in what segments?
- How should we allocate R&D efforts and funds?
- How successful will different product concepts be?
- How will product X fit into the markets five or ten years from now? . . .

A common objection to much long-range forecasting is that it is virtually impossible to predict with accuracy what will happen several years into the future. We agree that uncertainty increases when a forecast is made for a period more than two years out. However, at the very least, the forecast and a measure of its accuracy enable the manager to know his risks in pursuing a selected strategy and in this knowledge to choose an appropriate strategy from those available.

Systematic market research is, of course, a mainstay in this area. For example, priority pattern analysis can describe the consumer's preferences and the likelihood he will buy a product, and thus is of great value in forecasting (and updating) penetration levels and rates. But there are other tools as well, depending on the state of the market and the product concept.

FOR A DEFINED MARKET   While there can be no direct data about a product that is still a gleam in the eye, information about its likely performance can be gathered in a number of ways, provided the market in which it is to be sold is a known entity.

. . . one can compare a proposed product with competitors' present and planned products, ranking it on quantitative scales for different factors . . . .

If this approach is to be successful, it is essential that the (in-house) experts who provide the basic data come from different disciplines—marketing, R&D, manufacturing, legal, and so on—and that their opinions be unbiased . . . .

[Also], one can compare a projected product with an "ancestor" that has similar characteristics. In 1965, we disaggregated the market for color television by income levels and geographical regions and compared these submarkets with the historical pattern of black-and-white TV market growth. We justified this procedure by arguing that color TV represented an advance over black-and-white analogous to (although less intense than) the advance that black-and-white TV represented over radio. The analyses of black-and-white TV market growth also enabled us to estimate the variability to be expected—that is, the degree to which our projections would differ from actual as the result of economic and other factors . . . .

Our predictions of consumer acceptance of CORNING WARE® cookware, on the other hand, were derived primarily from one expert source, a manager who thoroughly understood consumer preferences and the housewares market. These predictions have been well borne out. This reinforces our belief that sales forecasts for a new product that will compete in an existing market are bound to be incomplete and uncertain unless one culls the best judgments of fully experienced personnel.

FOR AN UNDEFINED MARKET   Frequently, however, the market for a new product is weakly defined or few data are available, the product concept is still fluid, and history seems irrelevant. This is the case for gas turbines, electric and steam automobiles, modular housing, pollution measurement devices, and time-shared computer terminals.

Many organizations have applied the Delphi method of soliciting and consolidating experts' opinions under these circumstances. At CGW, in several instances, we have used it to estimate demand for such new products, with success . . . .

2. testing & introduction

Before a product can enter its (hopefully) rapid penetration stage, the market potential must be tested out and the product must be introduced —and then more market testing may be advisable. At this stage, management needs answers to these questions:

- What shall our marketing plan be—which markets should we enter and with what production quantities?
- How much manufacturing capacity will the early production stages require?
- As demand grows, where should we build this capacity?
- How shall we allocate our R&D resources over time?

Significant profits depend on finding the right answers, and it is therefore economically feasible to expend relatively large amounts of effort and money on obtaining good forecasts, short-, medium-, and long-range.

A sales forecast at this stage should provide three points of information: the date when rapid sales will begin, the rate of market penetration during the rapid-sales stage, and the ultimate level of penetration, or sales rate, during the steady-state stage.

USING EARLY DATA   The date when a product will enter the rapid-growth stage is hard to predict three or four years in advance (the usual horizon). A company's only recourse is to use statistical tracking methods to check on how successfully the product is being introduced, along with routine market studies to determine when there has been a significant increase in the sales rate.

Furthermore, the greatest care should be taken in analyzing the early sales data that start to accumulate once the product has been introduced into the market. For example, it is important to distinguish between sales to *innovators*, who will try anything new, and sales to *imitators*, who will buy a product only after it has been accepted by innovators, for it is the latter group that provides demand stability. Many new products have initially appeared successful because of purchases by innovators, only to fail later in the stretch.

Tracking the two groups means market research, possibly via opinion panels. A panel ought to contain both innovators and imitators, since innovators can teach one a lot about how to improve a product while imitators provide insight into the desires and expectations of the whole market.

The color TV set, for example, was introduced in 1954, but did not gain acceptance from the majority of consumers until late 1964. To be sure, the color TV set could not leave the introduction stage and enter the rapid-growth stage until the networks had substantially increased their color programming. However, special flag signals like "substantially increased network color programming" are likely to come after the fact, from the planning viewpoint; and in general, we find, scientifically designed consumer surveys conducted on a regular basis provide the earliest means of detecting turning points in the demand for a product.

SIMILAR-PRODUCT TECHNIQUE   Although statistical tracking is a useful tool during the early introduction stages, there are rarely sufficient data for statistical forecasting. Market research studies can naturally be useful, as we have indicated. But, more commonly, the forecaster tries to identify a similar, older product whose penetration pattern should be similar to that of the new product, since overall markets can and do exhibit consistent patterns.

Again, let's consider color television and the forecasts we prepared in 1965.

For the year 1947-1968, *Exhibit [III]* shows total consumer expenditures, appliance expenditures, expenditures for radios and TVs, and relevant percentages. Column 4 shows that total expenditures for appliances are relatively stable over periods of several years; hence, new appliances must compete with existing ones, especially during recessions (note the figures for 1948-1949, 1953-1954, 1957-1958, and 1960-1961).

Certain specific fluctuations in these figures are of special significance here. When black-and-white TV was introduced as a new product in 1948-1951, the ratio of expenditures on radio and TV sets to total expenditures for consumer goods (see column 7) increased about 33% (from 1.23% to 1.63%), as against a modest increase of only 13% (from 1.63% to 1.88%) in the ratio for the next decade. (A similar increase of 33% occurred in 1962-1966 as color TV made its major penetration.)

exhibit [III] . . . expenditures on appliances versus all consumer goods

[in billions of dollars]

Year (1)	All consumer goods* (2)	Household appliances† (3)	Radio, TV & other† (4)	Totals of columns 3 & 4 (5)	Column 5 ÷ Column 2 (6)	Column 4 ÷ Column 2 (7)
1947	110.9	3.18	1.43	4.61	4.16%	1.29%
1948	118.9	3.47	1.48	4.95	4.16	1.23
1949	119.1	3.13	1.70	4.83	4.06	1.43
1950	128.6	3.94	2.46	6.40	4.98	1.91
1951	138.4	3.87	2.26	6.13	4.43	1.63
1952	143.3	3.82	2.37	6.19	4.32	1.65
1953	150.0	3.99	2.61	6.60	4.40	1.74
1954	151.1	4.02	2.74	6.77	4.48	1.81
1955	162.9	4.69	2.79	7.48	4.59	1.71
1956	168.2	4.89	2.87	7.76	4.61	1.71
1957	176.4	4.63	3.00	7.63	4.33	1.70
1958	178.1	4.44	3.07	7.51	4.22	1.72
1959	190.9	4.86	3.42	8.28	4.34	1.79
1960	196.6	4.74	3.62	8.36	4.25	1.84
1961	200.1	4.77	3.76	8.53	4.26	1.88
1962	212.1	5.01	3.94	8.95	4.22	1.86
1963	222.5	5.24	4.54	9.78	4.40	2.04
1964	237.9	5.74	5.41	11.15	4.69	2.27
1965	257.4	6.03	6.01	12.04	4.68	2.33
1966	277.7	6.77	6.91	13.68	4.93	2.49
1967	288.1	7.09	7.41	14.50	5.03	2.57
1968	313.9	7.80	7.85	15.65	4.99	2.50

*Data obtained from Survey of Current Business, Personal Consumption Expenditure Tables (U.S. Department of Commerce, July issues).

†Data obtained from the Survey of Business Statistics (U.S. Department of Commerce, 1969 Biennial Edition).

Probably, the acceptance of black-and-white TV as a major appliance in 1950 caused the ratio of all major household appliances to total consumer goods (see column 6) to rise to 4.98%; in other words, the innovation of TV caused the consumer to start spending more money on major appliances around 1950.

Our expectation in mid-1965 was that the introduction of color TV would induce a similar increase. Thus, although this product comparison did not provide us with an accurate or detailed forecast, it did place an upper bound on the future total sales we could expect.

The next step was to look at the cumulative penetration curve for black-and-white TVs in U.S. households, shown in *Exhibit [IV]*. We assumed color-TV penetration would have a similar *S*-curve, but that it would take longer for color sets to penetrate the whole market (that is, reach steady-state sales). Whereas it took black-and-white TV 10 years to reach steady state, qualitative expert-opinion studies indicated that it would take color twice that long—hence the more gradual slope of the color-TV curve.

At the same time, studies conducted in 1964 and 1965 showed significantly different penetration sales for color TV in various income groups, rates that were helpful to us in projecting the color-TV curve and tracking the accuracy of our projection.

With these data and assumptions, we forecast retail sales for the remainder of 1965 through mid-1970 (see the dotted section of the lower curve in *Exhibit [IV]*. The forecasts were accurate through 1966 but too high in the following three years, primarily because of declining general economic conditions and changing pricing policies.

We should note that when we developed these forecasts and techniques, we recognized that additional techniques would be necessary at later times to maintain the accuracy that would be needed in subsequent periods. These forecasts provided acceptable accuracy for the time they were made, however, since the major goal then was only to estimate the penetration rate and the ultimate, steady-state level of sales. Making refined estimates of how the manufacturing-distribution pipelines will behave is an activity that properly belongs to the next life-cycle stage . . . .

PREDICTING RAPID GROWTH   To estimate the date by which a product will enter the rapid-growth stage is another matter. As we have seen, this date is a function of many factors: the existence of a distribution system, customer acceptance of or familiarity with the product concept, the need met by the product, significant events (such as color network programming), and so on.

As well as by reviewing the behavior of similar products, the date may be estimated through Delphi exercises or through rating and ranking schemes, whereby the factors important to customer acceptance are estimated, each competitor product is rated on each factor, and an overall score is tallied for the competitor against a score for the new product.

As we have said, it is usually difficult to forecast precisely when the turning point will occur; and, in our experience, the best accuracy that can be expected is within three months to two years of the actual time.

It is occasionally true, of course, that one can be certain a new product will be enthusiastically accepted. Market tests and initial customer reaction made it clear there would be a large market for CORNING WARE® cookware. Since the distribution system was already in existence, the

exhibit [IV] . . . long-term household penetration curves for color and black-and-white TV

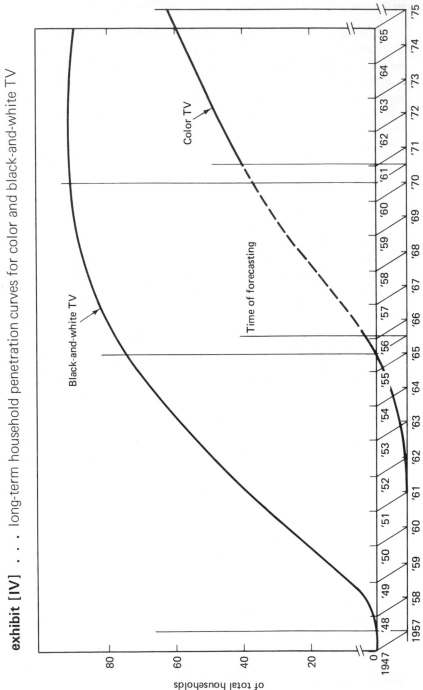

time required for the line to reach rapid growth depended primarily on our ability to manufacture it. Sometimes forecasting is merely a matter of calculating the company's capacity—but not ordinarily.

3. rapid growth

When a product enters this stage, the most important decisions relate to facilities expansion. These decisions generally involve the largest expenditures in the cycle (excepting major R&D decisions), and commensurate forecasting and tracking efforts are justified.

Forecasting and tracking must provide the executive with three kinds of data at this juncture:

- Firm verification of the *rapid-growth rate forecast* made previously.

- A hard date when sales will level to "normal," *steady-state growth.*

- For component products, the deviation in the growth curve that may be caused by characteristic *conditions along the pipeline*—for example, inventory blockages.

FORECASTING THE GROWTH RATE   Medium- and long-range forecasting of the market growth rate and of the attainment of steady-state sales requires the same measures as does the product introduction stage— detailed marketing studies (especially intention-to-buy surveys) and product comparisons . . . .

The growth rate for CORNING WARE® cookware, as we explained, was limited primarily by our production capabilities; and hence the basic information to be predicted in that case was the date of leveling growth. Because substantial inventories buffered information on consumer sales all along the line, good field data were lacking, which made this date difficult to estimate. Eventually we found it necessary to establish a better (more direct) field information system.

As well as merely buffering information, in the case of a component product, the pipeline exerts certain distorting effects on the manufacturer's demand; these effects, although highly important, are often illogically neglected in production or capacity planning.

SIMULATING THE PIPELINE   While the ware-in-process demand in the pipeline has an *S*-curve like that of retail sales, it may lag or lead sales by several months, distorting the shape of the demand on the component supplier.

Exhibit [V] shows the long-term trend of demand on a component supplier other than Corning as a function of distributor sales and distributor inventories. As one can see from this curve, supplier sales may grow relatively sharply for several months and peak before retail sales have leveled off. The implications of these curves for facilities planning and allocation are obvious . . . .

TRACKING & WARNING   This knowledge is not absolutely "hard," of course, and pipeline dynamics must be carefully tracked to determine if the various estimates and assumptions made were indeed correct. Statistical methods provide a good short-term basis for estimating and checking the growth rate and signaling when turning points will occur.

In late 1965 it appeared to us that the ware-in-process demand was increasing, since there was a consistent positive difference between actual TV bulb sales and forecasted bulb sales. Conversations with product managers and other personnel indicated there might have been a significant change in pipeline activity; it appeared that rapid increases in retail demand were boosting glass requirements for ware-in-process, which could create a hump in the *S*-curve like the one illustrated in *Exhibit [V]*. This humping provided additional profit for CGW in 1966 but had an adverse effect in 1967. We were able to predict this hump, but unfortunately we were unable to reduce or avoid it because the pipeline was not sufficiently under our control.

exhibit [V] . . . patterns for color-TV distributor sales, distributor inventories, and component sales

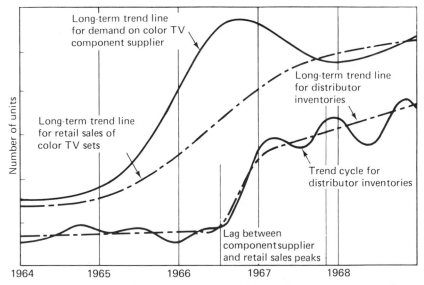

Note: Scales are different for component sales, distributor inventories, and distributor sales, with the patterns put on the same graph for illustrative purposes.

The inventories all along the pipeline also follow an *S*-curve (as shown in *Exhibit [V]*), a fact that creates and compounds two characteristic conditions in the pipeline as a whole: initial overfilling and subsequent shifts between too much and too little inventory at various points —a sequence of feast-and-famine conditions.

For example, the simpler distribution system for CORNING WARE® cookware had an *S*-curve like the ones we have examined. When the retail sales slowed from rapid to normal growth, however, there were no early indications from shipment data that this crucial turning point had been reached. Data on distributor inventories gave us some warning that the pipeline was overfilling, but the turning point at the retail level was still not identified quickly enough, as we have mentioned before, because of lack of good data at that level. We now monitor field information regularly to identify significant changes, and adjust our shipment forecasts accordingly.

MAIN CONCERNS   One main activity during the rapid-growth stage, then, is to check earlier estimates and, if they appear incorrect, to compute as accurately as possible the error in the forecast and obtain a revised estimate.

In some instances, models developed earlier will include only "macroterms"; in such cases, market research can provide information needed to break these down into their components. For example, the color-TV forecasting model initially considered only total set penetrations at different income levels, without considering the way in which the sets were being used. Therefore, we conducted market survey to determine set use more precisely.

Equally, during the rapid-growth stage, sub-models of pipeline segments should be expanded to incorporate more detailed information as it is received. In the case of color TV, we found we were able to estimate the overall pipeline requirements for glass bulbs, the CGW market-share factors, and glass losses, and to postulate a probability distribution around the most likely estimates. Over time, it was easy to check these forecasts against actual volume of sales, and hence to check on the procedures by which we were generating them.

We also found we had to increase the number of factors in the simulation model—for instance, we had to expand the model to consider different sizes of bulbs—and this improved our overall accuracy and usefulness . . . .

4. steady state

The decisions the manager makes at this stage are quite different from those he has made earlier. Most of the facilities planning has been squared away, and trends and growth rates have become reasonably stable. It is possible that swings in demand and profit will occur because of changing economic conditions, new and competitive products, pipeline dynamics, and so on, and the manager will have to maintain his tracking activities and even introduce new ones. However, by and large, he will concentrate his forecasting attention on these areas:

- Long- and short-term production planning.
- Setting standards to check the effectiveness of marketing strategies.
- Projections designed to aid profit planning.

He will also need a good tracking and warning system to identify significantly declining demand for the product (but hopefully that is a long way off).

To be sure, the manager will want margin and profit projection and long-range forecasts to assist planning at the corporate level. However, short- and medium-term sales forecasts are basic to these more elaborate undertakings, and we shall concentrate on sales forecasts.

ADEQUATE TOOLS AT HAND   In planning production and establishing marketing strategy for the short and medium term, the manager's first considerations are usually an accurate estimate of the present sales level and an accurate estimate of the rate at which this level is changing.

The forecaster thus is called on for two related contributions at this stage:

- He should provide estimates of *trends* and *seasonals*, which obviously affect the sales level. Seasonals are particularly important for both overall production planning and inventory control. To do this, he needs to apply time series analysis and projection techniques—that is, *statistical* techniques.
- He should relate the future sales level to factors that are more easily predictable, or have a "lead" relationship with sales, or both. To do this, he needs to build *causal models*.

The type of product under scrutiny is very important in selecting the techniques to be used.

For CORNING WARE® cookware, where the levels of the distribution system are organized in a relatively straightforward way, we use statistical methods to forecast shipments and field information to forecast changes in shipment rates. We are now in the process of incorporating special information—marketing strategies, economic forecasts, and so on—directly into the shipment forecasts. This is leading us in the direction of a causal forecasting model.

On the other hand, a component supplier may be able to forecast total sales with sufficient accuracy for broad-load production planning, but the pipeline environment may be so complex that his best recourse for short-term projections is to rely primarily on salesmen's estimates. We find this true, for example, in estimating the demand for TV glass by size and customer. In such cases, the best role for statistical methods is providing guides and checks for salesmen's forecasts.

In general, however, at this point in the life cycle, sufficient time series data are available and enough causal relationships are known from direct experience and market studies so that the forecaster can indeed apply these two powerful sets of tools. Historical data for at least the last several years should be available, and he will use all of it, one way or another.

We might mention a common criticism at this point. People frequently object to using more than a few of the most recent data points (such as sales figures in the immediate past) for building projections, since, they say, the current situation is always to dynamic and conditions are changing so radically and quickly that historical data from further back in time have little or no value.

We think this point of view has little validity. A graph of several years' sales data, such as the one shown in *Part A* of *Exhibit [VI]* gives an impression of a sales trend one could not possibly get if one were to look only at two or three of the latest data points.

In practice, we find, overall patterns tend to continue for a minimum of one or two quarters into the future, even when special conditions cause sales to fluctuate for one or two (monthly) periods in the immediate future.

For short-term forecasting for one to three months ahead, the effects of such factors as general economic conditions are minimal, and do *not* cause radical shifts in demand patterns. And because trends tend to change gradually rather than suddenly, statistical and other quantitative methods are excellent for short-term forecasting. Using one or only a few of the most recent data points will result in giving insufficient consideration of the nature of trends, cycles, and seasonal fluctuations in sales.

Granting the applicability of the techniques, we must go on to explain how the forecaster identifies precisely what is happening when sales fluctuate from one period to the next and how he forecasts such fluctuations.

SORTING TRENDS & SEASONALS   A trend and a seasonal are obviously two quite different things, and they must be handled separately in forecasting.

Consider what would happen, for example, if a forecaster were merely to take an average of the most recent data points along a curve, combine this with other, similar average points stretching backward into the immediate past, and use these as the basis for a projection. He might

exhibit [VI] . . . data plots of factory sales of color TV sets

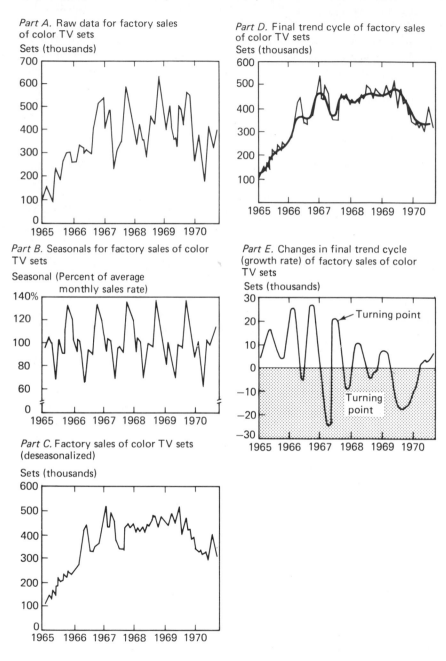

Part A. Raw data for factory sales of color TV sets

Sets (thousands)

Part B. Seasonals for factory sales of color TV sets

Seasonal (Percent of average monthly sales rate)

Part C. Factory sales of color TV sets (deseasonalized)

Sets (thousands)

Part D. Final trend cycle of factory sales of color TV sets

Sets (thousands)

Part E. Changes in final trend cycle (growth rate) of factory sales of color TV sets

Sets (thousands)

Turning point

Turning point

easily overreact to random changes, mistaking them for evidence of a pre-
vailing trend, he might mistake a change in the growth rate for a seasonal;
and so on.

To avoid precisely this sort of error, the moving average technique,
which is similar to the hypothetical one just described, uses data points
in such a way that the effects of seasonals (and irregularities) are eliminated.

Furthermore, the executive needs accurate estimates of trends *and*
accurate estimates of seasonality to plan broad-load production, to determine marketing efforts and allocations, and to maintain proper inventories—that is, inventories that are adequate to customer demand but are
not excessively costly.

Before going any further, it might be well to illustrate what such
sorting-out looks like. *Parts A, B,* and *C* of *Exhibit [VI]* show the initial
decomposition of raw data for factory sales of color TV sets between
1965 and mid-1970. *Part A* presents the raw data curve. *Part B* shows the
seasonal factors that are implicit in the raw data—quite a consistent pattern, although there is some variation from year to year. (In the next section we shall explain where this graph of the seasonals comes from.)

Part C shows the result of discounting the raw data curve by the seasonals of *Part B*; this is the so-called deseasonalized data curve. Next, in
Part D, we have drawn the smoothest or "best" curve possible through
the deseasonalized curve, thereby obtaining the *trend cycle*. (We might
further note that the differences between this trend-cycle line and the deseasonalized data curve represent the irregular or nonsystematic component that the forecaster must always tolerate and attempt to explain
by other methods.)

In sum, then, the objective of the forecasting technique used here is
to do the best possible job of sorting out trends and seasonalities. Unfortunately, most forecasting methods project by a smoothing process
analogous to that of the moving average technique, or like that of the
hypothetical technique we described at the beginning of this section, and
separating trends and seasonals more precisely will require extra effort
and cost.

Still, sorting-out approaches have proved themselves in practice. We
can best explain the reasons for their success by roughly outlining the
way we construct a sales forecast on the basis of trends, seasonals, and
data derived from them. This is the method:

• Graph the rate at which the trend is changing. For the illustration
given in *Exhibit [VI]* this graph is shown in *Part E*. This graph
describes the successive ups and downs of the trend cycle shown in
Part D.

- Project his growth rate forward over the interval to be forecasted. Assuming we were forecasting back in mid-1970, we should be projecting into the summer months and possibly into the early fall.

- Add this growth rate (whether positive or negative) to the present sales rate. This might be called the unseasonalized sales rate.

- Project the seasonals of *Part B* for the period in question, and multiply the unseasonalized forecasted rate by these seasonals. The product will be the forecasted sales rate, which is what we desired.

In special cases where there are no seasonals to be considered, of course, this process is much simplified, and fewer data and simpler techniques may be adequate.

We have found that an analysis of the patterns of change in the growth rate gives us more accuracy in predicting turning points (and therefore changes from positive to negative growth, and vice versa) than when we use only the trend cycle.

The main advantage of considering growth change, in fact, is that it is frequently possible to predict earlier when a no-growth situation will occur. The graph of change in growth thus provides an excellent visual base for forecasting and for identifying the turning point as well . . . .

forecasting in the future

In concluding an article on forecasting, it is appropriate that we make a prediction about the techniques that will be used in the short- and long-term future.

As we have already said, it is not too difficult to forecast the immediate future, since long-term trends do not change overnight. Many of the techniques described are only in the early stages of application, but still we expect most of the techniques that will be used in the next five years to be the ones discussed here, perhaps in extended form.

The costs of using these techniques will be reduced significantly; this will enhance their implementation. We expect that computer time-sharing companies will offer access, at nominal cost, to input-output data banks, broken down into more business segments than are available today. The continuing declining trend in computer cost per computation, along with computational simplifications, will make techniques such as the Box-Jenkins method economically feasible, even for some inventory-control applications. Computer software packages for the statistical techniques and some general models will also become available at a nominal cost.

At the present time, most short-term forecasting uses only statistical methods, with little qualitative information. Where qualitative information is used, it is only used in an external way and is not directly incorporated into the computational routine. We predict a change to total forecasting systems, where several techniques are tied together, along with a systematic handling of qualitative information . . . .

. . . Although the forecasting techniques have thus far been used primarily for sales forecasting, they will be applied increasingly to forecasting margins, capital expenditures, and other important factors. This will free the forecaster to spend most of his time forecasting sales and profits of new products. Doubtless, new analytical techniques will be developed for new-product forecasting, but there will be a continuing problem, for at least 10 to 20 years and probably much longer, in accurately forecasting various new-product factors, such as sales, profitability, and length of life cycle.

final word

The decision maker can help the forecaster formulate the forecasting problem properly, and he will have more confidence in the forecasts provided to him and use them more effectively, if he understands the basic features and limitations of the techniques. The forecaster, for his part, must blend the techniques he uses with the knowledge and experience of the managers.

The need today, we believe, is not for better forecasting methods, but for better application of the techniques at hand.

questions

1. List as many considerations as you can that might affect the choice of forecasting techniques by a local company familiar to you.

2. What is meant by forecasting "strategy"?

3. Explain the difference between the mean absolute deviation and the mean square error as criteria for judging the accuracy of a forecasting technique for a particular set of data.

4. If a company produces a "faddish" line of sporting goods equipment, how would its forecasting strategy differ from that of another company producing aluminum beverage containers?

5. In what situations would the identification of an underlying pattern in a set of historical data be of tremendous help to a forecaster?

6. If a graphical plot of cumulative forecast error results in large swings from negative errors to positive errors and has an average error near zero, what does this tell you about your forecasting technique?

7. Explain how the different stages of a product's life cycle will influence the choice of a forecasting strategy.

chapter 4 . . . forecasting based on regression techniques

introduction

A problem that is encountered in almost every field of study involves prediction of the value of a *response variable* from other known, related variables. When an individual without any background in forecasting attempts to use historical, numerical data to make a forecast, he will usually try to fit a curve to his data. This amounts to visually examining a graph of the data and then attempting to sketch a line through the data so that the error (mean absolute deviation or mean square error) is minimized. Regression is a statistical method of fitting a line through data to minimize squared error. It is exact whereas sketching is usually only an approximation. With linear regression, statistics can be used to obtain a forecast and a confidence interval for the forecast. For example, a forecaster who has used regression can forecast sales for a particular product for the next month to be $425,000 and can also state that he is 95% confident that actual sales will be between $390,000 and $460,000. This assumes that basic market conditions will remain the same.

Confidence intervals for least-square equations are useful in identifying a change in the trend of a set of data. If two or three consecutive observations fall outside these limits, the manager can be fairly confident that the basic relationship has changed since the historical data were gathered. This information may prove financially valuable by enabling the manager to react quickly to a change in trend. If the trend changes, however, the forecaster is advised to discard all data regarding the previous trend. This usually leaves the forecaster with an insufficient number of data to develop a new regression equation, and other forecasting techniques may have to be utilized.

In this chapter we consider these least-squares methods: simple linear regression, multiple linear regression, and nonlinear regression. The calculations for simple linear regression, which is the most commonly used regression technique, can easily be performed manually. However, the calculations for multiple linear and nonlinear regression are tedious to perform manually. Most computer centers have numerous software packages capable of executing all regression techniques described in this chapter. The forecaster should not apply these computer programs to a set of data without understanding what type of information they produce and how. Blindly supplying data to a computer frequently leads to disappointing results.

One of the limitations of regression is that numerous data points are required to develop a reliable forecast. The actual number required depends on the nature of the data and the economics of the situation. In general, a minimum of from 20 to 50 historical observations is desirable.

assumptions of regression

The objective of regression is to estimate the equation of a line through a set of data that minimizes the sum of the squared differences between the actual data and the line. To illustrate this, Figure 4-1 shows a linear equation that has been fit to a set of data. In this example our approximation is linear, i.e.,

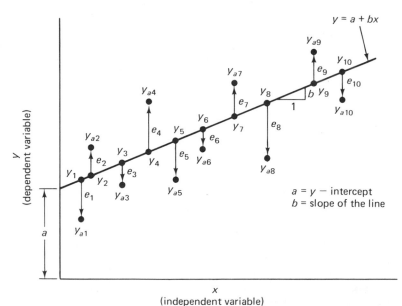

figure 4-1 . . . the regression relationship

$$y = a + bx$$

where a is the value of the equation when $x = 0$, and y increases b units for each one unit increase in x. *The actual response has been indicated by* y_a, *whereas* y *indicates the estimate calculated with the equation.* At a particular point, the actual response is represented by

$$y_{ai} = a + bx_i + e_i$$

where e_i is the difference between the actual data point, y_{ai}, and the point estimated by the equation. The term "e" is often referred to as the "residual." For n data points regression minimizes the value of total squared error:

$$\sum_{i-1}^{n} e_i^2 = e_1^2 + e_2^2 + e_3^2 + ---- + e_n^2$$

There are certain properties the e_i values must have before a regression equation can be considered valid in a statistical sense. Four of the most important properties are listed here:

1.   The average value of e_i must be zero, or near zero. (If an e_i is above the line, it is positive; if below it is negative.)

$$\frac{\Sigma e_i}{n} \approx 0$$

2.   The e_i values must be random. If the forecaster can find any pattern in the e_i values that can be used to predict future e_i values, they are not random. (Non-randomness often occurs when regression methods are applied to time-series data.)

3.   The e_i values must be distributed according to a normal, or Gaussian, probability model. In general if the majority of the data points are relatively close to the equation with a few scattered at slightly greater distances and the data are symmetrically scattered about the equation, this assumption will be satisfied.

4.   The variance of e_i about the equation must be constant. There cannot be a wide dispersion in residuals at one extreme of the equation (e.g., the lower end of the regression line) and very little dispersion about the equation at the other extreme.

the correct use of regression for forecasting

Regression is a valuable forecasting tool that can easily be misused. The objective of this discussion is to enable the reader to recognize different types of situations in which regression is helpful and to bring to your attention

CASE I Time independent causal data

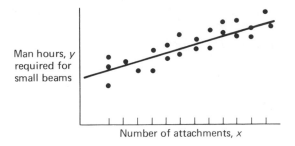

Man hours, *y*
required for
small beams

Number of attachments, *x*

CASE II Time lag causal data

Quarterly
carpet
sales, *y*
(square
yards)

Previous quarter's building
permits, *x*

CASE III Time-series

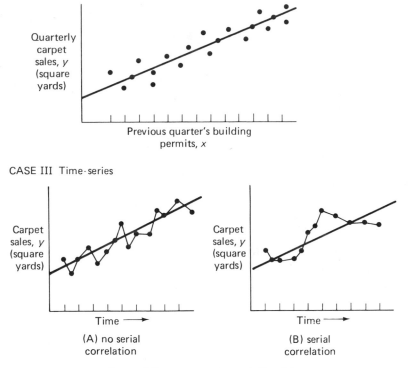

Carpet
sales, *y*
(square
yards)

Time ⟶

(A) no serial
correlation

Carpet
sales, *y*
(square
yards)

Time ⟶

(B) serial
correlation

figure 4-2 . . . regression relationships

some limitations of regression in forecasting. Regression applications are grouped into three cases for this purpose.

CASE I–TIME INDEPENDENT CAUSAL RELATIONSHIPS   An example of this use of regression is given by a steel company that is attempting to forecast man-hours of work in a proposed job so that a competitive contract can be bid on. The company has gathered data on man-hours of shop time expended as a function of the number of attachments for three different sizes of beams. An example plot of these data for small beams is shown in Figure 4-2 (Case I). There would be similar plots for medium and large beams. The forecaster determines the number of beams of each size (small, medium and large). For each small beam, he then estimates the man-hours of work content as a function of the attachments required on that beam. He repeats this process for the other sized beams and totals all of his estimates to prepare a final bid based on man-hours of work required.

In this case the data should be time-independent. If the number of attachments had increased over time and man-hours had increased because of additions of inexperienced personnel, then the data would be time-dependent and not as useful in making accurate forecasts with regression. If the observations had been gathered over a time period in which the number of attachments varied randomly and the quality of the work force had not changed, this application of regression would produce valid results.

The forecaster must exercise judgment to decide if a valid causal relationship or association exists between his variables. If both variables simultaneously increase (or decrease), the forecaster should be skeptical of the relationship because the variables may be dependent on a third variable not included in the equation. Large increases *and* decreases occurring simultaneously in both the measured indicator (x variable) and the response (y variable) are indicative of a good relationship.

In this example the response, man-hours, is expected to be caused by the indicator, number of attachments. (Refer to Figure 4-2.) Regression is also valid if there is a strong association between variables. For example, the number of telephones and the number of televisions in a community could be shown to be directly related by using regression, but there is no causal relationship between these two variables. In this case, it is recommended that the forecaster continue to search for an appropriate causal relationship. For instance, personal income of the community might be examined to determine if it is a better indicator for predicting the number of television sets.

In short, if a forecaster can identify a causal relationship that he believes to be time-independent and convenient for his purposes, then he should utilize it. Of course, the basic assumptions of regression must be satisfied, and *the results are valid over the interval of data observation and for the particular situation being investigated.* If Community X has more telephones per household than other communities studied from which the equation was derived, the regression equation is, at best, a crude approximation for making forecasts in Community X. At worst, it is completely useless for developing forecasts.

CASE II–TIME LAG CAUSAL RELATIONSHIPS   An example of this relationship is a carpet manufacturer who finds that his carpet sales in any quarter are related to the number of building permits for residential housing issued in the previous quarter for his marketing region. An example plot of this situation is shown in Figure 4-2 (Case II). It is important to note that here the independent variable (building permits) *leads* the dependent variable (carpet sales) by one quarter. A good discussion of leading indicators of national economic activity is provided in Appendix A.

Many of the comments made about Case I relationships are applicable here. The forecaster should determine if carpet sales and building permits have increased with general economic trends, or if there is a true causal relationship. Have there been accompanying increases and decreases in carpet sales and building permits over the period of observation? In many companies, advertising expenditures can be related to subsequent sales, but this could occur because increased sales have resulted in a decision to spend more money on advertising in hopes of further stimulating sales. The forecaster must satisfy himself that his indicator and forecasted response are causal or are so strongly associated that an increase or decrease in the indicator will be accompanied by a proportional change in the response. The previously noted assumptions of regression must be satisfied in this case, and again the relationship is valid only over the interval of observed data.

Causal relationships are valuable for making short-term forecasts since they can be used to predict future turning points in present trends. Success in basing forecasts on causal relationships depends on the wisdom and insight of the forecaster in identifying the best indicators for the desired response variable. Because causal relationships can be such an important part of a forecasting strategy and because they illustrate the ingenuity of some forecasters, they deserve special comment here. The successful use of causal relationships requires imagination and knowledge of the problem area to identify suitable predictors that can be quantified.

For example, a company manufacturing aluminum beverage containers attempts to forecast its annual sales of beer cans with an equation that relates sales to disposable income levels, number of drinking establishments per thousand persons, and age distribution of the population. In other instances, a pharmaceutical company has been successful at correlating its sales to national disposable income, and a manufacturer of televisions, radios, and phonographs considered more than 300 economic variables in determining a few that are good predictors of its sales. A meat-packing company predicts the number of cattle to be slaughtered in coming months by examining grazing conditions and ratios of the price of beef to the price of corn.

CASE III–TIME-SERIES RELATIONSHIP   An example of forecasting by using regression methods applied to time-series data is the carpet manufacturer who uses his previous quarterly carpet sales data to predict future sales more than one quarter into the future. Example plots of these data are shown in Figure 4-2 (Case III). Attempting to forecast with time-series data by using regression can lead to serious errors in the interpretation of results. This approach, however, is fairly common and is often referred to as *trend projection* or *trend analysis*. (Several examples of trend analysis are presented in Chapter 7.)

Referring to Case III(A) of Figure 4-2, the data satisfy the basic assumptions of regression. These data are randomly distributed about the line; there is no pattern to enable the forecaster to predict the next point. A pattern in the data about the regression line is referred to as *serial correlation*. Such an influence is definitely present in Case III(B) of Figure 4-2, for it is apparent that the data are *not* random. By examining this plot of data, a forecaster would not expect the next observation to lie above the line. There is a pattern in the data that allows the analyst to make a more accurate forecast than he could with regression by simply taking the last observation and adding or subtracting a small amount to it. A discussion of this general situation and an example problem are included in Appendix B where tests for serial correlation are presented. This appendix illustrates the application of the Von-Neuman test statistic and the Durbin-Watson test statistic to check for serial correlation in data.

When regression is used to forecast a time-series, the forecaster faces the question of whether to recalculate his equation when a new data point is obtained in each time period. If the forecaster decides to recalculate the regression equation every time he gets a new data point, a large volume of calculations is required (assuming forecasts are desired on a routine basis). If he does not recalculate the regression equation with every new data point, he is failing to use potentially valuable information in making forecasts. In addition, relatively large amounts of data must be stored with this procedure. If a large number of forecasts must be made, the economics of making calculations and storing data can become unfavorable to the use of regression.

Regression methods discussed in this chapter give every data point exactly the same weight. In our example, carpet sales in the first quarter of the year, five years ago, is weighted the same as that in the previous quarter. This is perhaps the major shortcoming in applying regression to historical time-series data. The exponential smoothing techniques covered in Chapter 5 typically place more emphasis on current data and less on data of the distant past. They also require fewer calculations and less storage of data. In general, moving averages and exponential smoothing techniques are more suitable for forecasting time-series relationships than regression is.

simple linear regression

In simple linear regression, the relationship that is used to fit the "n" data points ($1 \leqslant i \leqslant n$) is a linear equation in one variable:

$$y = a + bx$$

If the forecaster believes there is more than one independent variable that would be appropriate for making a more accurate forecast, he should consider multiple linear regression. Or if the trend line is not linear, then it may be advisable to apply nonlinear regression to the data. Both of these topics are treated later in this chapter.

A mathematical statement of expressions used to estimate "a" and "b" in the simple linear regression equation above is followed by an example that demonstrates the technique.

The parameters (a and b) of the above equation can be estimated as follows. (A summation over x_i, for example, is indicated by $\sum\limits_{i=1}^{n} x_i$ and equals $x_1 + x_2 + ---- + x_i + ---- + x_n$.)

$$b = \frac{\sum x_i y_{ai} - \overline{x} \sum y_{ai}}{\sum x_i^2 - \overline{x} \sum x_i}$$

$$a = \overline{y}_a - b\overline{x}$$

Here $\overline{x}$ and $\overline{y}_a$ are averages of the independent variable and dependent variable, respectively, for the n data points.

To calculate a confidence interval for our forecast, we must obtain the standard deviation of a single estimated value, $S(y)$. This quantity is a measure of the tightness of the individual data points about the regression line,

$$S(y) = \left[\frac{\sum (y_{ai} - y_i)^2}{n-2} \right]^{\frac{1}{2}} \cdot \left[1 + \frac{1}{n} + \frac{(x_0 - \overline{x})^2}{\sum (x_i - \overline{x})^2} \right]^{\frac{1}{2}}$$

Here x_0 is a value of the independent variable being used to obtain the forecast, y, and it lies in the range of observed x_i (i.e., $x_{min} \leqslant x_0 \leqslant x_{max}$):

$$y = a + bx_0$$

The 100 $(1 - \alpha)$ percent confidence interval for the forecast is defined to be:

$$y + (t_{\alpha/2,\, n-2})\, S(y) \qquad\qquad \text{(upper limit)}$$

to

$$y - (t_{\alpha/2,\, n-2})\, S(y) \qquad\qquad \text{(lower limit)}$$

The term, $t_{\alpha/2,\, n-2}$, is an appropriate value of the t-statistic. A table of t-values and instructions for using this table are given in Appendix C. For a 95% confidence interval ($\alpha = 0.05$, $\alpha/2 = 0.025$) and for n data points, there are $n - 2$ degrees of freedom. This means that with repeated forecasts involving n data points, approximately 95% of the confidence intervals calculated with the above equation will contain the true value of the response variable if the underlying causal relationship does not change.

example

A carpet manufacturer has found residential building permits in a given quarter to be strongly related to his carpet sales in the following quarter. These data are listed and summarized in Table 4-1 and plotted in Figure 4-3.

table 4-1 . . . calculations for simple linear regression

y_a = quarterly carpet sales (1000's sq. ft)

x = building permits in preceding quarter

Data Point i ($1 \leqslant i \leqslant n$)	y_{ai}	x_i	$x_i y_{ai}$	x_i^2
1	360	121	43,560	14,641
2	260	118	30,680	13,924
3	440	271	119,240	73,441
4	400	190	76,000	36,100
5	360	75	27,000	5,625
6	500	263	131,500	69,169
7	580	334	193,720	111,556
8	560	368	206,080	135,424
9	505	305	154,025	93,025
10	480	210	100,800	44,100
11	602	387	232,974	149,769
12	540	270	145,800	72,900
13	415	218	90,470	47,524
14	590	342	201,780	116,964
15	492	173	85,116	29,929
16	660	370	244,200	136,900
17	360	170	61,200	28,900
18	410	205	84,050	42,025
19	680	339	230,520	114,921
20	594	283	168,102	80,089
Totals	9,788	5,012	2,626,817	1,416,926

$$\Sigma x_i = 5,012 \qquad \Sigma y_{ai} = 9,788 \qquad \Sigma x_i^2 = 1,416,926$$

$$\bar{x} = \frac{\Sigma x_i}{20} \qquad\qquad \Sigma x_i y_{ai} = 2,626,817$$

$$= \frac{5012}{20} = 250.6$$

$$\bar{y}_a = \frac{\Sigma y_{ai}}{n} = \frac{9788}{20} = 489.4$$

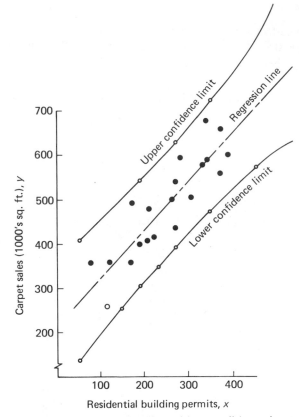

figure 4-3 . . . a regression line with a confidence interval

Because the plot indicates a linear relationship between the dependent variable (on the y-axis) and the independent variable (on the x-axis), linear regression is used to fit an equation to the data. The data summarized in Table 4-1 are utilized below to calculate the linear regression equation.

$$b = \frac{\Sigma x_i y_{ai} - \bar{x} \Sigma y_{ai}}{\Sigma x_i^2 - \bar{x} \Sigma x_i} = \frac{2,626,817 - 250.6 \,(9,788)}{1,416,926 - 250.6 \,(5,012)}$$

$$= \frac{173,944.2}{160,918.8} = 1.081$$

$$a = \bar{y}_a - b\bar{x} = 489.4 - 1.081 \,(250.6) = 218.5$$

Thus,

$$y = 218.5 + 1.081x$$

Suppose there are 310 building permits issued this quarter. Then our forecast of carpet sales in the coming quarter is

table 4-2 . . . calculations for a confidence interval

y_a = quarterly carpet sales (1000's sq. ft)

x = building permits in preceding quarter

y_i = 218.5 + 1.081x_i and $\bar{x}$ = 250.6 and $\bar{y}_a$ = 489.4

Data Point i ($1 \leqslant i \leqslant n$)	y_{ai}	x_i	y_i	$(y_{ai} - y_i)^2$	$(x_i - \bar{x})^2$	$(y_{ai} - \bar{y}_a)^2$
1	360	121	349.3	114.5	16,796.2	16,744
2	260	118	346.1	7413.2	17,582.8	52,624
3	440	271	511.4	5098.0	416.2	2440
4	400	190	423.9	571.2	3672.4	7992
5	360	75	299.6	3648.2	30,835.4	16,744
6	500	263	502.8	7.8	153.8	112
7	580	334	580.0	0.0	6955.6	8208
8	560	368	616.3	3169.7	13,782.8	4984
9	505	305	548.2	1866.2	2959.4	243
10	480	210	445.5	1190.2	1648.4	88
11	602	387	636.8	1211.0	18605.0	12,679
12	540	270	510.4	876.2	376.4	2560
13	415	218	454.2	1536.6	1062.8	5535
14	590	342	588.2	3.2	8354.0	10,120
15	492	173	405.5	7482.2	6021.8	7
16	660	370	618.5	1722.2	14,256.4	29,104
17	360	170	402.3	1789.3	6496.4	16,744
18	410	205	440.1	906.0	2079.4	6304
19	680	339	585.0	9025.0	7814.6	36,328
20	594	283	524.4	4844.2	1049.8	10,941
Totals				52,482.8	160,919.6	240,501

y = 218.5 + 1.081 (310) = 553.6   or   553,600 square feet

The information necessary to determine the confidence interval for this forecast is summarized in Table 4-2 and is used to perform the following calculations.

$$S(y) = \left[\frac{\Sigma(y_{ai} - y_i)^2}{n - 2} \right]^{1/2} \cdot \left[1 + \frac{1}{n} + \frac{(x_0 - \bar{x})^2}{\Sigma(x_i - \bar{x})^2} \right]^{1/2}$$

$$= \left[\frac{52,482.8}{18} \right]^{1/2} \cdot \left[1 + \frac{1}{20} + \frac{(310 - 250.6)^2}{160,919.6} \right]^{1/2}$$

$$= 55.88$$

(Recall that $[52{,}482.8/18]^{\frac{1}{2}} = \sqrt{\dfrac{52{,}482.8}{18}}$, etc.)

For a 95% confidence interval we have

$$t_{0.025,18} = 2.1009$$

and

$$y + (t_{\alpha/2,\,n-2})S(y) = 553.6 + 2.1009\,(55.88) = 671 \qquad \text{(upper limit)}$$

$$y - (t_{\alpha/2,\,n-2})S(y) = 553.6 - 2.1009\,(55.88) = 436 \qquad \text{(lower limit)}$$

To summarize, our forecast of next quarter's carpet sales is 553,600 square feet, and we are 95% confident that the true value of y will lie between 436,000 and 671,000 square feet. Again, the appropriate value of the t-statistic can be found in Appendix C.

The forecaster should not confuse statistical validity with real-world usefulness. For instance, the above confidence interval may be statistically sound and yet so wide that it is of little usefulness in a real-world situation. A forecaster may be able to draw upon his experience and judgment to evaluate a myriad of tangible and intangible factors and arrive at a forecast on which he places more confidence. Or, the confidence interval may seem wide to a statistician and yet to the practical forecaster it represents a tremendous improvement in forecasting precision.

In Figure 4-3 the data from Table 4-2 are plotted, the regression line is drawn and 95% confidence intervals are sketched. It can be seen that the interval is wider near the extreme ends of the observed values of x. This means that as x_0 (the point at which a forecast is desired) moves away from the average value of x, our estimate becomes more uncertain.

Statisticians often have a field day with numerous statistical tests associated with regression. A common problem is that such a volume of statistical results is presented to a decision maker who has little statistical training that he becomes confused, abandons regression, and returns to arbitrary forecasting. In the interest of keeping our discussion straightforward, we suggest that the *forecast* and its *confidence interval* are the two most important pieces of information obtained from regression analysis. An oversimplified, yet useful, rule for the manager without statistical training to keep in mind is "Get the forecast and the confidence interval, use common sense to examine both, and forget everything else."

Some of the most commonly used computer programs for regression analysis are not written to calculate a confidence interval. However, confidence intervals can be easily calculated by modifying the computer code, and the decision maker should insist on obtaining this piece of information. Various statistical tests used in connection with regression analysis are discussed in Appendix C to make you aware of their possible applications. At this point, we shall mention some of them before moving into multiple linear regression.

A *t-test* is used to determine if we can be confident that no parameters of our equation are zero; i.e., does *a* or *b* equal 0 in $y = a + bx$? If this test indicates that we are not confident that our *a* and *b* values are nonzero, there is nothing we can do to improve our *a* and *b* estimates, and the utility of the regression equation becomes questionable.

An *F-test* is used to determine if we can be statistically confident about the *strength* of the relationship between our variables (e.g., carpet sales and building permits). The confidence interval can be intuitively examined for this information. If there is no relationship, the confidence interval will be ridiculously wide; if the relationship is excellent, the confidence interval will be relatively narrow.

The correlation coefficient is a measure of the strength of the relationship between the variables. Again, the confidence interval gives the forecaster much of the information he or she needs about the strength of the relationship. However, because the correlation coefficient will be useful later in multiple linear regression when formulating and testing a set of causal relationships, it is discussed briefly at this point.

The correlation coefficient, *r*, can be determined as follows:

$$r = \sqrt{1.0 - \frac{\Sigma(y_{ai} - y_i)^2}{\Sigma(y_{ai} - \overline{y}_a)^2}}$$

If every y_{ai} value equals that calculated from our equation (namely, $y_i = a + bx_i$), then $y_{ai} = y_i$ and $r = 1.0$, and we have a perfect fit. If there is no relationship at all (a shotgun effect) between the dependent and independent variable, the second term under the radical will be one, or nearly one, and *r* will be zero, or nearly zero. The r^2 value is called the *coefficient of determination*; *r* is the correlation coefficient and $-1 \leqslant r \leqslant 1$. A negative value of *r* indicates that one variable decreases as the other increases, while the variables both increase (or decrease) at the same time when *r* is positive. The coefficient of determination and the correlation coefficient for data in Table 4-1 are, respectively,

$$r^2 = 1.0 - \frac{\Sigma(y_{ai} - y_i)^2}{\Sigma(y_{ai} - \overline{y}_a)^2} = 1.0 - \frac{52,483}{240,501}$$

$$= 1 - 0.2182 = 0.7818$$

$$r = \sqrt{0.7818} \cong 0.88$$

multiple linear regression

Multiple linear regression involving three or more variables is an important extension of the theory and techniques of simple linear regression. The correlation between two variables in simple regression can be misleading and spurious when the two variables are both dependent on a third variable not included in the analysis. In some cases this excluded variable may be time— the result being that the dependent variable and independent variable in simple regression both increase or decrease regularly, even though there is no direct causal relationship between them. By including more independent variables in the analysis, it may be possible to develop an equation that permits a more accurate estimate of the dependent variable, y, to be made.

If the forecaster believes there is more than one independent variable that can be measured and used to predict a response of the dependent variable, then multiple linear regression (MLR) may be useful. The general equation for MLR has the following form when there are p independent variables.

$$y = a + b_1 x_1 + b_2 x_2 + --- + b_k x_k + --- + b_p x_p$$

The large number of calculations required with multiple linear regression makes this method very tedious to apply manually. Additional variables in the equation do not represent an insurmountable barrier, however, because there are numerous computer programs available for solving multiple linear regression problems. Later in this section an example problem having two independent variables is analyzed with one of the widely used computer programs.

First let us review various approaches to deciding which variables to include in a multiple linear regression analysis. A carpet manufacturer may initially consider several independent variables such as number of residential building permits in the previous quarter or year (x_1), previous quarter's (or year's) sales (x_2), disposable personal income in his market area (x_3), number of houses sold (x_4), and building permits for office space (x_5). The forecaster could, for example, gather these data for the past five years (if forecasting by quarters, this would give 20 data points) and calculate the a and b_k $(1 \leq k \leq p)$ values for his equation.

It is recommended that the forecaster examine the equation, calculate a confidence interval for a particular forecast, and use common sense in eliminating variables that are not meaningful. In this particular situation, the forecaster can begin by calculating five regression equations, each expressed in terms of a different combination of four out of the five independent variables given above. For each of the five equations expressed in four independent variables, he can obtain a forecast and develop a confidence interval. If the confidence interval is tighter, or just as tight, for any of the equations when compared to the original equation expressed in five independent variables, the forecaster can conclude that the variable eliminated in the associated equation is not contributing to a better forecast.

In addition, the forecaster can also examine the $b_k x_k$ values. If some of these values are near zero, or insignificant in comparison to the other terms, this is an indication that the corresponding variables can be eliminated without adversely affecting the forecast.

If any of the b_k are negative, this should be a signal to the forecaster's common sense that something *could* be wrong. For example, if b_3 were negative, this would mean that carpet sales declined with increased personal disposable income. Unless the forecaster could find some reason for this effect, he should eliminate $b_3 x_3$ from the equation. When a variable is eliminated, the forecaster must go back and develop an entirely new multiple linear regression equation in terms of the remaining variables.

The cost of gathering data and using the computer in a regression analysis is usually insignificant in comparison to the potential value of the forecast to company operations. A variable should *not* be discarded unless the forecaster believes it is meaningless, or unless its inclusion in the equation widens the confidence interval appreciably.

Another approach to eliminating variables in multiple linear regression is the use of a *correlation matrix*. A hypothetical correlation matrix is presented in Table 4-3. Each entry in this matrix is the correlation coefficient between variables in the corresponding row and column. For example, the correlation coefficient between y and x_1 is

$$r = 0.88$$

as calculated in the previous section (page 71) dealing with simple linear regression. By examining Table 4-3, we see that the relationship between y and x_3 is poor. This indicates that x_3, home sales, should not be considered in de-

table 4-3 . . . a correlation matrix

	y	x_1	x_2	x_3	x_4
y	1.00	0.88	0.75	0.46	0.70
x_1	0.88	1.00	0.68	0.75	0.72
x_2	0.75	0.68	1.00	0.61	0.42
x_3	0.46	0.75	0.61	1.00	0.51
x_4	0.70	0.72	0.42	0.51	1.00

y = quarter's sales (1000's sq. ft.)

Previous Quarter's Data

x_1 = residential building permits

x_2 = carpet sales

x_3 = home sales

x_4 = permits for office construction

veloping the forecast. Further examination reveals that x_1 and x_3 are correlated more than any other pair of independent variables. When two of our forecasting variables are highly or even moderately correlated, this indicates that we may eliminate one of them without losing accuracy in our forecast.

The equations for determining estimates of parameters for a linear regression equation in *three variables* (two independent variables) appear on page 75. We next demonstrate how these expressions are applied to an example problem.

example

In the carpet manufacturing problem of the previous section, suppose the company also sells carpeting to an automobile manufacturer for use in a particular model of car. The carpet manufacturer wishes to develop an equation that gives this quarter's sales in terms of previous quarter's building permits and sales of the automobile for which he supplies carpet. The data are presented and calculations are performed in Table 4-4.

$$b_1 = \frac{173,945(238.2) - 6060.7(3650)}{160,918(238.2) - (3650)^2}$$

$$= \frac{41,433,699 - 22,121,555}{38,330,667 - 13,322,500} = 0.772$$

$$b_2 = \frac{6060.7(160,918) - 173,945(3650)}{160,918(238.2) - (3650)^2}$$

$$= \frac{975,275,723 - 634,899,250}{38,330,667 - 13,322,500} = 13.61$$

$$a = 489.4 - 0.772(250.6) = 13.6(26.42) = -63.79$$

$$y = -63.79 + 0.772x_1 + 13.61x_2$$

If there are 310 building permits issued in the previous quarter and 2,500 cars sold, our forecast of carpet sales is:

$$y = -63.79 + 0.772(310) + 13.61(25) = 515.8$$

or

$$y = 515,800 \text{ square feet of carpet}$$

Manually calculating a confidence interval for our forecast above involves a time-consuming procedure, even though the multiple linear regression equation has only three variables in it. Because the relative tightness of the confidence interval will tell us whether adding x_2 (automobile sales) improves the accuracy of our forecast, we have computed the 95% confidence interval:

equations for estimating coefficients in multiple linear regression analysis for two independent variables

$$b_1 = \frac{\left\{\left[\sum_{i=1}^{n}(y_{ai}-\bar{y}_a)(x_{1i}-\bar{x}_1)\right]\left[\sum_{i=1}^{n}(x_{2i}-\bar{x}_2)^2\right]\right\} - \left\{\left[\sum_{i=1}^{n}(y_{ai}-\bar{y}_a)(x_{2i}-\bar{x}_2)\right]\left[\sum_{i=1}^{n}(x_{1i}-\bar{x}_1)(x_{2i}-\bar{x}_2)\right]\right\}}{\left\{\left[\sum_{i=1}^{n}(x_{1i}-\bar{x}_1)^2\right]\left[\sum_{i=1}^{n}(x_{2i}-\bar{x}_2)^2\right]\right\} - \left\{\left[\sum_{i=1}^{n}(x_{1i}-\bar{x}_1)(x_{2i}-\bar{x}_2)\right]^2\right\}}$$

$$b_2 = \frac{\left\{\left[\sum_{i=1}^{n}(y_{ai}-\bar{y}_a)(x_{2i}-\bar{x}_2)\right]\left[\sum_{i=1}^{n}(x_{1i}-\bar{x}_1)^2\right]\right\} - \left\{\left[\sum_{i=1}^{n}(y_{ai}-\bar{y}_a)(x_{1i}-\bar{x}_1)\right]\left[\sum_{i=1}^{n}(x_{1i}-\bar{x}_1)(x_{2i}-\bar{x}_2)\right]\right\}}{\left\{\left[\sum_{i=1}^{n}(x_{1i}-\bar{x}_1)^2\right]\left[\sum_{i=1}^{n}(x_{2i}-\bar{x}_2)^2\right]\right\} - \left\{\left[\sum_{i=1}^{n}(x_{1i}-\bar{x}_1)(x_{2i}-\bar{x}_2)\right]^2\right\}}$$

$$a = \bar{y}_a - b_1\bar{x}_1 - b_2\bar{x}_2$$

The basic equation is:

$$y = a + b_1 x_1 + b_2 x_2$$

table 4-4 . . . data and calculations for multiple linear regression

i	y_a	x_1	x_2	$y_a - \bar{y}_a$	$x_1 - \bar{x}_1$	$x_2 - \bar{x}_2$	$(x_1 - \bar{x}_1)^2$	$(x_2 - \bar{x}_2)^2$	$(y_a - \bar{y}_a)$ $\cdot (x_1 - \bar{x}_1)$	$(y_a - \bar{y}_a)$ $\cdot (x_2 - \bar{x}_2)$	$(x_1 - \bar{x}_1)$ $\cdot (x_2 - \bar{x}_2)$	$(y_a - \bar{y}_a)^2$
1	360	121	26.0	-129.4	-129.6	-0.42	16,796	0.2	16,770	54.3	54.4	16,744
2	260	118	20.5	-229.4	-132.6	-5.92	17,583	35.0	30,418	1,358.0	785.0	52,624
3	440	271	21.5	-49.4	20.4	-4.92	416	24.2	-1,008	243.0	-100.4	2,440
4	400	190	23.5	-89.4	-60.6	-2.92	3,672	8.5	5,418	261.0	177.0	7,992
5	360	75	21.5	-129.4	-175.6	-4.92	30,835	24.2	22,723	636.6	863.9	16,744
6	500	263	26.25	10.6	12.4	-0.17	154	0	131	-1.8	-2.1	112
7	580	334	28.5	90.6	83.4	2.08	6,956	4.3	7,556	188.4	173.5	8,208
8	560	368	29.5	70.6	117.4	3.08	13,783	9.5	8,288	217.4	361.6	4,984
9	505	305	24.5	15.6	54.4	-1.92	2,959	3.7	849	-30.0	-104.4	243
10	480	210	29.5	-9.4	-40.6	3.08	1,648	9.5	382	-29.0	-125.0	88
11	602	387	26.1	112.6	136.4	-0.32	18,605	0.1	15,359	-36.0	-43.6	12,679
12	540	270	27.25	50.6	19.4	0.83	376	0.7	982	42.0	16.1	2,560
13	415	218	22.3	-74.4	-32.6	-4.12	1,063	17.0	2,425	306.5	134.3	5,535
14	590	342	31.0	100.6	91.4	4.58	8,354	21.0	9,195	460.7	418.6	10,120
15	492	173	28.0	2.6	-77.6	1.58	6,022	2.5	-202	4.1	-122.6	7
16	660	370	28.5	170.6	119.4	2.08	14,256	4.3	20,370	354.8	248.4	29,104
17	360	170	23.1	-129.4	-80.6	-3.32	6,496	11.0	10,430	429.6	267.6	16,744
18	410	205	27.0	-79.4	-45.6	0.58	2,079	0.3	3,621	-46.1	-26.4	6,304
19	680	339	32.0	190.6	88.4	5.58	7,815	31.1	16,849	1,063.5	493.3	36,328
20	594	283	32.0	104.6	32.4	5.58	1,050	31.1	3,389	583.7	180.8	10,941
TOTALS							160,918	238.2	173,945	6,060.7	3,650.0	240,506

$\bar{y}_a = 489.4$ y_a = carpet sales (1000's sq. ft.)

$\bar{x}_1 = 250.6$ x_1 = building permits previous quarter

$\bar{x}_2 = 26.42$ x_2 = auto sales previous quarter (100's)

Upper limit = 596,800 square feet

Lower limit = 435,400 square feet

The equations that were employed to calculate this confidence interval can be found in the following book: William Volk, *Applied Statistics for Engineers* (McGraw-Hill Book Company, New York, 1958), p. 278.

After referring back to page 70, you can see that the confidence interval for carpet sales was 436,000 to 671,000 square feet based on simple linear regression analysis. When we add x_2 and determine the parameters and forecast of the multiple linear regression equation, the confidence interval is reduced to 435,400 to 596,800 square feet. Thus, the confidence interval is tighter after including x_2 as an independent variable, and the manager would probably conclude that y = 515,800 square feet of carpet is a more reliable forecast.

To illustrate how a multiple linear regression computer code can be used to determine the parameters (a, b_1, and b_2) in the previous example, the data of Table 4-4 were analyzed with the MLR portion of the *Statistical Package for the Social Sciences (SPSS)*.* A stepwise procedure is utilized by SPSS in which a simple linear regression equation is initially determined for each independent variable. Then the independent variable most highly correlated (i.e., having the largest correlation coefficient) with the dependent variable is entered as the first term in the MLR equation being developed. For the SPSS computer run, a partial listing of results for this first step are shown below:

DEPENDENT VARIABLE.. Y

VARIABLE(S) ENTERED ON STEP NUMBER 1..   X1

MULTIPLE R	0.88418
R SQUARE	0.78178
STANDARD ERROR	53.99736

VARIABLES IN THE EQUATION

VARIABLE	B	STD ERROR B
X1	1.08094	0.13461
(CONSTANT)	218.51545	

*A reference to the SPSS user's manual, and references to two other widely used MLR computer codes, are given here:
1. Norman H. Nie et al, Statistical Package for the Social Sciences (SPSS), 2nd ed. (New York: McGraw-Hill Book Company, 1970).
2. W.J. Dixon, (ed.), Biomedical Computer Programs, (Los Angeles: University of California Press, 1973).
3. IBM S/360 Scientific Subroutine Package, Version 3 Programmer's Manual, 5th ed., (New York: IBM Corporation, 1970).

Here the variable x_1 was entered, and its correlation coefficient is seen to be 0.88418. The simple linear regression equation is

$$y = 218.51545 + 1.08094x_1$$

Other measures involving statistics beyond the scope of this discussion are also automatically computed by SPSS, but they have been deleted above.

The second step is next performed by including x_2 in the MLR analysis. The resultant equation with two independent variables has a multiple correlation coefficient of 0.94953, which improves upon the value obtained at Step 1. Results of Step 2 appear below.

VARIABLE(S) ENTERED ON STEP NUMBER 2..   X2

MULTIPLE R	0.94953
R SQUARE	0.90160
STANDARD ERROR	37.31101

VARIABLES IN THE EQUATION

VARIABLE	B	STD ERROR B
X1	0.77214	0.11514
X2	13.60917	2.99119
(CONSTANT)	-63.78968	

MAXIMUM STEP REACHED

If the coefficient of determination had decreased rather than increased because of x_2's introduction into the equation, the final equation would have involved only x_1 at the termination of Step 2. Thus, our final equation is $y = -63.78968 + 0.77214x_1 + 13.60917x_2$, which is the same as we calculated earlier by hand. A matrix of correlation coefficients for the data in Table 4-4 is shown below as calculated by SPSS:

	y	x_1	x_2
y	1.0000	0.8842	0.8008
x_1	0.8842	1.0000	0.5895
x_2	0.8008	0.5895	1.0000

Thus, we see that x_1 and x_2 are moderately correlated ($r = 0.5895$).

If the reader has occasion to use one of the many computer codes available for multiple linear regression, he or she is advised to read the user's manual carefully. In this regard, you will discover that the statistical tests performed by computer software packages in common use often vary considerably from one code to another. Furthermore, the interpretation of output measures that are calculated normally requires the user to be knowledgeable with the statistical theory that underlies each test. Therefore, additional study may be required to understand fully the information generated by MLR computer codes.

nonlinear regression

If data appear to follow a curve instead of a straight line, then nonlinear regression can possibly be applied. A widely-used model has this form:

$$y = a + b_1 x_1 + b_2 x_1{}^2$$

In developing this model, we define a new variable $x_2 = x_1{}^2$ and our equation becomes

$$y = a + b_1 x_1 + b_2 x_2$$

Thus, to solve this type of problem, equations from multiple linear regression (2 independent variables) can be utilized.

To illustrate nonlinear regression, the example used with simple linear regression is recalled (page 67). Examination of Figure 4-3 indicates the data can be relatively well represented by a straight line, so we might expect the $b_2 x_2$ term to be relatively insignificant in the final results.

Basic information that is used in calculating the nonlinear regression equation is presented in Table 4-5. Note that x_2 always equals $x_1{}^2$. Rather than repeating all the computations required as shown previously in Table 4-4, the results of nonlinear regression for data in Table 4-5 are summarized in Table 4-6. These results are compared to those obtained previously by applying simple linear regression to the same data. Both approaches result in practically the same forecast. There is very little improvement in the confidence interval with nonlinear regression, as we expected, because the data can be approximated with a straight line. A curvilinear pattern in the data as illustrated in Figure 3-1(D) of the previous chapter would have favored the successful application of nonlinear regression.

This concludes our discussion of linear and nonlinear regression. When a causal relationship between a response variable and an independent variable can be identified, regression techniques are well suited for making forecasts within the range of observations on x. To forecast over time, the independent variable must be a good leading indicator of the desired response. The amount of time by which x leads y is the time period for which a forecast can be made.

questions

1. Suppose you own an automobile dealership. Over the past several years you have found that quarterly new car sales tend to lag the prime interest rate by three months. You would like to make a forecast of next

table 4-5 . . . data for nonlinear regression

Data point No.	y_a	x_1	$x_2 = x_1{}^2$
1	360	121	14,641
2	260	118	13,924
3	440	271	73,441
4	400	190	36,100
5	360	75	5,625
6	500	263	69,169
7	580	334	111,556
8	560	368	135,424
9	505	305	93,025
10	480	210	44,100
11	602	387	149,769
12	540	270	72,900
13	415	218	47,524
14	590	342	116,964
15	492	173	29,929
16	660	370	136,900
17	360	170	28,900
18	410	205	42,025
19	680	339	114,921
20	594	283	80,089

table 4-6 . . . comparison of linear regression and nonlinear regression

	Linear Regression	Nonlinear Regression
Basic equation	$y = a + bx$	$y = a + b_1 x_1 + b_2 x_1{}^2$
Equation fitting the data of Table 4-5	$y = 218.51 + 1.081x$	$y = 238.84 + 0.88x + 0.0004x^2$
Forecast for $x = 310$	$y = 553.6$	$y = 550.1$
The 95% confidence interval	436 to 671	333 to 768

quarter's car sales so the size of your sales force can be anticipated. The following data are gathered:

Yr.	Qtr.	Interest Rate	Sales		Yr	Qtr	Interest Rate	Sales
1	1	8.00%	23		4	1	7.00%	25
	2	8.25%	17			2	7.50%	26
	3	8.50%	18			3	7.50%	17
	4	8.25%	20			4	8.25%	20
2	1	7.75%	21		5	1	8.75%	15
	2	7.25%	25			2	8.50%	18
	3	7.70%	24			3	7.50%	22
	4	7.25%	29			4	7.00%	23
3	1	7.50%	24		6	1	7.50%	?
	2	7.75%	23					
	3	7.25%	26					
	4	7.00%	30					

a. Calculate a simple regression equation for these data, assuming the interest rate is the independent variable.

b. Calculate the correlation coefficient.

c. Calculate the standard error of the forecast.

d. Make a forecast of sales for next quarter based on this quarter's prime interest rate of 7.50%. What is the confidence interval for this forecast when $\alpha = 0.05$?

e. Plot the residuals (error terms), and see if you can determine a pattern in them. (Statistical tests for checking for serial correlation in these data could be applied—see Appendix B.)

2. List and explain three assumptions that underlie regression analysis. Can you describe a simple means of checking the validity of each assumption for a set of data?

3. What problems might be encountered when simple regression is used to make a linear projection based on time-series data? (See Appendix B.)

4. In multiple linear regression analysis, how would you decide which variables in the equation could be dropped? Also explain how a matrix of cross correlation coefficients could be used to improve the results of your analysis.

5. In problem 1a, check to see whether b is significantly different than zero.

chapter 5 . . . moving averages and exponential smoothing

introduction

The techniques presented in this chapter are applicable to time-series data, and in many situations they are more appropriate and easier to use than are regression methods. One of the chief difficulties in applying regression is the need to update coefficients of the least-squares equation whenever a new data point is obtained. Because a relatively large number of calculations is required to update the equation, more suitable forecasting techniques such as those described in the present chapter have been developed. In addition, various difficulties may be experienced when regression methods are called upon to analyze time-series data. As noted previously, these potential problems are discussed in Appendix B.

With moving averages and exponential smoothing, forecasting equations can be quickly revised with a relatively small number of calculations as each new data point is collected. Another advantage of exponential smoothing over regression is that it permits the forecaster to place more weight on current data rather than treating all data points with equal importance. Exponential smoothing also minimizes data storage requirements when calculations are performed manually or with a computer. Furthermore, moving averages and exponential smoothing are able to deal directly with serial correlation in time-series data while regression techniques are not.

The main disadvantage of moving averages and exponential smoothing methods concerns the basic assumption that trends and patterns of the past will continue into the future. Because time-series analysis cannot predict turning points in the future, expert judgment and/or analysis of suspected causal factors should be used in interpreting results of forecasting methods included in this chapter. A second disadvantage to time-series techniques is that no statistical confidence interval for the forecast can be estimated as with the regression methods of Chapter 4.

With all of the techniques described in this chapter, the forecaster must make a decision as to how much importance should be given to current data. In this regard one of the basic problems is illustrated in Figure 5-1. Here we see that demand has been relatively stable over time, and then a data point is experienced that is unusually high. Often such a point is referred to as an *outlier*. Management can give no simple explanation for this outcome and they might ask: "Could this occurrence be the result of an unexplainable effect, or does it represent a true shift in level of demand?"

An unusual one-time-only occurrence that is not related to the true trend is called an outlier, while random variation in the data about the true trend is termed *noise*. Noise is caused by uncontrollable factors, and there will always be some noise in real data. Our dilemma is to decide if the new data point in Figure 5-1 is noise or an outlier, or whether it represents the beginning of a new level of demand. What should our forecast be for the next time period? How can we develop a forecasting technique to deal with this situation? There are two extremes to the courses of action that the forecaster can take. The actual approach will usually be somewhere between these extremes:

1. The forecaster can adopt a model that reacts very quickly to dramatic changes.* If the outlier data point indicates the beginning of a new demand level, the model will detect it immediately and give it considerable weight as additional forecasts are developed. If this last data point is only noise or a human error in measurement, for example, the forecaster could be making a serious error by reacting too quickly.

2. The forecaster can develop a very stable, conservative model that is affected very little by noise. If the pattern of the data does change, the model will not react until several data points have been experienced at the new level. A very slow, overly cautious reaction to a true shift in the response variable can be disastrous in many highly competitive industries.

One way of selecting the "best" model, in terms of how quickly it reacts to abrupt changes in the data, involves applying several models having different reaction rates to historical data and measuring the mean square error of each. The one that minimizes mean square error for a given set of data is often regarded as the best model to use in forecasting future responses. This will be demonstrated later in an example problem.

A model here is a mathematical expression that is designed to emulate, or copy, the process by which data points are determined in a time-series.

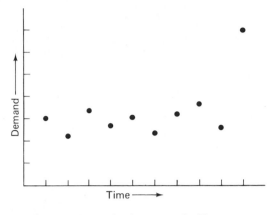

figure 5-1 . . . the forecaster's dilemma

A straightforward "working level" discussion of moving averages and exponential smoothing is often not presented in introductory texts such as this one. We have chosen to pursue this type of discussion here for one basic reason. Over the years, we have observed many instances in which the output of computer programs for time-series analysis cannot be correctly interpreted because the user has little understanding of how the various techniques work. To help remedy this situation, we have included mathematical expressions and calculations in our explanation of moving averages and exponential smoothing. Several examples are worked manually to familiarize the reader with how the equations are applied to data. Then we offer a computer program for preparing forecasts with these techniques. In this manner we hope to provide the necessary background for the correct application and interpretation of time-series tools treated in Chapter 5.

In view of the comments above, the reader who is interested in only an overview of moving averages and exponential smoothing is encouraged to consider the first four sections of this chapter. The remainder of the chapter can be omitted without adversely affecting an understanding of forecasting techniques presented in subsequent chapters.

simple moving averages

A moving average is simply a numerical average of the last N data points that are used for purposes of making a forecast. As each new data point is acquired it is included in calculating the average, and the data point for the Nth period preceding the new data point is discarded. As an example, the data in Table 5-1 are plotted in Figure 5-2. By using an $N = 5$, the moving average at the end of the fifth period is

table 5-1 . . . single moving averages applied to typical data

Period Number t	Demand, x_t (1000 units)	$M_t^{[1]}$ $N=5$*	$M_t^{[1]}$ $N=10$
1	50	—	—
2	45	—	—
3	60	—	—
4	52	—	—
5	45	50.4	—
6	51	50.6	—
7	60	53.6	—
8	43	50.2	—
9	57	51.2	—
10	40	50.2	50.3
11	56	51.2	50.9
12	87	56.6	55.1
13	49	57.8	54.0
14	43	55.0	53.1
15	52	57.4	53.8
16	85	63.2	57.2
17	98	65.4	61.0
18	90	73.6	65.7
19	97	84.4	69.7
20	86	91.2	74.3
21	91	92.4	77.8
22	83	89.4	77.4
23	97	90.8	82.2
24	86	88.6	86.5
25	89	89.2	90.2

*For example, $M_6^{[1]} = (45 + 60 + 52 + 45 + 51)/5 = 50.6$. It represents our forecast of future demand in period 7, 8, 9, ———. When the demand in period 7 is actually observed, the absolute error is seen to be 60.0 - 50.6 = 9.4.

$$M_5^{[1]} = \frac{50 + 45 + 60 + 52 + 45}{5} = 50.4$$

With the assumption of a constant pattern in the data, $M_5^{[1]}$ is used as the forecast of future demand. In general, the moving average at time t, taken over N periods, is

$$M_t^{[1]} = \frac{x_t + x_{t-1} + \text{———} + x_{t-N+1}}{N} \qquad (5\text{-}1)$$

where x_t is the observed response at time t. Another way of stating the above equation to minimize required calculations is

$$M_t^{[1]} = M_{t-1}^{[1]} + \frac{x_t - x_{t-N}}{N} \tag{5-2}$$

or

$$M_6^{[1]} = M_5^{[1]} + \frac{x_6 - x_1}{5} = 50.4 + \frac{51 - 50}{5} = 50.6$$

Thus, after the sixth data point has been collected, our forecast of demand in subsequent periods is 50.6.

The moving averages for $N=5$ and $N=10$ are calculated in Table 5-1 and plotted in Figure 5-2. The values of 5 and 10 for N are fairly low. They were chosen to illustrate the characteristics of moving averages with a relatively small amount of data. At period 12 a data point occurs ($x_{12} = 87$) that should be considered noise. The mean of the data, excluding x_{12}, is 50.2 up through period 15. This anomolous point x_{12} causes the moving average with $N=5$ to

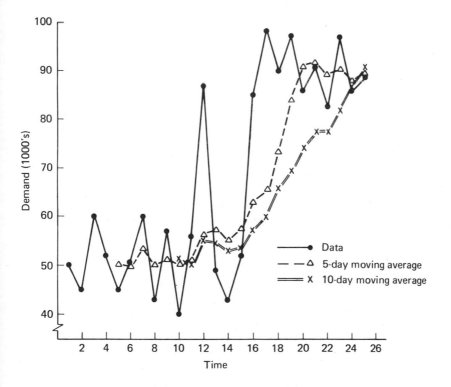

figure 5-2 . . . a comparison of 5-day and 10-day moving averages

increase to a high of 57.8 in period 13, while the $N=10$ model increases to a high of only 55.1 in period 12.

From Figure 5-2 it can be seen that a new level of demand begins in period 16. As expected, the moving average with $N=5$ adjusts to the new level in 5 periods, while the model with $N=10$ requires 10 periods. *As N is increased, the moving average is less sensitive to noise and requires longer to adjust to a new response level.* In general, N typically varies from 6 to 200 but the forecaster should not hesitate to use an N outside of these limits if it gives superior results when applied to representative historical data.

double moving averages

The data of Table 5-1 are basically constant and have no trend. That is, the model for the response in period t is $y_t = a + \epsilon_t$, where a represents a constant and ϵ_t is the error term. The simple moving average is intended for data of this nature. If the data have a linear or quadratic trend, the simple moving average will be misleading. A new situation is illustrated in the data of Table 5-2 that are plotted in Figure 5-3. Here the data are perfectly stable for 10 periods with no noise. Then a linear trend is introduced after period 10 that increases by 3 (1000's) units of demand in each time period. It can be seen from Figure 5-3 that the moving average $M_t^{[1]}$ will continue to lag the data. The amount of this lag is called the bias which equals $\dfrac{N-1}{2}\, b$, where b is the slope of the linear trend in Figure 5-3. In this example the bias is 6:

$$\frac{(N-1)b}{2} = \frac{(5-1)3}{2} = 6$$

In order to correct for the bias and develop an improved forecasting equation, the double moving average $M_t^{[2]}$ can be calculated. To calculate $M_t^{[2]}$, simply treat the moving average $M_t^{[1]}$ as an individual data point and obtain a moving average of these averages (i.e., determine an average of the moving average):

$$M_t^{[2]} = \frac{M_t^{[1]} + M_{t-1}^{[1]} + \text{---} + M_{t-N+1}^{[1]}}{N} \tag{5-3}$$

For the data given in Table 5-2 with $N=5$,

$$M_{11}^{[2]} = \frac{50 + 50 + 50 + 50 + 50.6}{5} = 50.12$$

$$M_{12}^{[2]} = \frac{50 + 50 + 50 + 50.6 + 51.8}{5} = 50.48$$

$$M_{13}^{[2]} = \frac{50 + 50 + 50.6 + 51.8 + 53.6}{5} = 51.20$$

table 5-2 . . . single and double moving averages with a linear trend

Period Number t	Demand, x_t (1000 units)	$M_t^{[1]}$ N=5	$M_t^{[2]}$ N=5*
1	50	—	—
2	50	—	—
3	50	—	—
4	50	—	—
5	50	50.0	—
6	50	50.0	—
7	50	50.0	—
8	50	50.0	—
9	50	50.0	50.00
10	50	50.0	50.00
11	53	50.6	50.12
12	56	51.8	50.48
13	59	53.6	51.20
14	62	56.0	52.40
15	65	59.0	54.20
16	68	62.0	56.48
17	71	65.0	59.12
18	74	68.0	62.00
19	77	71.0	65.00
20	80	74.0	68.00

*Double moving averages do not constitute forecasts. Both $M_t^{[1]}$ and $M_t^{[2]}$ are used in Equations (5-4) and (5-5) to determine a_t and b_t. The forecast T periods ahead is then calculated as follows: $y_{t+T} = a_t + b_t \cdot T$.

The results of Table 5-2 may now be used to determine an equation for forecasting future demand. The equation will be of the form $y_{t+T} = a_t + b_t \cdot T$, where T is the number of time periods from the present time, t, to the period we are forecasting, and

$$a_t = 2M_t^{[1]} - M_t^{[2]} \tag{5-4}$$

$$b_t = \left(\frac{2}{N-1}\right)(M_t^{[1]} - M_t^{[2]}) \tag{5-5}$$

As an example suppose that we are currently in period 20 and wish to develop a forecast for period 25. Based on Table 5-2, we find that our forecast for period 25 is 95:

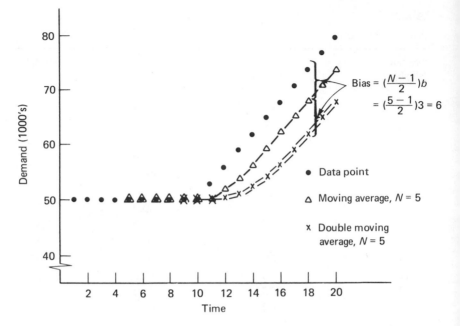

figure 5-3 . . . the reaction of a moving average to a linear trend

$$a_{20} = 2(74) - 68 = 80$$

$$b_{20} = \frac{2}{5-1}(74 - 68) = 3$$

$$y_{t+T} = a_t + b_t T$$

$$y_{20+5} = 80 + 3(5) = 95$$

The reader may verify that the forecast is accurate if the present trend continues. Since there is no noise in the data illustrated in Figure 5-3 and the trend is linear, double moving averages give a perfect forecast when used after the demand in period 18 has been observed. That is, if this linear trend continues, perfect forecasts will be obtained for $T = 1, 2, 3$ - - - after $t = 18$.

The double moving average is appropriate for linear trends but will not give accurate results when there is curvature in the data. However, a triple moving average can be used in developing an equation to fit a trend having curvature. Because triple exponential smoothing is most commonly used in this situation, discussion of this type of data pattern is deferred to a later section.

fundamental exponential smoothing

The moving average overcomes some of the difficulties encountered with regression because with moving averages it is relatively easy to take each new data point into consideration in developing forecasts. Current data can be given increased importance in the forecast by making N smaller. The moving average technique, however, requires a relatively large amount of data storage. For example, if a financial institution is using a moving average with $N = 200$ to forecast 1,000 stock prices, then 200,000 data points must be stored. Exponential smoothing has many of the same advantages as moving averages but requires a minimum amount of data storage.

In our example that illustrated moving averages, we saw the following

$$M_6^{[1]} = M_5^{[1]} + \frac{x_6 - x_1}{5}$$

If we stored none of the data, a value of x_1 would not be available. Our best estimate of x_1 would then be $M_5^{[1]}$. By using this in our equation, we get

$$M_6^{[1]} = M_5^{[1]} + \frac{x_6 - M_5^{[1]}}{5}$$

or

$$M_6^{[1]} = M_5^{[1]} - \frac{1}{5}M_5^{[1]} + \frac{x_6}{5}$$

$$M_6^{[1]} = \frac{4}{5}M_5^{[1]} + \frac{x_6}{5}$$

For the general case,

$$M_t^{[1]} = \frac{1}{N}x_t + \left(1 - \frac{1}{N}\right)M_{t-1}^{[1]} \qquad (5\text{-}6)$$

The above equation could be used to calculate $M_t^{[1]}$ if no data were stored. If we let $\alpha = \frac{1}{N}$ and $S_t^{[1]} = M_t^{[1]}$ and substitute these into Equation (5-6), we arrive at the basic exponential smoothing model:

$$S_t^{[1]} = \alpha x_t + (1 - \alpha)S_{t-1}^{[1]} \qquad (5\text{-}7)$$

or

$$\frac{\text{New}}{\text{estimate}} = \alpha\binom{\text{new}}{\text{data}} + (1 - \alpha)\binom{\text{previous}}{\text{estimate}}$$

This term, α, is called the smoothing constant. In general α should lie between 0.01 and 0.30, but the forecaster should not hesitate to use a value outside this range if it gives better results with representative historical data. *A large α value is similar to a small N with the moving average, because a large α and a small N both place the most importance on the most current data.* If we are searching for an α that will give an exponential smoothing model having similar response characteristics to a moving average with a certain N, we may use the following expression to determine the value of such a smoothing constant.

$$\alpha = \frac{2}{N + 1} \tag{5-8}$$

If we have a moving average with $N=5$, then a smoothing constant of a $\alpha = \frac{2}{5+1} = 0.333$ in a single exponential smoothing model will give about the same results.

Single exponential smoothing is illustrated with data listed in Table 5-3 that are graphed in Figure 5-4. The following are example calculations for $S_t^{[1]}$, which are termed "smoothed statistics" for period t.

table 5-3 . . . exponential smoothing applied to data

Period Number t	Demand, x_t (1000 units)	$S_t^{[1]}$ $\alpha=0.30$	$S_t^{[2]}$ $\alpha=0.30$
0	—	50.00	50.00
1	50	50.00	50.00
2	52	50.60	50.18
3	47	49.52	49.98
4	51	49.96	49.98
5	49	49.67	49.88
6	48	49.17	49.67
7	51	49.72	49.68
8	40	46.80	48.82
9	48	47.16	48.32
10	52	48.61	48.41
11	51	49.33	48.68
12	59	52.23	49.75
13	57	53.66	50.92
14	64	56.76	52.67
15	68	60.13	54.91
16	67	62.19	57.09
17	69	64.23	59.23
18	76	67.76	61.79
19	75	69.93	64.23
20	80	72.95	66.85

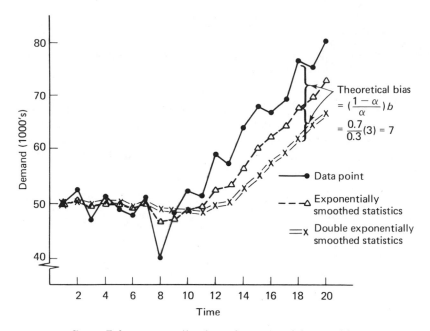

figure 5-4 . . . an application of exponential smoothing

$$S_t^{[1]} = \alpha x_t + (1-\alpha)\, S_{t-1}^{[1]}$$

$$S_1^{[1]} = 0.3(50) + 0.7(50) = 50$$

$$S_2^{[1]} = 0.3(52) + 0.7(50) = 50.6$$

$$S_3^{[1]} = 0.3(47) + 0.7(50.6) = 49.52$$

$$S_4^{[1]} = 0.3(51) + 0.7(49.52) = 49.96$$

In determining $S_1^{[1]}$ above, a value of $S_0^{[1]}$ must be estimated. If there is no trend in the initial data, an estimate based on the average of the first few data points is adequate. Here $S_0^{[1]}$ was estimated to be 50.

To better understand the meaning of exponential smoothing, the following expression shows how each value of $x_t, x_{t-1}, x_{t-2}, ----$ is included in the forecast.

$$S_t^{[1]} = \alpha x_t + (1-\alpha)S_{t-1}^{[1]}$$

where

$$S_{t-1}^{[1]} = \alpha x_{t-1} + (1-\alpha)S_{t-2}^{[1]}$$

and then

$$S_t^{[1]} = \alpha x_t + \alpha(1-\alpha)x_{t-1} + (1-\alpha)^2 S_{t-2}^{[1]} \qquad (5\text{-}9)$$

It is possible to continue substituting smoothed values in the same fashion until we get this:

$$S_t^{[1]} = \alpha x_t + \alpha(1-\alpha)x_{t-1} + \alpha(1-\alpha)^2 x_{t-2} + \alpha(1-\alpha)^3 x_{t-3} \tag{5-10}$$
$$+ \text{---} + (1-\alpha)^t S_0^{[1]}$$

As you can see, every previous value of x is included in $S_t^{[1]}$. The x values are weighted so that the values most distant in time have the smallest weighting factors. A large α will place very little weight on remote data. The following calculations illustrate the weighting of the different data points included in $S_4^{[1]}$ above as described by Equation (5-10).

$$S_4^{[1]} = 0.3(51) + 0.3(0.7)\, 47 + 0.3(0.7)^2\, 52 + 0.3(0.7)^3\, 50 + (0.7)^4\, 50$$

$$= 0.30(51) + 0.21(47) + 0.147(52) + 0.1029(50) + 0.2401(50)$$

$$= 49.96$$

This agrees with our calculation of $S_4^{[1]}$ on page 93.

double exponential smoothing

To develop an equation that takes account of a linear trend in data, we must calculate double exponentially smoothed statistics, $S_t^{[2]}$, where

$$S_t^{[2]} = \alpha S_t^{[1]} + (1-\alpha)\, S_{t-1}^{[2]} \tag{5-11}$$

Note that values of $S_0^{[1]}$ and $S_0^{[2]}$ must be assumed in these calculations. If a relatively large amount of data is available, then their initial estimates are not important. As exponential smoothing is applied to the data, the initial estimate of $S_0^{[1]}$ is discounted and becomes a negligible part of $S_t^{[1]}$. The same is true of $S_0^{[2]}$. If we only have a few data points (less than 15 or 20) then these initial estimates will influence our forecasts and special procedures should be used to estimate $S_0^{[1]}$ and $S_0^{[2]}$. (These procedures are presented in the next section.) An initial value of $S_0^{[1]} = S_0^{[2]} = 50$ is used in the example of Table 5-3 since the data have no initial trend and have an average value of about 50.

As an example of required calculations, consider the data given for periods 11, 12 and 13 in Table 5-3:

$$S_{12}^{[2]} = 0.3(52.23) + 0.7(48.68) = 49.75$$
$$S_{13}^{[2]} = 0.3(53.66) + 0.7(49.75) = 50.92$$

Notice that the smoothed and the doubly smoothed data have been plotted in Figure 5-4. Because of the linear trend in the raw data, these smoothed statistics are utilized further to obtain a forecast.

Various quantities from Table 5-3 are now utilized in an equation for forecasting future demand. The equation is of the form $y_{t+T} = a_t + b_t T$, where T is the number of time units from the present period, t, to the period we are forecasting and

$$a_t = 2S_t^{[1]} - S_t^{[2]} \tag{5-12}$$

$$b_t = \frac{\alpha}{1-\alpha}\left[S_t^{[1]} - S_t^{[2]}\right] \tag{5-13}$$

Note that x_t has been used to denote an observation at time t in a time-series; y_{t+T} is a term representing a forecast of the response variable T periods into the future.

As an example, suppose that we are currently in period 20 and we wish to develop a forecast for period 30. From Table 5-3, we calculate the following quantities in developing our forecast for period 30, y_{30}.

$$a_{20} = 2(72.95) - 66.85 = 79.05$$

$$b_{20} = \frac{0.3}{0.7}[72.95 - 66.85] = 2.61$$

$$y_{20+10} = 79.05 + 2.61(10) = 105.15$$

The smoothed and doubly smoothed statistics of Table 5-3 were used in the above manner to develop forecasts for one time period into the future ($T = 1$). These forecasts and the actual data are compared in Figure 5-7. (This figure is included later in connection with another illustrative problem.)

triple exponential smoothing

If the data we are dealing with exhibit curvature, then double exponential smoothing is inadequate and we must resort to triple exponential smoothing. Triple exponentially smoothed data are sufficient for almost all practical applications. There is not normally any advantage in higher-order smoothing. The triple exponentially smoothed statistics are calculated as follows:

$$S_t^{[3]} = \alpha S_t^{[2]} + (1-\alpha)S_{t-1}^{[3]} \tag{5-14}$$

The model we are developing is of the form

$$y_{t+T} = a_t + b_t T + c_t T^2$$

where

$$a_t = 3S_t^{[1]} - 3S_t^{[2]} + S_t^{[3]} \tag{5-15}$$

$$b_t = \frac{\alpha}{2(1-\alpha)^2}\left[(6-5\alpha)S_t^{[1]} - 2(5-4\alpha)S_t^{[2]} + (4-3\alpha)S_t^{[3]}\right] \tag{5-16}$$

$$c_t = \frac{\alpha^2}{2(1-\alpha)^2}\left[S_t^{[1]} - 2S_t^{[2]} + S_t^{[3]}\right] \tag{5-17}$$

These equations are used to develop a forecast in the next section.

developing initial estimates for moving averages and exponential smoothing

When exponential smoothing is used for forecasting, values of $S_0^{[1]}$, $S_0^{[2]}$ and $S_0^{[3]}$ must be initially estimated ($S_0^{[1]}$ and $S_0^{[2]}$ were discussed previously and $S_0^{[3]}$ applies to triple exponential smoothing). If we have many data points (50 or more), then the initial estimates are not critical since $S_0^{[1]}$, $S_0^{[2]}$, and $S_0^{[3]}$ are "corrected for" after applying exponential smoothing to the data. After 50 or more calculations, these initial estimates will have a very small weighting as indicated by equation 5-10. If we have only a small number of data points (less than 15 or 20), the equations we develop are very sensitive to these initial estimates.

The following is a brief summary of the approach that should be followed to apply exponential smoothing to a limited amount of data.

1. Graph the data and use trial and error calculations to obtain an equation that generally fits the data ($y = a_{est} + b_{est}t + c_{est}t^2$ for a quadratic model).

2. Use the parameters that you have estimated (a_{est}, b_{est}, c_{est}) to calculate values of $S_0^{[1]}$, $S_0^{[2]}$, and $S_0^{[3]}$.

3. Apply exponential smoothing in the standard manner, using the smoothed values in the equations (given below) to prepare forecasts.

Equations are given in this section that enable the forecaster to make accurate initial estimates of $S_0^{[1]}$, $S_0^{[2]}$, and $S_0^{[3]}$. To use these equations we must examine the data and make an estimate of the equation that fits the data. For the linear model, a_{est} and b_{est} are our estimated parameters for $y = a_{est} + b_{est}t$. For the quadratic model a_{est}, b_{est}, and c_{est} are the estimated parameters for $y = a_{est} + b_{est}t + c_{est}t^2$. The estimated parameters can be derived by using trial-and-error procedures until an equation of a curve is determined that gives a reasonable fit for the historical data. A high degree of accuracy is not necessary initially. The equations required to develop estimates of $S_0^{[1]}$, $S_0^{[2]}$, and $S_0^{[3]}$ from a_{est}, b_{est} and c_{est} are presented here.

Linear Model, $y = a_{est} + b_{est} \cdot t$

$$S_0^{[1]} = a_{est} - \left[\frac{(1-\alpha)}{\alpha}\right] \cdot b_{est} \tag{5-18}$$

$$S_0^{[2]} = a_{est} - \left[\frac{2(1-\alpha)}{\alpha}\right] \cdot b_{est} \tag{5-19}$$

Quadratic Model, $y = a_{est} + b_{est}t + c_{est}t^2$

$$S_0 = a_{est} - \left[\frac{(1-\alpha)}{\alpha}\right] \cdot b_{est} + \left[\frac{(1-\alpha)\,(2-\alpha)}{\alpha^2}\right] \cdot c_{est} \qquad (5\text{-}20)$$

$$S_0^{[2]} = a_{est} - \left[\frac{2(1-\alpha)}{\alpha}\right] \cdot b_{est} + \left[\frac{2(1-\alpha)(3-2\alpha)}{\alpha^2}\right] \cdot c_{est} \qquad (5\text{-}21)$$

$$S_0^{[3]} = a_{est} - \left[\frac{3(1-\alpha)}{\alpha}\right] \cdot b_{est} + \left[\frac{3(1-\alpha)\,(4-3\alpha)}{\alpha^2}\right] \cdot c_{est} \qquad (5\text{-}22)$$

To illustrate the application of these equations, data that are utilized for this purpose have been listed in Table 5-4 and graphed in Figure 5-5. After plotting the data, the forecaster can use different values of a_{est}, b_{est}, and c_{est} to develop the equation of a curve that approximately fits the data. For purposes of illustration, the actual values of a, b, and c that were utilized to derive the data of Figure 5-5 are used as the initial estimates. These values are $a=50$, $b=0.5$, and $c=0.2$. Therefore the data listed in Table 5-4 fall directly on a curve calculated by the equation $y = 50 + 0.5t + 0.2t^2$. The purpose of using this example without considering noise is to emphasize clearly that initial estimates of the smoothing statistics are not readily apparent. We must perform several calcuations to obtain these estimates. The example below also demonstrates that the equations for triple exponential smoothing produce forecasts exactly equal to observed data when there is no noise present in the data.

Let $a_{est} = 50$, $b_{est} = 0.5$, and $c_{est} = 0.2$. Then

$$S_0^{[1]} = 50 - \left[\frac{(1-0.3)}{0.3}\right] 0.5 + \left[\frac{(1-0.3)\,(2-0.3)}{(0.3)^2}\right] 0.2 = 51.478$$

$$S_0^{[2]} = 50 - \left[\frac{2(1-0.3)}{0.3}\right] 0.5 + \left[\frac{2(1-0.3)\,(3-0.6)}{(0.3)^2}\right] 0.2 = 55.134$$

$$S_0^{[3]} = 50 - \left[\frac{3(1-0.3)}{0.3}\right] 0.5 + \left[\frac{3(1-0.3)\,(4-0.9)}{(0.3)^2}\right] 0.2 = 60.967$$

These smoothed statistics are utilized as our initial estimates in Table 5-4. The data are exponentially smoothed as shown in Table 5-4, and in period $t = 10$ the estimates of the parameters are calculated. These estimates are calculated below in developing a forecast for period $t = 20$.

At $t = 10$,

$$a_{10} = 3S_{10}^{[1]} - 3S_{10}^{[2]} + S_{10}^{[3]} \qquad \text{[from (5-15)]}$$

$$= 3(67.144) - 3(61.466) + 57.966 = 75.0$$

table 5-4 . . . forecasting a trend with curvature

Period Number t	Demand, x_t (1000 Units)	$S_t^{[1]}$	$S_t^{[2]}$	$S_t^{[3]}$
0	—	51.478	55.134	60.967
1	50.7	51.245	53.967	58.867
2	51.8	51.411	53.200	57.167
3	53.3	51.978	52.833	55.867
4	55.2	52.944	52.866	54.966
5	57.5	54.311	53.300	54.466
6	60.2	56.078	54.133	54.366
7	63.3	58.244	55.366	54.666
8	66.8	60.811	57.000	55.366
9	70.7	63.778	59.033	56.466
10	75.0	67.144	61.466	57.966

$$b_{10} = \frac{\alpha}{2(1-\alpha)^2} [(6-5\alpha)S_{10}^{[1]} - 2(5-4\alpha)S_{10}^{[2]} + (4-3\alpha)S_{10}^{[3]}] \quad \text{[from (5-16)]}$$

$$= \frac{0.3}{2(0.7)^2} [(4.5(67.144) - 7.6(61.466) + 3.1(57.966)]$$

$$= 4.5$$

$$c_{10} = \frac{\alpha^2}{2(1-\alpha)^2} [S_t^{[1]} - 2S_t^{[2]} + S_t^{[3]}] \quad \text{[from (5-17)]}$$

$$= \frac{0.3^2}{2(0.7)^2} [67.144 - 2(61.466) + 57.966]$$

$$= 0.2$$

Our forecasting equation in period 10 is

$$y_{10} = 75 + 4.5T + 0.2T^2$$

and our forecast for period 20 is

$$y_{10+10} = 75 + 4.5(10) + 0.2(10)^2 = 140$$

The original equation used to develop this data was $y = 50 + 0.5t + 0.2t^2$. The response for period 20, using this equation, is $y = 50 + 0.5(20) + 0.2(20)^2 = 140$ which is identical to the forecast based on a_{10}, b_{10}, and c_{10}. This illustrates that we may utilize the above equations to obtain initial estimates of $S_0^{[1]}$, $S_0^{[2]}$, and $S_0^{[3]}$. The problem also demonstrates triple exponential smoothing calculations, the use of equations to obtain a_{est}, b_{est} and c_{est}, and the development of a forecast for a period T time units in the future.

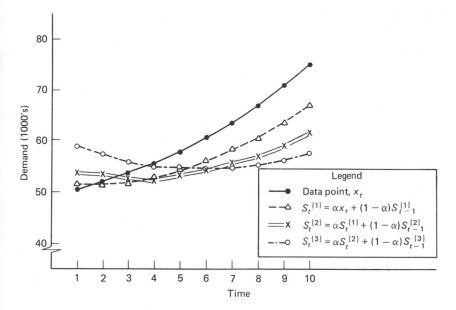

figure 5-5 . . . use of exponential smoothing to forecast a trend having curvature

winters' method

Many forecasted quantities exhibit a seasonal influence in addition to a linear trend. An example of this is beer sales, toy sales, many food item sales and even some stock prices. Example data for such a quantity are listed in Table 5-5 and illustrated in Figure 5-6. Simple techniques for graphing and analyzing the available data are first discussed in this section because these techniques are often sufficient to make a forecast with only a few calculations. Winters' method of forecasting is then presented. Winters' method is a procedure for revising the forecasting equations as new information becomes available.

The first step in analyzing seasonal data is to plot the data and visually sketch a trend line on the graph. This is illustrated in Figure 5-6. The trend line should pass through the center of the data and should express the general long-term trend. It is not usually necessary to use regression to obtain a good estimate of the trend line. The next step is to read the value from the trend line that corresponds to each time period, and compare it to the actual observation. In Figure 5-6, the trend line intersects the y-axis (demand) at 50.0. In period 24 the trend line has a value of 64, so the slope of the trend line is $\dfrac{(64-50)}{24 \text{ periods}} = 0.583$, and the equation of the line is $y = 50.0 + 0.583t$, where t is the period number. In period 1 the value from the trend line is 50.0 +

table 5-5 . . . data for a linear trend with a seasonal effect

Period Number t	(A) Demand, x_t (1000 Units)	(B) Value From Trend Line in Figure 5-6	(C) (A)÷(B)
1	59.1	50.6	1.17
2	55.0	51.2	1.07
3	50.2	51.7	0.97
4	46.9	52.3	0.90
5	46.2	52.9	0.87
6	46.1	53.5	0.86
7	46.5	54.1	0.86
8	47.2	54.7	0.86
9	49.5	55.2	0.90
10	58.1	55.8	1.04
11	64.4	56.4	1.14
12	66.2	57.0	1.16
13	65.6	57.6	1.14
14	63.2	58.2	1.09
15	59.2	58.7	1.01
16	55.7	59.3	0.94
17	54.3	59.9	0.91
18	53.7	60.5	0.89
19	54.0	61.1	0.88
20	54.8	61.7	0.89
21	56.3	62.2	0.91
22	62.6	62.8	1.00
23	69.1	63.4	1.09
24	71.9	64.0	1.12

0.583(1) = 50.583 which is rounded to 50.6 and entered in Table 5-5. Column B of Table 5-5 is obtained by making these same calculations for each period. The actual data in Column A are then divided by the values of the trend line in Column B to obtain the multiplicative seasonal factors of Column C. In Column C of Table 5-5 it can be seen that demand in the first January (period 1) was 1.17 times the value of the trend line, and in the second January (period 13) it was 1.14 times the value of the trend line. In Table 5-6, these factors are averaged for each month to obtain an initial estimate of the multiplicative seasonal factors. The seasonal effect of this example occurs over a length of time equal to 12 months, or 12 data points, which is quite common in practice. This *periodicity* of 12 months, however,

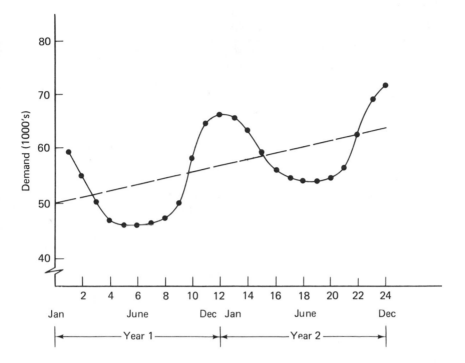

figure 5-6 . . . an illustration of a linear trend with a seasonal effect

is not a prerequisite for applying these procedures (i.e., the periodicity might be 4, 16, etc., depending on the nature of the data).

Based on this simple analysis, the forecaster has sufficient information to forecast demand for any future period. For example, if we wish to forecast demand for July in year 5 and we are presently at time zero, our forecast is 55 months $(12 \frac{\text{months}}{\text{year}} \times 4 \text{ years} + 7 \text{ months} = 55 \text{ months})$ into the future. The value of the trend line in July 1975 is $50 + 0.583(55) = 82.1$. The multiplicative seasonal factor for July from Table 5-6 is 0.87 so our estimated demand for July 1975 is $0.87(82.1) = 71.4$.

Winters' method begins with this initial information and then incorporates exponential smoothing to update estimates of the intercept, the slope of the trend line, and the seasonal factors. The basic equations for doing this are presented first, and then they are applied to an example problem.

At time t we utilize these relationships prior to actually making a forecast:

A. The estimate of the current intercept is:

$$a_t = \alpha \left(\frac{x_t}{F_{t-N'}} \right) + (1-\alpha)(a_{t-1} + b_{t-1}) \tag{5-23}$$

table 5-6 . . . calculations for winters' method

Position of Data Point in the Cycle	Average of Historical Multiplicative Seasonal Factors
1—Jan	(1.17 + 1.14)/2 = 1.16
2—Feb	(1.07 + 1.09)/2 = 1.08
3—March	(0.97 + 1.01)/2 = 0.99
4—April	(0.90 + 0.94)/2 = 0.92
5—May	(0.87 + 0.91)/2 = 0.89
6—June	(0.86 + 0.89)/2 = 0.88
7—July	(0.86 + 0.88)/2 = 0.87
8—Aug	(0.86 + 0.89)/2 = 0.88
9—Sept	(0.90 + 0.91)/2 = 0.91
10—Oct	(1.04 + 1.00)/2 = 1.02
11—Nov	(1.14 + 1.09)/2 = 1.12
12—Dec	(1.16 + 1.12)/2 = 1.17

At time $t = 24$, the best estimates of the multiplicative seasonal factors are the above averages:

$$F_{13} = 1.16 \qquad F_{19} = 0.87$$
$$F_{14} = 1.08 \qquad F_{20} = 0.88$$
$$F_{15} = 0.99 \qquad F_{21} = 0.91$$
$$F_{16} = 0.92 \qquad F_{22} = 1.02$$
$$F_{17} = 0.89 \qquad F_{23} = 1.12$$
$$F_{18} = 0.88 \qquad F_{24} = 1.17$$

B. The estimate of the slope of the trend line is:

$$b_t = \beta(a_t - a_{t-1}) + (1-\beta)b_{t-1} \tag{5-24}$$

C. The updated seasonal factor is:

$$F_t = \sigma\left(\frac{x_t}{a_t}\right) + (1-\sigma)\,F_{t-N}' \tag{5-25}$$

D. The forecast developed at time t for a period T time units into the future is:

$$y_{t+T} = (a_t + b_t T)F^* \tag{5-26}$$

The individual terms in the above equations are defined as follows:

1. x_t is the actual observation of time t.

2. a_t is the estimated intercept of the trend line at time t.

3. b_t is the estimated slope of the trend line at time t.

4. N' is the number of observations comprising the periodicity of the data.

5. F_t is the estimate of the multiplicative seasonal factor for period t.

6. $F_{t-N'}$ is the estimate of the seasonal factor N' periods in the past. For example if we are in June of year 3, then we are in period $t = 30$ ($2 \times 12 + 6 = 30$) when $N' = 12$. It is clear that $t-N' = 30-12 = 18$, which is June of year 2. In Equation (5-25), $F_{t-N'}$ simply indicates that to update our estimate of the June seasonal factor we must utilize the previous best estimate of the June seasonal factor.

7. F^* is used to denote our best estimate of the seasonal factor in period $t+T$. If we are forecasting for some future June, we must use our current best estimate of the June seasonal factor as F^*.

8. α, β, and σ are exponential smoothing constants, where $0 < \alpha, \beta, \sigma < 1$. It is common for forecasters to assume the same values for all three of these constants. However, it may be desirable to have the estimates of the intercept, the slope, and the seasonal factors react at different rates to changes in the data.

The use of these equations can be best explained through an example. Referring to the data of Table 5-5, let us assume that we are in January of year 3 (i.e., period 25) and have just experienced a demand of 75 so that $x_{25} = 75$. Our best estimate of the slope at the end of the previous period is 0.583 which was obtained from the trend line, $b_{24} = 0.583$. Our best estimate of the value of the trend line in the previous period $a_{24} = 50 + 0.583(24) = 64.0$. The best estimates of the seasonal factors are given in Table 5-6. We shall let $\alpha = \beta = \sigma = 0.3$, which places heavy weight on current data. In practice the forecaster should experiment with different values of these smoothing constants to develop a model that minimizes the mean square error.

The following calculations illustrate Winters' method in terms of Equations (5-23), (5-24), and (5-25) to determine a_{25}, b_{25} and F_{25}.

$$a_{25} = \alpha\left(\frac{x_{25}}{F_{25-12}}\right) + (1 - \alpha)(a_{24} + b_{24})$$

$$= 0.3\left(\frac{75}{1.16}\right) + 0.7(64.0 + 0.583)$$

$$= 64.60$$

$$b_{25} = \beta(a_{25} - a_{24}) + (1 - \beta)b_{24}$$

$$= 0.3(64.60 - 64.0) + 0.7(0.583)$$

$$= 0.588$$

$$F_{25} = \sigma\left(\frac{x_{25}}{a_{25}}\right) + (1 - \sigma)F_{13}$$

$$= 0.3\left(\frac{75}{64.60}\right) + 0.7 \ (1.16)$$

$$= \mathbf{1.16}$$

F_{25} will be stored and used the next time a January forecast is required. F_{13} is discarded. When x_{26} becomes available, a_{26}, b_{26} and F_{26} can then be calculated. The values of a_{25} and b_{25} obtained above and the previously estimated F_{14} are required in making these revisions.

By using the information available in period 25, our forecast of June's demand is

$$y_{25+5} = (a_{25} + b_{25} \cdot 5)F^*$$

$$= [64.60 + 5(0.588)] \ 0.88 = \mathbf{59.43}$$

Here we let $T = 5$ because June is 5 months into the future from January of the same year.

Winters' method is a direct, simple, computationally tractable technique for forecasting seasonal data. It can be applied to data with periodicity of any number of data points and to data with an unusual pattern if a cycling trend can be observed.

choosing a smoothing constant

A simple example is provided at this point to illustrate a procedure for choosing a smoothing constant. A random number generator provided 10 data points that fell in an interval of 40 to 60, inclusive. These hypothetical data could represent many real-world processes such as inventory levels, a stock price, or the ash content of a pound of coal. The data are listed in Table 5-7, and single exponential smoothing is used to forecast one period into the future. At first, two values of the smoothing constant, $\alpha = 0.1$ and $\alpha = 0.3$, are applied to the data. It is assumed that the forecast for period 1 is 50. The forecast and the mean square error for these two α values are shown in Table 5-7.

Examining these results, we see that the smaller α value, $\alpha = 0.1$, has a slightly smaller MSE. In searching for an improved α, the MSE for $\alpha = 0.05$ is evaluated and found to be smaller. Out of curiosity, an $\alpha = 0$ is evaluated and found to have the least MSE of any α evaluated. This indicates that the best forecast for this set of random data having a horizontal pattern is a constant that is not updated with each new data point. For this type of situation the forecaster might use a very small α that results in a low MSE but that would still detect a change in the data pattern. *In general, if the underlying pattern of the data does not change often, a small α is appropriate. If there are frequent changes in the basic data pattern, then a large α is selected so the model can react quickly to the change.*

table 5-7 . . . . choosing a smoothing constant

Time Period	Data Point	α = 0.10 Forecast	Squared Error	α = 0.20 Forecast	Squared Error	α = 0.05 Forecast	Squared Error	α = 0.00 Forecast	Squared Error
0	50	—	—	—	—	—	—	—	—
1	59	50.0	81.0	50.0	81.0	50.0	81.0	50.0	81.0
2	44	50.9	47.6	51.8	60.8	50.4	41.0	50.0	36.0
3	50	50.2	0.0	50.2	0.0	50.1	0.0	50.0	0.0
4	60	50.2	96.0	50.2	96.0	50.1	98.0	50.0	100.0
5	52	51.2	0.6	52.2	0.0	50.6	2.0	50.0	4.0
6	47	51.2	17.6	52.1	26.0	50.7	13.7	50.0	9.0
7	41	50.8	96.0	51.1	102.0	50.5	90.3	50.0	81.0
8	43	49.8	46.2	49.1	37.2	50.0	49.0	50.0	49.0
9	48	49.2	1.4	47.9	0.0	49.7	2.9	50.0	4.0
10	52	49.0	9.0	47.9	16.8	49.6	5.8	50.0	4.0
			395.4		419.8		383.7		368.0

$\alpha = 0.10$

$$MSE = \frac{395.4}{10} = 39.54$$

$\alpha = 0.20$

$$MSE = \frac{419.8}{10} = 41.98$$

$\alpha = 0.05$

$$MSE = \frac{383.7}{10} = 38.4$$

$\alpha = 0.00$

$$MSE = \frac{368.0}{10} = 36.8$$

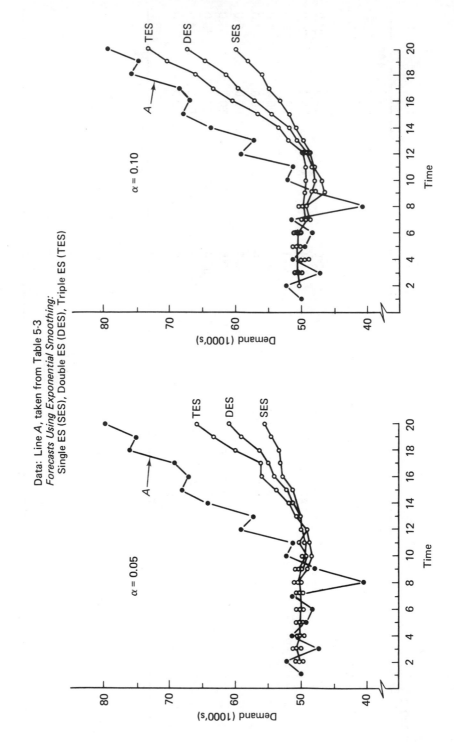

Data: Line A, taken from Table 5-3
Forecasts Using Exponential Smoothing:
Single ES (SES), Double ES (DES), Triple ES (TES)

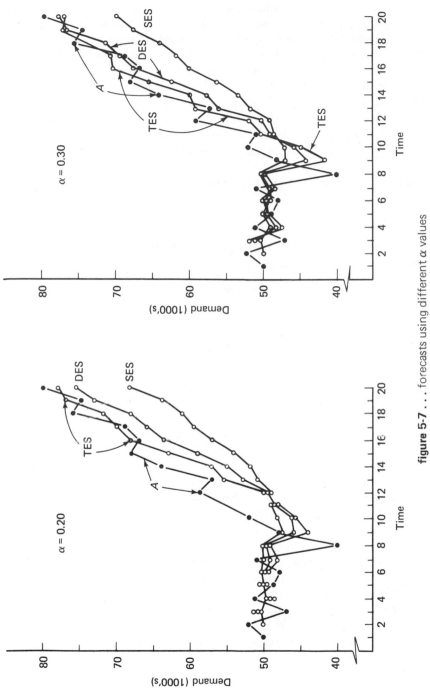

figure 5-7 . . . forecasts using different α values

A second example illustrating the effects of various α values is illustrated in Figure 5-7. These are the same data that were used earlier to illustrate the single and double exponentially smoothed values in Figure 5-4. Each graph in Figure 5-7 shows the raw data and actual forecasts developed for one period in the future (T = 1) with single, double and triple exponential smoothing. There is no appreciable difference in the first portion of the graphs among single, double, and triple exponential smoothed forecasts. Nor are there large differences brought about by different α values. When a linear trend is introduced, the forecasts developed with triple exponential smoothing react more quickly than do the other methods. Forecasts made with larger α values also respond quickly to the linear trend. However, when α is large, forecasts are quite sensitive to noise and may overreact to random influences in the data.

a computer program for making forecasts with techniques described in chapters 4 and 5

In this section a computer program is presented that will take a set of data and calculate forecasts with these methods:

1. Simple regression
2. Moving averages (single and double)
3. Exponential smoothing (single, double and triple)
4. Winters' method of exponential smoothing

The purpose of the program is twofold: (1) To permit the user to compare forecasting techniques for a particular set of data so that the one having the smallest mean square error can be identified, and (2) To enable the user to prepare forecasts T periods into the future without having to perform the calculations manually. The potential user is advised to read Chapters 4 and 5 before utilizing this program, if he has not already done so. The program is written in FORTRAN IV and can be run on most computer systems.

We first review briefly *how* the computer calculates forecasts, residuals, etc. for each of the techniques listed above. (A more detailed explanation of *why* forecasts are prepared as they are in the program has been given in Chapters 4 and 5.) Then we describe how various data and parameters are keypunched onto standard computer cards, and what changes must be made in the program deck to accommodate desired modifications in the manner forecasts are calculated. Finally, two different sets of data are utilized to demonstrate how the output appears and to explain column headings of various quantities that are computed. A listing of the entire program is given later so that the reader may reproduce it if he desires to make forecasts with any one, or all, of the aforementioned techniques.

I. *General description of each part of the program.*

A. **Simple regression.** The method of least squares is employed to fit a line through the data. Then the program uses the equation for the line to determine the predicted value of the dependent variable for observed values of the independent variable, and the prediction error is calculated by comparing the forecasts with the actual data. The Y-intercept (A^*) and the slope (B^*) of the regression line are also calculated and printed in the output of the program.

B. **Moving averages and exponential smoothing.**

1. *Single moving averages.* The program reads the number of periods (NUM*) from a data card that are to be employed to calculate single moving averages (SMA*). These moving averages are the "Forecasted Values" and are compared with actual data to determine the error terms. These residuals are printed in the output.

2. *Double moving averages.* The program uses the number of periods in the moving average (NUM*) to calculate double moving averages (DMA*). The DMA values are then utilized to determine the corresponding a_t (MA*) and b_t (MB*) terms for the forecasting equation. Then the forecasting equation, $y_{t+T} = a_t + b_t \cdot T$ (FDMA* = MA + MB * 1), is used to determine the forecasting value for each period when $T = 1$. Forecasts are compared with actual data in deriving forecasting error, and the results are printed in the output.

3. *Simple exponential smoothing.* The program uses the second data point ($Y(2)^*$) as the smoothed statistic for the first period. Then smoothed statistics (SES*) in subsequent periods are calculated by using the desired α (ALPHA*) value, where $0 \leqslant \alpha \leqslant 1$. The smoothed statistics are regarded as the forecasted values (FSES*) for following periods. Comparisons between actual observations and forecasted values are made for purposes of calculating the mean square error. Results are printed in the output.

4. *Double exponential smoothing.* The program uses the second point ($Y(2)^*$) as the double smoothed statistic (DES*) for the first period. Doubly smoothed statistics (DES*) are calculated for each succeeding time period based on the specified α (ALPHA*) value. Then the coefficients of the forecasting equation (EA*, EB*) are calculated so that next period's prediction can be determined. The forecast for each period is compared to

---

Note: When an asterisk (*) appears next to a symbol such as A, B, SMA, etc., this means that the same symbol is used in the computer program to represent the variable or parameter being described.

the actual value (observation) so that a mean square error for the double exponential smoothing technique can be computed.

5. *Triple exponential smoothing.* The program uses the second data point ($Y(2)*$) as the triple smoothed statistic (TES*) for the first period. A value of TES is calculated as each new data point is taken into account. Again, α (ALPHA*) is used in making this calculation. Then the coefficients of the forecasting equation (TA*, TB*, TC*) are calculated for each period so that next period's forecast may be determined. The forecast for each period is compared to the actual observation in that period to permit the mean square error to be evaluated.

C. **Winters' method.** The regression line that was determined in the first part of this program is used as the initial trend line in Winters' method. Then the program utilizes the first 2L data points (periodicity of L*) to find the initial multiplicative seasonal factors (SF1*, SF2*). For example, if L = 4, the first eight data points are used to make these initial estimates. After the initial multiplicative seasonal factors are calculated for two cycles, they are averaged and used to make initial estimates of the "future seasonal factors (SF*)." Next the program uses exponential smoothing to update estimates of the intercept (AA*), slope (BB*), and multiplicative seasonal factors (SSF*) as additional data points are evaluated. These estimates are needed to make a forecast for the following period. The forecast (FW*) is calculated and compared with the actual observation so that the mean square error can be obtained for this method.

II. *Description of data input cards.*

A. **Card-by-card explanation of the input data.**

1. *Number of data points.* This card serves to read into the computer the number of observations that comprises your time-series. An example of how this card would be punched when 60 data points were available is shown here.

2. *Period numbers and corresponding observations.* This group of cards feeds in the historical data that are available for all time

periods. The number of pairs of values read into the computer must correspond to the integer that appears on the first data card (above). An example of the card for period 4 which has a value of 51.0 is shown below.

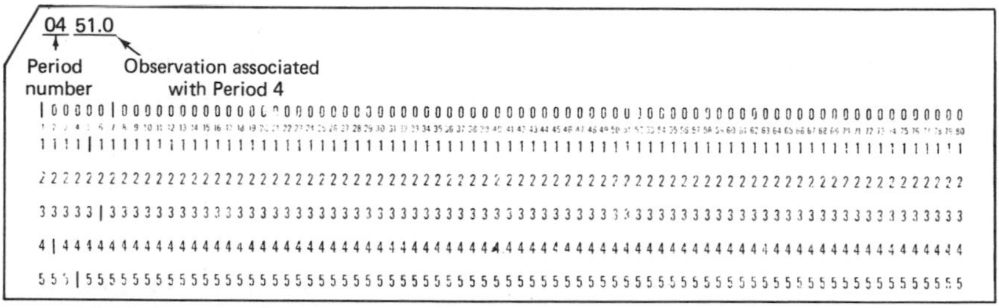

04 51.0

Period number

Observation associated with Period 4

3. *Number of periods in the single and double moving averages.* This card reads the NUM value that the user wishes to utilize for the number of periods in calculating the single and double moving average. An example of the card with NUM = 6 is shown below.

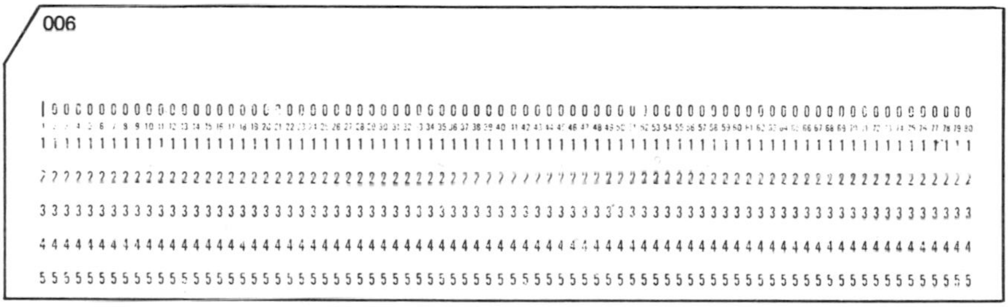

006

4. *Alpha value for exponential smoothing.* This card reads in the ALPHA value that the user wishes to utilize in all three exponential smoothing techniques. An example of the card with ALPHA = 0.3 is shown below.

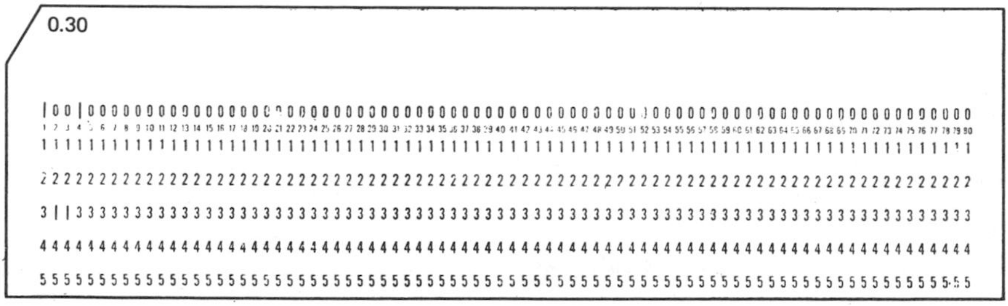

0.30

5. *Value of* T *utilized for making forecasts.* This card specifies the number of periods into the future at which time the user desires

a forecast. An example of T = 10 periods from now that the user wants a forecast is shown below.

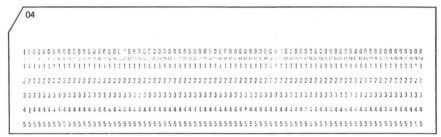

6. *Value of* L *(Periodicity) for Winters' method.* This card reads the value of L to be used in making forecasts with Winters' method. For quarterly data the periodicity L should be 4. For this situation the card is shown below.

7. *Smoothing constants for Winters' method.* This card inputs the alpha, beta, and sigma values that the user chooses for Winters' method of exponential smoothing. Recall that $0 \leqslant \alpha, \beta, \sigma \leqslant 1$. An example of the card is shown below.

B. Input data format summary.

Data Cards	Column	Format	Parameter	Explanation
1. Number of data points	1-2	I2	N	Number of data points available.

2. Period numbers   1-2   I2   X(I)   Period number.
   and correspond-   4-7   F4.1   Y(I)   Value associated with
   ing observations   each time period.
3. Number of per-   1-3   I3   NUM   Number of data points
   iods for moving   to be used in calculat-
   averages   ing moving averages.
4. ALPHA value   1-4   F5.3 ALPHA α value for exponen-
   for exponential   tial smoothing.
   smoothing
5. Value of *T*   1-2   I2   T   Number of periods
   utilized for   ahead that you want
   making fore-   to forecast.
   casts
6. Value of *L*   1-2   I2   L   Number of data points
   (periodicity)   that comprise one
   for Winters'   cycle of seasonal in-
   method   fluences.
7. Smoothing
   constants for   1-4   F4.2 WALPHA α for Winters' method
   Winters'   6-9   F4.2 WBETA β for Winters' method
   method   11-14 F4.2 WSIGMA σ for Winters' method

C.   General layout of the program deck and data cards.

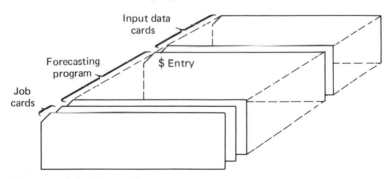

III. Printout of the Source Program.

```
      INTEGER X,T,REM,SM1,SM2,DM1,DM2                                     1
      DIMENSION X(61),Y(61),DX(61),DY(61),DXSQ(61),DYSQ(61),              2
     *EST(61,E(61),ESQ(61),SMA(62),DES(62),YESTSQ(61),YEST(61),           3
     *DMA(62),MA(62),MB(62),FDMA(62),SES(62),EA(62),EB(62),FDES(62),      4
     *ESMA(62),ESMASQ(62),EDMA(62),EDMASQ(62),ESES(62),ESESSQ(62),        5
     *EDES(62),ESESSQ(62),SMASQ(62),FDMASQ(62),SESSQ(62),FDESSQ(62),      6
     *SF1(61),SF2(61),SF(61),AA(61),BB(61),SSF(61),FW(62),                7
     *EFW(61),EFWSQ(61),FWSQ(61),EMA(61),EES(61),EW(61),                  8
     *TES(62),TA(62),TB(62),TC(62),FTES(62),ETES(62),FTESSQ(62),          9
     *ETESSQ(62),FSES(62)                                                 10
      SUMY=0.                                                             11
      SUMDY=0.                                                            12
```

```
          SUMX=0.                                                        13
          SDYSQ=0.                                                       14
          SDXSQ=0.                                                       15
          SUMXY=0.                                                       16
          SUMXSQ=0.                                                      17
          S1=0.                                                          18
          S2=0.                                                          19
          S3=0.                                                          20
          S4=0.                                                          21
          S5=0.                                                          22
          S6=0.                                                          23
          S7=0.                                                          24
          S8=0.0                                                         25
          SS1=0.                                                         26
          SS2=0.                                                         27
          SS3=0.                                                         28
          SS4=0.                                                         29
          SS5=0.                                                         30
          SS6=0.                                                         31
          SS7=0.                                                         32
          SS8=0.                                                         33
          SS9=0.                                                         34
          SS10=0.                                                        35
          SS11=0.                                                        36
          SS12=0.0                                                       37
          SS13=0.0                                                       38
C    READ IN NUMBER OF DATA POINTS                                       39
          READ(5,7)N                                                     40
        7 FORMAT(I2)                                                     41
C                                                                        42
C    READ IN PERIOD AND CORRESPONDING DATA                              43
          J=N+1                                                          44
          X(1)=0
          Y(1)=0.0
          READ(5,10) (X(I),Y(I),I=2,J)                                   45
       10 FORMAT(I2,1X,F4.0)                                             46
C                                                                        47
C    INPUT NUMBER OF PERIOD FOR MOVING AVERAGE
          READ(5,470)NUM
      470 FORMAT(I3)
C    READ IN ALPHA VALUE                                                 48
          READ(5,9)ALPHA                                                 49
        9 FORMAT(F4.3)                                                   50
C                                                                        51
C    READ IN THE NUMBER OF PERIODS AHEAD THAT THE FORECAST SHOULD BE MADE  52
          READ(5,19)T                                                    53
       19 FORMAT(I2)                                                     54
C    READ IN VALUE OF L(PERIODICITY) FOR WINTERS' METHOD
          READ(5,41)L
       41 FORMAT(I2)
C    READ IN SMOOTHING CONSTANTS FOR WINTERS' METHOD
          READ(5,42)WALPHA, WBETA,WDELTA
       42 FORMAT(F4.2,1X,F4.2,1X,F4.2)
C   ***************************                                          55
C   SIMPLE REGRESSION                                                    56
C   ***********************                                              57
C                                                                        58
          DO 2 I=2,J                                                     59
          SUMY=SUMY+Y(I)                                                 60
```

```
       2 SUMX=SUMX+X(I)                                              61
         AVGY=SUMY/N                                                 62
         AVGX=SUMX/N                                                 63
         DO 3 I=2,J                                                  64
         DY(I)=Y(I)-AVGY                                             65
         SUMDY=SUMDY+DY(I)                                           66
         DX(I)=X(I)-AVGX                                             67
         DYSQ(I)=DY(I)**2                                            68
         SDYSQ=SDYSQ+DYSQ(I)                                         69
         DXSQ(I)=DX(I)**2                                            70
         SDXSQ=SDXSQ+DXSQ(I)                                         71
         SUMXY=SUMXY+(X(I)*Y(I))                                     72
       3 SUMXSQ=SUMXSQ+X(I)**2                                       73
C                                                                    74
C   COEFFICIENTS OF SIMPLE REGRESSION                                75
C   SIMPLE LINEAR REGRESSION LINE IS ' Y(I)=A + BX(I)'               76
C                                                                    77
         B=(SUMXY-(AVGX*SUMY))/(SUMXSQ-(AVGX*SUMX))                  78
         A=AVGY-(B*AVGX)                                             79
C                                                                    80
C   ESTIMATED VALUES AND RESIDUALS                                   81
C   YEST(I) = ESTIMATED Y VALUE AT TIME I                            82
C   E(I) = DIFFERENCE BETWEEN ESTIMATED Y VALUE AND ACTUAL VALUE     83
C   AT TIME I                                                        84
C                                                                    85
         DO 4 I=2,J                                                  86
         YEST(I)=A+B*X(I)                                            87
         YESTSQ(I)=YEST(I)**2                                        88
         E(I)=Y(I)-YEST(I)                                           89
         ESQ(I)=E(I)**2                                              90
       4 CONTINUE                                                    91
         WRITE(6,12)                                                 92
      12 FORMAT(//,4X,'*** SIMPLE REGRESSION ***')                   93
         WRITE(6,15)                                                 94
      15 FORMAT(//,4X,'X',4X,'Y',7X,' FORECAST',4X,'E',11X,'ESQ')    95

         DO 5 I=2,J                                                  97
         WRITE(6,16) X(I),Y(I),YEST(I),E(I),ESQ(I)                   98
      16 FORMAT(3X,I2,2X,F5.0,3X,F10.4,2X,F9.4,2X,F13.4)             99
       5 CONTINUE                                                   100
C                                                                   101
C   SS1 = SUM OF SQUARES OF RESIDUALS IN SIMPLE REGRESSION          102
C                                                                   103
         DO 6 I=2,J                                                 104
         S1=S1+YEST(I)                                              105
         S2=S2+YESTSQ(I)                                            106
       6 SS1=SS1+ESQ(I)                                             107
         WRITE(6,17) S1,SS1                                         108
      17 FORMAT('0',/,9X,F15.4,11X,F15.3)                           109
         WRITE(6,18)AVGX,AVGY,A,B                                   110
      18 FORMAT('0',///,'0AVERAGE X= ',F8.4,/,'0AVERAGE Y= ',F12.4,/, 111
        *'0A OF SIMPLE REGRESSION= ',F10.4,/,                       112
        *'0B OF SIMPLE REGRESSION= ',F10.4)                         113
C                                                                   114
C                                                                   115
C                                                                   116
C   *********************************************                   117
C   MOVING AVERAGES AND EXPONENTIAL SMOOTHING                       118
C   *********************************************                   119
```

```
C                                                                     120
C    SMA = SIMPLE MOVING AVERAGES                                     121
C    DMA = DOUBLE MOVING AVERAGES                                     122
C    FDMA = FORECAST WITH DOUBLE MOVING AVERAGES                      123
C                                                                     124
     NP1=N+2                                                          125
     NUM1=NUM
     NUM=NUM1+2
     SM1=1
     SM2=NUM1
     DO 8 I=NUM,NP1
     SM =0.0
     DO 450 M=SM1,SM2
     SM=SM+Y(M+1)
 450 CONTINUE
     SM1=SM1+1
     SM2=SM2+1
     SMA(I)=SM /NUM1
     SMASQ(I)=SMA(I)**2                                               128
   8 CONTINUE                                                         129
     NUM=NUM1*2+1
     DM1=1
     DM2=NUM1
     DO 45 I=NUM,NP1
     DM =0.0
     DO 460 M=DM1,DM2
     DM =DM +SMA(M+1+NUM1)
 460 CONTINUE
     DM1=DM1+1
     DM2=DM2+1
     DMA(I)=DM /NUM1
     MA(I)=SMA(I)*2.−DMA(I)                                           132
     MB(I)=(SMA(I)−DMA(I))*2/3                                        133
     FDMA(I+1)=MA(I)+MB(I)                                            134
     FDMASQ(I+1)=FDMA(I+1)**2                                         135
  45 CONTINUE                                                         136
     FORDMA=MA(J)+MB(J)*T
C                                                                     137
C    SES = SMOOTHED STATISTIC FOR SINGLE EXPONENTIAL SMOOTHING        138
C    DES = SMOOTHED STATISTIC FOR DOUBLE EXPONENTIAL SMOOTHING.       139
C    TES= SMOOTHED STATISTIC FOR TRIPLE EXPONENTIAL SMOOTHING         140
C    EA,EB ARE THE COEFFICIENTS IN THE FORECASTING EQUATION FOR DOUBLE 141
C       EXPONENTIAL SMOOTHING.
C    TA,TB,TC ARE THE COEFFICIENTS IN THE FORECASTING EQUATION FOR    142
C       TRIPLE EXPONENTIAL SMOOTHING.
C    FDES = FORECAST WITH DOUBLE EXPONENTIAL SMOOTHING                143
C    FTES=FORECAST WITH TRIPLE EXPONENTIAL SMOOTHING                  144
C                                                                     145
     SES(1)=Y(2)                                                      146
     DO 46 I=2,J                                                      147
     SES(I)=ALPHA*(Y(I)−SES(I−1))+SES(I−1)                           148
  46 CONTINUE                                                         151
     DO 410 I=3,J
     FSES(I)=SES(I−1)                                                 149
     SESSQ(I)=FSES(I)**2                                              150
 410 CONTINUE
     SESFOR=SES(J)
     DES(1)=Y(2)                                                      152
     DO 55 I=2,J                                                      153
```

```
        DES(I)=ALPHA*SES(I)+(1.−ALPHA)*DES(I−1)                        154
        EA(I)=2.*SES(I)−DES(I)                                         155
        EB(I)=(SES(I)−DES(I))*ALPHA/(1.−ALPHA)                         156
     55 CONTINUE                                                       159
        DO 420 I=3,J
        FDES(I)=EA(I−1)+EB(I−1)
        FDESSQ(I)=FDES(I)**2                                           158
    420 CONTINUE
        DESFOR=EA(J)+T*EB(J)                                           160
        TES(1)=Y(2)                                                    161
        DO 51 I=2,J                                                    162
        TES(I)=ALPHA*DES(I)+(1.−ALPHA)*TES(I−1)                        163
        TA(I)=3.*SES(I)−3.*DES(I)+TES(I−1)                             164
        TB(I)=(ALPHA/(2.*(1.−ALPHA)**2))*((6.−5.*ALPHA)*SES(I)−(10.−8.* 165
       *ALPHA)*DES(I)+(4.−3.*ALPHA)*TES(I))                            166
        TC(I)=(ALPHA/(1.−ALPHA))**2*(SES(I)−2.0*DES(I'+TES(I))         167
     51 CONTINUE                                                       170
        DO 430 I=3,J
        FTES(I)=TA(I−1)+TB(I−1)+TC(I−1)/2.
        FTESSQ(I)=FTES(I)**2                                           169
    430 CONTINUE
        TESFOR=TA(J)+TB(J)*T+TC(J)/2.0*T**2                            171
C                                                                      172
C ESMA,EDMA,ESES,EDES = DIFFERENCE BETWEEN ESTIMATED AND ACTUAL VALUE  173
C IN SIMPLE,DOUBLE MOVING AVERAGES AND SINGLE,DOUBLE EXPONENTIAL       174
C SMOOTHING.
C ETES=DIFFERENCE BETWEEN ESTIMATED AND ACTUAL VALUE IN TRIPLE         175
C         EXPONENTIAL SMOOTHING.                                       176
C                                                                      177
        NUM=NUM1+2
        DO 11 I=NUM,J                                                  178
        ESMA(I)=SMA(I)−Y(I)                                            179
        ESMASQ(I)=ESMA(I)**2                                           180
     11 CONTINUE                                                       181
        NUM=NUM1+2
        DO 47 I=NUM,J                                                  182
        EDMA(I)=FDMA(I)−Y(I)                                           183
        EDMASQ(I)=EDMA(I)**2                                           184
     47 CONTINUE                                                       185
        DO 48 I=3,J                                                    186
        ESES(I)=FSES(I)−Y(I)                                           187
        ESESSQ(I)=ESES(I)**2                                           188
        EDES(I)=FDES(I)−Y(I)                                           189
        EDESSQ(I)=EDES(I)**2                                           190
        ETES(I)=FTES(I)−Y(I)                                           191
        ETESSQ(I)=ETES(I)**2                                           192
     48 CONTINUE                                                       193
        WRITE(6,20)                                                    194
     20 FORMAT(//,4X,'*** MOVING AVERAGES ***')                        195
        WRITE(6,22)                                                    196
     22 FORMAT(4X,'PERIOD',2X,'ACTUAL',2X,'SIMPLE MOVING AVERAGE',     197
       *27X,'DOUBLE MOVING AVERAGE')                                   198
        WRITE(6,23)                                                    199
     23 FORMAT(19X,'FORECAST',2X,'RESIDUAL',2X,'RESIDUAL−SQ',          200
       *15X,'M(2)' 4X,'FORECAST',2X,'RESIDUAL',2X,                     201
       *'RESIDUAL−SQ'                                                  202
        DO 98 I=2,J                                                    203
        WRITE(6,24) X(I),Y(I),SMA(I),ESMA(I),SMASQ(I),DMA(I),          204
       *FDMA(I),EDMA(I),EDMASQ(I)                                      205
```

```
24 FORMAT(7X,I2,3X,F5,0,2X,F8,3,2X,F8.3,15X,F11.3,2X,F8.3.         206
  *2X,F8.3,2X,F8.3,2X,F11.3)                                        207
98 CONTINUE                                                         208
   NUM=NUM1+2
   DO 13 I=NUM ,J                                                   209
   S3=S3+SMA(I)                                                     210
   SS2=SS2+ESMASQ(I)                                                211
13 SS3=SS3+SMASQ(I)                                                 212
   NUM=NUM1*2+2
   DO 49 I=NUM,J                                                    213
   S4=S4+FDMA(I)                                                    214
   SS4=SS4+EDMASQ(I)                                                215
49 SS5=SS5+FDMASQ(I)                                                216
   WRITE(6,25) S3,SS2,S4,SS4                                        217
25 FORMAT('0',/,12X,F15.3,12X,F11.3,22X,F15.3,3X,F15.3)            218

   WRITE(6,59)T,FORDMA
59 FORMAT(/,64X,' FORECAST FOR',1X,I2,1X,'PERIOD(S) AHEAD IS',1X,
  *F8.3)
   WRITE(6,26)                                                      220
26 FORMAT(///,4X,'*** EXPONENTIAL SMOOTHING ***')                  221
   WRITE (6.27)                                                     222
27 FORMAT(//,20X,'SINGLE EXPONENTIAL SMOOTHING')                    223
   WRITE(6,28)                                                      224
28 FORMAT(4X,'PERIOD',2X,'ACTUAL',4X,'SES',4X,'FORECAST',2X,        225
  *'RESIDUAL',2X,'RESIDUAL—SQ')                                     226
   DO 14 I=1,J                                                      227
   WRITE(6,29)X(I),Y(I),SES(I),FSES(I),FSES(I),FSESSQ(I)            228
29 FORMAT(7X,I2,3X,F5.0,2X,F8.3,2X,F8.3,2X,F8.3,2X,F11.3,2X,F11.3)  229

14 CONTINUE                                                         231
   DO 38 I=3,J                                                      232
   S5=S5+FSES(I)                                                    233
   S6=S6+FDES(I)                                                    234
   S8=S8+FTES(I)                                                    235
   SS6=SS6+ESESSQ(I)                                                236
   SS7=SS7+SESSQ(I)                                                 237
   SS8=SS8+EDESSQ(I)                                                238
   SS12=ETESSQ(I)+SS12                                              239
   SS13=SS13+FTESSQ(I)                                              240
38 SS9=SS9+FDESSQ(I)                                                241
   WRITE(6,35) S5,SS6                                               242
35 FORMAT('0',/,21X,F15.3,12X,F11.3)                               243
   WRITE(6,21)T,SESFOR
   WRITE(6,74)                                                      244
74 FORMAT(///,20X,'DOUBLE EXPONENTIAL SMOOTHING')                   245
   WRITE(6,76)                                                      246
76 FORMAT(4X,'PERIOD',2X,'ACTUAL',4X,'DES',8X,'EA',8X,'FR',6X,      247
  *'FORECAST',3X,'RESIDUAL',2X,'RESIDUAL—SQ')                       248
   DO 77 I=1,J                                                      249
   WRITE(6,78)X(I),Y(I),DES(I),EA(I),EB(I),FDES(I),EDES(I),EDESSQ(I) 250

78 FORMAT(7X,I2,3X,F5.0,1X,F8.3,3X,F8.3,2X,F8.3,4X,F8.3,3X,F8.3,2X, 252
  *F11.3)                                                           253
77 CONTINUE                                                         254
   WRITE(6,79)S6,SS8                                                255
79 FORMAT('0',/,41X,F11.3,12X,F11.3)                               256
   WRITE(6,21)T,DESFOR                                              257
21 FORMAT(/,' FORECAST FOR'.1X.I2,1X,'PERIOD(S) AHEAD IS',1X,F8.3)
   WRITE(6,31)                                                      259
```

```
   31 FORMAT(//,20X,'TRIPLE EXPONENTIAL SMOOTHING')                            260
      WRITE(6,32)                                                              261
   32 FORMAT(4X,'PERIOD',2X,'ACTUAL',4X,'TES',6X,'TA',8X,'TB',6X,'TC',         262
     *4X,'FORECAST',2X,'RESIDUAL',2X,'RESIDUAL—SQ')                            263
      DO 97 I=1,J                                                              264
      WRITE (6,33)X(I),Y(I),TES(I),TA(I),TB(I),TC(I),FTES(I),ETES(I),          265
     *ETESSQ(I)                                                                266
   33 FORMAT(7X,I2,3X,F5.0,2X,F8.3,1X,F8.3,1X,F7.3,1X,F7.3,3X,F8.3,2X,         267
     *F8.3,2X,F11.3)                                                           268
   97 CONTINUE                                                                 269
      WRITE(6,36)S8,SS12                                                       270
   36 FORMAT('0',/,48X,F15.3,12X,F11.3)                                        271
      WRITE(6,30)T,TESFOR                                                      272
   30 FORMAT(/,' FORECAST FOR',1X,I2,1X,'PERIOD(S) AHEAD IS',1X,F8.3)
C   **********************                                                     274
C   WINTERS' METHOD                                                           275
C   **********************                                                     276
C                                                                             277
C   FOR INITIAL TREND LINE, WE USE SIMPLE LINEAR REGRESSION                   278
C   YEST(I)=A + BX(I)                                                         279
C   INITIAL MULTIPLICATIVE SEASONAL FACTORS ( 'MSF' ) BY USING THE 1ST        280
C   AND 2ND YEAR IN THE DATA                                                  281
C                                                                             282
C   1. FOR THE 1ST YEAR                                                       283
C                                                                             284
      L=L+1                                                                    285
      DO 170 I=2,L                                                             286
  170 SF1(I)=Y(I)/YEST(I)                                                      287
C                                                                             288
C   2. FOR THE 2ND YEAR                                                       289
C                                                                             290
      LP1=1+L                                                                  291
      LT2=2*L—1                                                                292
      DO 175 I=LP1,LT2                                                         293
  175 SF2(I)=Y(I)/YEST(I)                                                      294
C                                                                             295
C   INITIAL ESTIMATES OF THE FUTURE SEASONAL FACTORS ( 'SF' )                 296
C                                                                             297
      DO 180 I=2,L                                                             298
      M=I+L—1                                                                  299
      SF(I)=(SF1(I)+SF2(M))/2                                                  300
  180 SF(M)=SF(I)                                                             301
      WRITE(6,345)                                                            302
  345 FORMAT(//,4X,'*** WINTERS' METHOD ***')                                 303
      WRITE(6,350)                                                            304
  350 FORMAT(/,4X,'PERIOD',6X,'ACTUAL',2X,'VALUE FROM TREND LINE',2X,         305
     *'MULT.SEASONAL FACTOR')                                                  306
      DO 185 I=2,L                                                             307
      WRITE(6,355) X(I),Y(I),YEST(I),SF1(I)                                    308
  355 FORMAT(7X,I2,7X,F5.0,10X,F10.4,17X,F4.2)                                 309
  185 CONTINUE                                                                 310
      DO 190 I=LP1,LT2                                                         311
      WRITE(6,360) X(I),Y(I),YEST(I),SF2(I)                                    312
  360 FORMAT (7X,I2,7X,F5.0,10X,F10.4,17X,F4.2)                                313
  190 CONTINUE                                                                 314
      WRITE (6,365)                                                            315
  365 FORMAT(///,4X,'PERIOD',2X,'AVG.OF MULT.SEASONAL FACTORS')                316
      DO 195 I=2,L                                                             317
      WRITE(6,370) X(I),SF(T)                                                  318
  370 FORMAT(7X,I2,15X,F5.2)                                                   319
```

```
195 CONTINUE                                                          320
C                                                                     321
C   UPDATING THE ESTIMATE OF THE INTERCEPT,SLOPE,AND MULT.SEASONAL    322
C   FACTOR BY USING EXPONENTIAL SMOOTHING                             323
C                                                                     324
C   AA(I)  =  ESTIMATED VALUE OF THE TREND LINE AT PERIOD I           325
C   BB(I)  =  ESTIMATED SLOPE OF THE TREND AT PERIOD I                326
C   SSF(I) =  REVISED ESTIMATE OF SEASONAL FACTOR                     327
C   FW(I)  =  FORECAST BY WINTERS' METHOD                             328
C                                                                     329
       LP3=1+LT2                                                      334
       LT3=3*L−2                                                      335
       K=LT3−1                                                        336
       DO 200 I=LP3,K                                                 337
       AA(LT2)=YEST(LT2)                                              338
       BB(LT2)=B                                                      339
       AA(I)=WALPHA*Y(I)/SF(I+1−L) + (1.−WALPHA)*(AA(I−1)+BR(I−1))    340
       BB(I)=WBETA*(AA(I)−AA(I−1)) + (1.−WBETA)*BB(I−1)               341
       SSF(I)=WDELTA*Y(I)/AA(I) + (1.−WDELTA)*SF(I+1−L)               342
       FW(I+1)=(AA(I)+BB(I)*1.)*SF(I+2−L)                             343
200 CONTINUE                                                          344
       DO 205 I=LT3,J                                                 345
       SSF(LT2)=SF(LT2)                                               346
       AA(I)=WALPHA*Y(I)/SSF(I+1−L) + (1.−WALPHA)*(AA(I−1)+BB(I−1))   347
       BB(I)=WBETA*(AA(I)−AA(I−1)) + (1.−WBETA)*BB(I−1)               348
       SSF(I)=WDELTA*Y(I)/AA(I) + (1.−WDELTA)*SSF(I+1−L)              349
       FW(I+1)=(AA(I)+BB(I)*1.)*SSF(I+2−L)                            350
205 CONTINUE                                                          351
       MOA=J+T−1
       MOB=L−1
       REM= MOD(MOA,MOB)
       WINFOR= (AA(J)+BB(J)*T)*SSF(REM+LT2)
       LP5=1+LP3                                                      352
       DO 210 I=LP5,J                                                 353
       EFW(I)=FW(I)−Y(I)                                              354
       EFWSQ(I)=EFW(I)**2                                             355
       FWSQ(I)=FW(I)**2                                               356
210 CONTINUE                                                          357
       DO 215 I=LP5,J                                                 358
       S7=S7+FW(I)                                                    359
       SS10=SS10+EFWSQ(I)                                             360
       SS11=SS11+FWSQ(I)                                              361
215 CONTINUE                                                          362
       WRITE(6,375)                                                   363
375 FORMAT(//,4X,'*** FORECAST BY WINTERS METHOD ***')               364
       WRITE(6,380)                                                   365
380 FORMAT(//,4X,'PERIOD',6X,'ACTUAL',3X,'FORECAST',5X,'RESIDUAL',2X, 366
      *'RESIDUAL−SQ')                                                 367
       DO 220 I=LP3,J                                                 368
       WRITE(6,385) X(I),Y(I),FW(I),EFW(I),EFWSQ(I)                   369
385 FORMAT(7X,I2,7X,F5.0,4X,F8.3,4X,F8.3,4X,F10.4)                    370
220 CONTINUE                                                          371
       WRITE(6,390) S7,SS10                                           372
390 FORMAT(/,22X,F11.3,13X,F14.3)                                     373
       WRITE(6,21)T,WINFOR                                            374
       RETURN
       END
```

IV. Example Problems for Computer Analysis

example 1

The objective of Example 1 is to use the computer program that is listed in Section III to analyze the following data with different forecasting techniques and to choose the one that appears to be most appropriate for the data.

The table shown below contains 36 months of data regarding ambulance calls responded to by the EMS Company from January 1973 through December 1975. The data are plotted on a graph on the following page.

Month	1973	Year 1974	1975
January	1056	1302	1785
February	1002	1271	1582
March	1217	1440	1685
April	1156	1468	1706
May	1295	1482	1948
June	1231	1401	1785
July	1342	1641	1839
August	1382	1761	1976
September	1287	1697	1890
October	1402	1772	2153
November	1365	1752	2154
December	1441	1822	1891
Total	**15176**	**18810**	**22394**

The purpose of determining the best forecasting method for the above data is to obtain accurate estimates of future numbers of ambulance calls so that the company's plans for the coming months can be formulated. Based on these forecasts, management of this company can decide whether present facilities are adequate to meet future demands, whether certain vehicles should be pulled out of service for preventive maintenance, and so forth.

The results of computer analysis of the ambulance data are presented on the following pages. Simple linear regression results are listed primarily because this technique is utilized later in Winters' method of exponential smoothing. (The reader should recall from Chapter 4 some of the problems associated with using linear regression in making forecasts involving time-series data.) Forecasts with moving averages (single and double) were based on $N=6$. With moving averages and exponential smoothing, a forecast 10 periods ahead ($T=10$) is indicated below to illustrate this feature of the computer program and to demonstrate numerical differences in forecasts among the various techniques.

Forecasting Method	Forecast 10 periods ahead
Single Moving Average	1966.167
Double Moving Average	2874.000
Single Exponential Smoothing	1930.910
Double Exponential Smoothing	2312.029
Triple Exponential Smoothing	2269.488
Winters' Method	2371.568

After the computer program has been run, we should be concerned with choosing the best forecasting model for our data. The method that we employ here involves the minimization of the mean square error (MSE). The

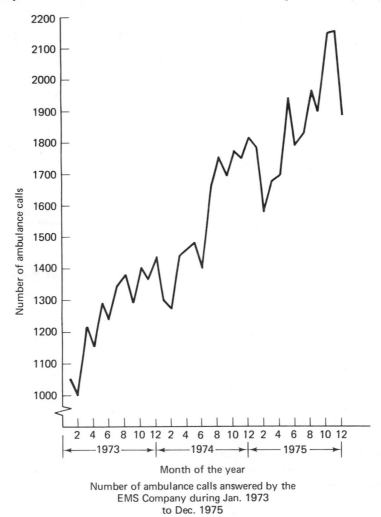

Number of ambulance calls answered by the
EMS Company during Jan. 1973
to Dec. 1975

equation for computing MSE of a particular forecasting technique is shown below:

$$\text{MSE} = \frac{1}{n} \sum_{i=1}^{n} (\text{Forecast}_i - \text{Actual}_i)^2$$

Here n is the number of periods used in the summation operation and can be found by counting the number of entries under the column headed by "Residual-SQ" on the computer printouts.

The mean square error gives equal emphasis to overestimates and underestimates but it considers large errors to be more serious than the small errors. This is indicated by the squaring of the errors in the above equation.

Now let us calculate the mean square error of each forecasting method and select the model that has the smallest mean square error. The regression model is not considered because it is generally not suitable for time-series analysis of data such as we have in this example problem.

Simple Moving Average with 6 periods (30 forecasts are made):

$$\text{Mean Square Error} = \frac{1}{n} \sum_{i=1}^{n} (\text{Forecast}_i - \text{Actual}_i)^2$$

$$= \frac{1}{n} (\text{Sum of Residuals})^2$$

$$= \frac{1}{30} (689,139.800)$$

$$= 22,971.33$$

Double Moving Average with 12 periods (24 forecasts are made):

$$\text{Mean Square Error} = \frac{1}{n} \sum_{i=1}^{n} (\text{Forecast}_i - \text{Actual}_i)^2$$

$$= \frac{1}{24} (748,431.000)$$

$$= 31,184.625$$

Single Exponential Smoothing (35 forecasts are made):

$$\text{Mean Square Error} = \frac{1}{n} \sum_{i=1}^{n} (\text{Forecast}_i - \text{Actual}_i)^2$$

$$= \frac{1}{35} (947,502.300)$$

$$= 27,071.49$$

SIMPLE REGRESSION†

X	Y	FORECAST	ERROR	ESQ
1	1056.	1096.9410	−40.9414	1676.1980
2	1002.	1123.7490	−121.7495	14822.9400
3	1217.	1150.5570	66.4424	4414.5890
4	1156.	1177.3650	−21.3657	456.4939
5	1295.	1204.1730	90.8262	8249.3900
6	1231.	1230.9810	0.0181	0.0003
7	1342.	1257.7900	84.2100	7091.3160
8	1382.	1284.5980	97.4019	9487.1210
9	1287.	1311.4060	−24.4063	595.6650
10	1402.	1338.2140	63.7856	4068.6080
11	1365.	1365.0220	−0.0225	0.0005
12	1441.	1391.8300	49.1694	2417.6330
13	1302.	1418.6380	−116.6387	13604.5700
14	1271.	1445.4460	−174.4468	30431.6700
15	1440.	1472.2540	−32.2549	1040.3770
16	1468.	1499.0620	−31.0630	964.9092
17	1482.	1525.8710	−43.8711	1924.6720
18	1401.	1552.6790	−151.6792	23006.5700
19	1641.	1579.4870	61.5127	3783.8110
20	1761.	1606.2950	154.7046	23933.5000
21	1697.	1633.1030	63.8965	4082.7600
22	1772.	1659.9110	112.0884	12563.8000
23	1752.	1686.7190	65.2803	4261.5110
24	1822.	1713.5270	108.4722	11766.2100
25	1785.	1740.3350	44.6641	1994.8780
26	1582.	1767.1440	−185.1440	34278.3100
27	1685.	1793.9520	−108.9521	11870.5700
28	1706.	1820.7600	−114.7603	13169.9100
29	1948.	1847.5680	100.4316	10086.5100
30	1785.	1874.3760	100.4316	10086.1520
31	1839.	1901.1840	−62.1846	3866.9200
32	1976.	1927.9920	48.0073	2304.7030
33	1890.	1954.8000	−64.8008	4199.1400
34	2153.	1981.6080	171.3911	29374.9100
35	2154.	2008.4160	145.5830	21194.4100
36	1891.	2035.2250	−144.2251	20800.8700

56378.9400   345773.000

AVERAGE X= 18.5000
AVERAGE Y= 1566.0830
A OF SIMPLE REGRESSION= 1070.1330
B OF SIMPLE REGRESSION=   26.8081

†A is the y intercept
B is the slope of the regression line.
ESQ is the square of the error term.

MOVING AVERAGES†

PERIOD	ACTUAL	SINGLE MOVING AVERAGE FORECAST	RESIDUAL	RESIDUAL−SQ
1	1056.	UUUUUUUU	UUUUUUUU	UUUUUUUUUUU
2	1002.	UUUUUUUU	UUUUUUUU	UUUUUUUUUUU
3	1217.	UUUUUUUU	UUUUUUUU	UUUUUUUUUUU
4	1156.	UUUUUUUU	UUUUUUUU	UUUUUUUUUUU
5	1295.	UUUUUUUU	UUUUUUUU	UUUUUUUUUUU
6	1231.	UUUUUUUU	UUUUUUUU	UUUUUUUUUUU
7	1342.	1159.500	−182.500	33306.250
8	1382.	1207.167	−174.833	30566.750
9	1287.	1270.500	−16.500	272.250
10	1402.	1282.167	−119.833	14360.060
11	1365.	1323.167	−41.833	1750.041
12	1441.	1334.833	−106.167	11271.370
13	1302.	1369.833	67.833	4601.348
14	1271.	1363.167	92.167	8494.664
15	1440.	1344.667	−95.333	9088.473
16	1468.	1370.167	−97.833	9571.391
17	1482.	1381.167	−100.833	10167.390
18	1401.	1400.667	−0.333	0.111
19	1641.	1394.000	−247.000	61009.000
20	1761.	1450.500	−310.500	96410.250
21	1697.	1532.167	−164.833	27170.070
22	1772.	1575.000	−197.000	38809.000
23	1752.	1625.667	−126.333	15960.140
24	1822.	1670.667	−151.333	22901.820
25	1785.	1740.833	−44.167	1950.701
26	1582.	1764.833	182.833	33427.990
27	1685.	1735.000	50.000	2500.000
28	1706.	1733.000	27.000	729.000
29	1948.	1722.000	−226.000	51076.000
30	1785.	1754.667	−30.333	920.121
31	1839.	1748.500	−90.500	8190.250
32	1976.	1757.500	−218.500	47742.250
33	1890.	1823.167	−66.833	4466.715
34	2153.	1857.333	−295.667	87418.810
35	2154.	1931.833	−222.167	49358.060
36	1891.	1966.167	75.167	5650.000
		46589.790		689139.800

†In calculating the single moving average, N=6 was used. FORECAST FOR 10 PERIODS AHEAD IS 1966.167.

		DOUBLE MOVING AVERAGE			
PERIOD	ACTUAL	(M2)†	FORECAST	RESIDUAL	RESIDUAL-SQ
1	1056.	UUUUUUUU	UUUUUUUU	UUUUUUUU	UUUUUUUUUU
2	1002.	UUUUUUUU	UUUUUUUU	UUUUUUUU	UUUUUUUUUU
3	1217.	UUUUUUUU	UUUUUUUU	UUUUUUUU	UUUUUUUUUU
4	1156.	UUUUUUUU	UUUUUUUU	UUUUUUUU	UUUUUUUUUU
5	1295.	UUUUUUUU	UUUUUUUU	UUUUUUUU	UUUUUUUUUU
6	1231.	UUUUUUUU	UUUUUUUU	UUUUUUUU	UUUUUUUUUU
7	1342.	UUUUUUUU	UUUUUUUU	UUUUUUUU	UUUUUUUUUU
8	1382.	UUUUUUUU	UUUUUUUU	UUUUUUUU	UUUUUUUUUU
9	1287.	UUUUUUUU	UUUUUUUU	UUUUUUUU	UUUUUUUUUU
10	1402.	UUUUUUUU	UUUUUUUU	UUUUUUUU	UUUUUUUUUU
11	1365.	UUUUUUUU	UUUUUUUU	UUUUUUUU	UUUUUUUUUU
12	1441.	1262.888	UUUUUUUU	UUUUUUUU	UUUUUUUUUU
13	1302.	1297.943	1453.000	151.000	22801.000
14	1271.	1323.943	1488.000	217.000	47089.000
15	1440.	1336.304	1428.000	−12.000	144.000
16	1468.	1350.971	1358.000	−110.000	12100.000
17	1482.	1360.637	1401.000	−81.000	6561.000
18	1401.	1371.610	1414.000	13.000	169.000
19	1641.	1375.638	1448.000	−193.000	37249.000
20	1761.	1390.194	1424.000	−337.000	113569.000
21	1697.	1421.443	1550.000	−147.000	21609.000
22	1772.	1455.583	1715.000	−57.000	3249.000
23	1752.	1496.332	1773.000	21.000	441.000
24	1822.	1541.332	1841.000	19.000	361.000
25	1785.	1599.137	1886.000	101.000	10201.000
26	1582.	1651.527	1976.000	394.000	155236.000
27	1685.	1685.333	1953.000	268.000	71824.000
28	1706.	1711.666	1817.000	111.000	12321.000
29	1948.	1727.722	1768.000	−180.000	32400.000
30	1785.	1741.721	1713.000	−72.000	5184.000
31	1839.	1742.999	1775.000	−64.000	4096.000
32	1976.	1741.777	1757.000	−219.000	47961.000
33	1890.	1756.471	1783.000	−107.000	11449.000
34	2153.	1777.193	1933.000	−220.000	48400.000
35	2154.	1812.165	1990.000	−164.000	26896.000
36	1891.	1847.415	2130.000	239.000	57121.000

| | | | | | |
| | | 40774.000 | | | 748431.000 |

FORECAST FOR 10 PERIOD(S) AHEAD IS 2874.000

†M(2) is the double moving average when N=6.

EXPONENTIAL SMOOTHING

SINGLE EXPONENTIAL SMOOTHING

PERIOD	ACTUAL	SES	FORECAST	RESIDUAL	RESIDUAL-SQ.
0	0.	1056.000	UUUUUUU	UUUUUUU	UUUUUUUUUU
1	1056.	1056.000	UUUUUUU	UUUUUUU	UUUUUUUUUU
2	1002.	1045.200	1056.000	54.000	2916.000
3	1217.	1079.560	1045.200	−171.800	29515.250
4	1156.	1094.848	1079.560	−76.440	5843.102
5	1295.	1134.878	1094.848	−200.152	40060.950
6	1231.	1154.102	1134.878	−96.122	9239.449
7	1342.	1191.682	1154.102	−187.898	35305.540
8	1382.	1229.745	1191.682	−190.318	36221.070
9	1287.	1241.196	1229.745	−57.255	3278.122
10	1402.	1273.357	1241.196	−160.804	25857.910
11	1365.	1291.685	1273.357	−91.643	8398.496
12	1441.	1321.548	1291.685	−149.315	22294.870
13	1302.	1317.638	1321.548	19.548	382.128
14	1271.	1308.311	1317.638	46.638	2175.143
15	1440.	1334.648	1308.311	−131.689	17342.100
16	1468.	1361.318	1334.648	−133.352	17782.700
17	1482.	1385.455	1361.318	−120.682	14564.050
18	1401.	1388.563	1385.455	−15.545	241.660
19	1641.	1439.051	1388.563	−252.437	63724.190
20	1761.	1503.440	1439.051	−321.949	103651.400
21	1697.	1542.152	1503.440	−193.560	37465.390
22	1772.	1588.122	1542.152	−229.848	52830.050
23	1752.	1620.897	1588.122	−163.878	26856.130
24	1822.	1661.118	1620.897	−201.103	40442.320
25	1785.	1685.894	1661.118	−123.882	15346.820
26	1582.	1665.115	1685.894	103.894	10793.960
27	1685.	1669.092	1665.115	−19.885	395.404
28	1706.	1676.473	1669.092	−36.908	1362.197
29	1948.	1730.779	1676.473	−271.527	73726.680
30	1785.	1741.623	1730.779	−54.221	2939.964
31	1839.	1761.098	1741.623	−97.377	9482.316
32	1976.	1804.076	1761.098	−214.902	46182.800
33	1890.	1821.262	1804.078	−85.922	7382.523
34	2153.	1887.610	1821.262	−331.738	110049.700
35	2154.	1940.888	1887.610	−266.390	70963.680
36	1891.	1930.910	1940.888	49.888	2488.782

                                  50948.370   947502.300

FORECAST FOR 10 PERIOD(S) AHEAD IS 1930.910

		DOUBLE EXPONENTIAL SMOOTHING	
PERIOD	ACTUAL	DES†	EA†
0	0.	1056.000	UUUUUUUU
1	1056.	1056.000	1056.000
2	1002.	1053.840	1036.560
3	1217.	1058.983	1100.136
4	1156.	1066.156	1123.539
5	1295.	1079.900	1189.856
6	1231.	1094.740	1213.464
7	1342.	1114.128	1269.235
8	1382.	1137.251	1322.239
9	1287.	1158.040	1324.352
10	1402.	1181.103	1365.610
11	1365.	1203.219	1380.151
12	1441.	1226.885	1416.211
13	1302.	1245.035	1390.241
14	1271.	1257.690	1358.931
15	1440.	1273.082	1396.215
16	1468.	1290.729	1431.908
17	1482.	1309.674	1461.236
18	1401.	1325.451	1451.676
19	1641.	1348.171	1529.930
20	1761.	1379.225	1627.656
21	1697.	1411.810	1672.494
22	1772.	1447.072	1729.171
23	1752.	1481.837	1759.958
24	1822.	1517.693	1804.542
25	1785.	1551.333	1820.455
26	1582.	1574.089	1756.141
27	1685.	1593.090	1745.094
28	1706.	1609.766	1743.181
29	1948.	1633.968	1827.589
30	1785.	1655.499	1827.747
31	1839.	1676.619	1845.578
32	1976.	1702.110	1906.046
33	1890.	1725.941	1916.584
34	2153.	1758.274	2016.946
35	2154.	1794.787	2086.979
36	1891.	1822.019	2039.801

FORECAST FOR 10 PERIOD(S) AHEAD IS 2312.029

†Note: For double exponential smoothing, DES is the doubly smoothed statistic. EA, EB are the coefficients in the forecasting equation for the double exponential smoothing technique. For triple exponential smoothing, TES is the triply smoothed statistic. TA, TB, TC are the coefficients in the forecasting equation for the triple exponential smoothing technique.

EB†	FORECAST	RESIDUAL	RESIDUAL-SQ
UUUUUUUU	UUUUUUUU	UUUUUUUU	UUUUUUUUUUU
0.000	UUUUUUUU	UUUUUUUU	UUUUUUUUUUU
−2.160	1056.000	54.000	2916.026
5.144	1034.400	−182.600	33342.610
7.173	1105.280	−50.720	2572.490
13.744	1130.712	−164.288	26990.490
14.841	1203.600	−27.400	750.755
19.388	1228.305	−113.695	12926.620
23.123	1288.623	−93.377	8719.207
20.789	1345.362	58.362	3406.130
23.063	1345.141	−56.859	3232.961
22.117	1388.674	23.674	560.438
23.666	1402.268	−38.732	1500.181
18.151	1439.877	137.877	19010.120
12.655	1408.392	137.392	18876.580
15.392	1371.586	−68.414	4680.480
17.647	1411.606	−56.394	3180.233
18.945	1449.555	−32.445	1052.651
15.778	1480.181	79.181	6269.574
22.720	1467.453	−173.547	30118.420
31.054	1552.650	−208.350	43409.860
32.585	1658.709	−38.291	1466.183
35.262	1705.080	−66.920	4478.340
34.765	1764.433	12.433	154.582
35.856	1794.722	−27.278	744.067
33.640	1840.398	55.398	3068.987
22.756	1854.095	272.095	74035.750
19.001	1778.897	93.897	8816.730
16.677	1764.095	58.095	3374.997
24.203	1759.857	−188.143	35397.620
21.531	1851.791	66.791	4461.070
21.120	1849.277	10.277	105.624
25.492	1866.697	−109.303	11947.080
23.830	1931.538	41.538	1725.433
32.334	1940.415	−212.585	45192.570
36.523	2049.279	−104.721	10966.420
27.223	2123.501	232.501	54056.920
	54642.000		483507.100

TRIPLE EXPONENTIAL SMOOTHING

PERIOD	ACTUAL	TES†	TA†	TB†
0	0.	1056.000	UUUUUUUU	UUUUUUUU
1	1056.	1056.000	1056.001	−0.000
2	1002.	1055.567	1030.081	−5.832
3	1217.	1056.250	1117.297	14.623
4	1156.	1058.231	1142.325	18.205
5	1295.	1062.565	1223.165	33.742
6	1231.	1069.000	1240.651	32.702
7	1342.	1078.025	1301.660	41.409
8	1382.	1089.870	1355.506	47.089
9	1287.	1103.504	1339.338	35.993
10	1402.	1119.023	1380.265	39.093
11	1365.	1135.863	1384.422	33.331
12	1441.	1154.067	1419.853	35.271
13	1302.	1172.260	1371.876	18.059
14	1271.	1189.346	1324.121	3.239
15	1440.	1206.093	1374.046	12.511
16	1468.	1223.020	1417.862	19.178
17	1482.	1240.350	1450.362	22.375
18	1401.	1257.370	1429.683	13.138
19	1641.	1275.530	1530.005	32.408
20	1761.	1296.269	1648.178	52.972
21	1697.	1319.376	1687.292	52.724
22	1772.	1344.915	1742.525	55.923
23	1752.	1372.299	1762.099	50.449
24	1822.	1401.378	1802.573	50.258
25	1785.	1431.368	1805.061	41.394
26	1582.	1459.912	1704.447	10.457
27	1685.	1486.548	1687.916	2.775
28	1706.	1511.191	1686.669	−0.254
29	1948.	1535.746	1801.621	23.452
30	1785.	1559.697	1794.117	16.389
31	1839.	1583.081	1813.134	16.307
32	1976.	1606.886	1888.987	29.074
33	1890.	1630.697	1892.851	23.871
34	2153.	1656.212	2018.705	46.822
35	2154.	1683.929	2094.486	55.235
36	1891.	1711.547	2010.605	26.382

FORECAST FOR 10 PERIOD(S) AHEAD IS 2269.488

†Note: For double exponential smoothing, DES is the doubly smoothed statistic. EA, EB are the coefficients in the forecasting equation for the double exponential smoothing technique. For triple exponential smoothing, TES is the triply smoothed statistic. TA, TB, TC are the coefficients in the forecasting equation for the triple exponential smoothing technique.

TC†	FORECAST	RESIDUAL	RESIDUAL-SQ
UUUUUUUU	UUUUUUUU	UUUUUUUU	UUUUUUUUUUU
0.000	UUUUUUUU	UUUUUUUU	UUUUUUUUUUU
−0.432	1056.000	54.000	2916.053
1.115	1024.032	−192.968	37236.550
1.298	1132.477	−23.523	553.341
2.353	1161.179	−133.821	17907.930
2.101	1258.082	27.082	733.449
2.591	1274.403	−67.597	4569.344
2.820	1344.364	−37.636	1416.486
1.789	1404.005	117.005	13690.140
1.886	1376.225	−25.775	664.345
1.319	1420.301	55.301	3058.149
1.365	1418.412	−22.588	510.213
−0.011	1455.806	153.806	23656.170
−1.108	1389.929	118.929	14144.150
−0.339	1326.806	−113.194	12812.950
0.180	1386.387	−81.613	6660.645
0.404	1437.130	−44.870	2013.327
−0.311	1472.938	71.938	5175.141
1.140	1442.666	−198.334	39336.460
2.579	1562.983	−198.017	39210.570
2.369	1702.440	5.440	29.596
2.431	1741.200	−30.800	948.613
1.845	1799.664	47.664	2271.816
1.694	1813.470	−8.530	72.766
0.912	1853.678	68.678	4716.664
−1.447	1846.911	264.911	70178.000
−1.909	1714.180	29.180	851.468
−1.992	1689.737	−16.263	264.491
−0.088	1685.419	−262.581	68948.750
−0.605	1825.029	40.029	1602.305
−0.566	1810.203	−28.797	829.246
0.421	1829.158	−146.842	21562.510
0.005	1918.271	28.271	799.277
1.705	1916.724	−236.276	55826.280
2.201	2066.379	−87.621	7677.496
−0.099	2150.821	259.821	67506.930

| | 54707.350 | | 530350.800 |

*** WINTERS' METHOD ***

PERIOD	ACTUAL	VALUE FROM TREND LINE	MULT. SEASONAL FACTOR
1	1056.	1096.9410	0.96
2	1002.	1123.7490	0.89
3	1217.	1150.5570	1.06
4	1156.	1177.3650	0.98
5	1295.	1204.1730	1.08
6	1231.	1230.9810	1.00
7	1342.	1257.7900	1.07
8	1382.	1284.5980	1.08
9	1287.	1311.4060	0.98
10	1402.	1338.2140	1.05
11	1365.	1365.0220	1.00
12	1441.	1391.8300	1.04
13	1302.	1418.6380	0.92
14	1271.	1445.4460	0.88
15	1440.	1472.2540	0.98
16	1468.	1499.0620	0.98
17	1482.	1525.8710	0.97
18	1401.	1552.6790	0.90
19	1641.	1579.4870	1.04
20	1761.	1606.2950	1.10
21	1697.	1633.1030	1.04
22	1772.	1659.9110	1.07
23	1752.	1686.7190	1.04
24	1822.	1713.5270	1.06

PERIOD	AVG. OF MULT. SEASONAL FACTORS
1	0.94
2	0.89
3	1.02
4	0.98
5	1.02
6	0.95
7	1.05
8	1.09
9	1.01
10	1.06
11	1.02
12	1.05

*** FORECAST BY WINTERS' METHOD ***

PERIOD	ACTUAL	FORECAST	RESIDUAL	RESIDUAL-SQ
25	1785.	UUUUUUUU	UUUUUUUU	UUUUUUUUUUU
26	1582.	1580.183	−1.817	3.3029
27	1685.	1845.644	160.644	25806.5000
28	1706.	1788.751	82.751	6847.6830
29	1948.	1884.731	−63.269	4002.9400
30	1785.	1782.991	−2.009	4.0352
31	1839.	2002.050	163.050	26585.1500
32	1976.	2075.440	99.440	9888.3980
33	1890.	1945.731	55.731	3105.9390
34	2153.	2056.040	−96.960	9401.2300
35	2154.	2016.021	−137.979	19038.2600
36	1891.	2116.659	225.659	50922.0600
		21094.220		155605.400

FORECAST FOR 10 PERIOD(S) AHEAD IS 2371.568

Double Exponential Smoothing (35 forecasts are made):

$$\text{Mean Square Error} \; = \; \frac{1}{n} \sum_{i=1}^{n} (\text{Forecast}_i - \text{Actual}_i)^2$$

$$= \; \frac{1}{35} \, (483,507.100)$$

$$= \; 13,814.49$$

Triple Exponential Smoothing (35 forecasts are made):

$$\text{Mean Square Error} \; = \; \frac{1}{n} \sum_{i=1}^{n} (\text{Forecast}_i - \text{Actual}_i)^2$$

$$= \; \frac{1}{35} \, (530,350.800)$$

$$= \; 15,152.88$$

Winters' Method (11 forecasts are made):

$$\text{Mean Square Error} \; = \; \frac{1}{n} \sum_{i=1}^{n} (\text{Forecast}_i - \text{Actual}_i)^2$$

$$= \; \frac{1}{11} \, (155,605.400)$$

$$= \; 14,145.95$$

summary

Forecasting Method	Mean Square Error
Simple Moving Average	22,971.33
Double Moving Average	31,184.63
Single Exponential Smoothing	27,071.49
Double Exponential Smoothing	13,814.49
Triple Exponential Smoothing	15,152.88
Winters' Method	14,145.95

From the above table we observe that the best model for the ambulance data is double exponential smoothing. Winters' method is second best.

example 2

Let us consider the problem of forecasting national plant and equipment expenditures during the next quarter ($T=1$). A keen interest in business capital expenditures is maintained by many individuals and corporations because of its dual role in the economy: (1) capital spending creates new production capacity and (2) capital spending generates additional income. These two considerations influence spending patterns in many other areas of the economy, so a firm that produces consumer goods, for instance, could benefit by having a reliable forecast of next quarter's capital expenditures. In Appendix A more is said about this lagging indicator of general business activity.

The purpose of Example 2 is to illustrate how the computer program listed in Section III might be used to select a suitable technique for this particular time-series. Quarterly data for plant and equipment expenditures for 1960-1973 are listed below, followed by a graph of the data on page 136.

$ billions spent on plant and equipment from the first
quarter 1960 through the fourth quarter 1973

Year	Quarter	$ Billion	Year	Quarter	$ Billion
1960	1	9.27	1967	1	15.61
	2	8.98		2	15.40
	3	9.53		3	17.05
	4	7.57		4	14.25
1961	1	8.61	1968	1	15.86
	2	8.65		2	16.02
	3	9.54		3	17.95
	4	8.02		4	16.04
1962	1	9.50	1969	1	18.81
	2	9.62		2	19.25
	3	10.18		3	21.46
	4	8.25		4	17.47
1963	1	9.74	1970	1	20.33
	2	10.14		2	20.26
	3	11.09		3	21.66
	4	9.40		4	17.68
1964	1	11.11	1971	1	20.60
	2	11.54		2	20.14
	3	12.84		3	22.79
	4	10.79		4	19.38
1965	1	12.81	1972	1	22.01
	2	13.41		2	21.86
	3	14.95		3	25.20
	4	12.77		4	21.50
1966	1	15.29	1973	1	24.73
	2	15.57		2	25.04
	3	17.00		3	28.48
	4	13.59		4	24.10

SOURCE: *Survey of Current Business*, U.S. Department of Commerce, Washington, D.C.

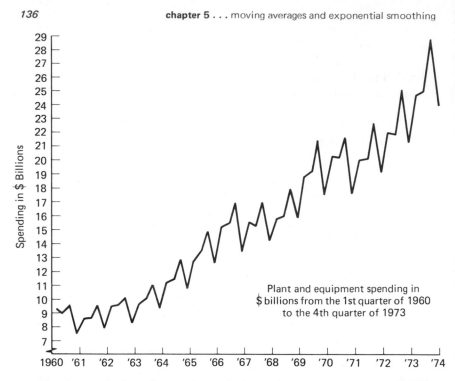

Plant and equipment spending in $ billions from the 1st quarter of 1960 to the 4th quarter of 1973

To choose the best forecasting technique, the mean square error (MSE) criterion is used. That is, we compare the mean square error of each technique and choose the one with the smallest value. (Calculation of the mean square error was shown in the previous example.) The following table shows the mean square error for various time-series analysis methods. Note that different values of α have been evaluated for single, double and triple exponential smoothing by making several computer runs. For Winters' method of exponential smoothing, the smoothing constants were all set at either 0.05, 0.10, 0.20, or 0.30.

	Mean Square Error			
	$\alpha = 0.05$	$\alpha = 0.10$	$\alpha = 0.20$	$\alpha = 0.30$
Single Moving Averages ($N = 8$)	—	—	4.56	—
Double Moving Averages ($N = 8$)	—	—	3.32	—
Single Exponential Smoothing	19.98	9.18	4.38	3.31
Double Exponential Smoothing	6.01	2.72	2.48	2.83
Triple Exponential Smoothing	3.02	2.42	2.88	3.66
Winters' Method	1.78	1.19	0.85	0.59

From the above table, Winters' method is the preferred technique for these data. If you examine the data closely it should be apparent that the data have a positive linear and seasonal trend, and Winters' method is ideally suited for data having this underlying pattern.

The following table provides forecasts for 1 period ahead ($T = 1$) to demonstrate numerical differences among the various techniques.

Forecasting Methods	Forecast 1 Period Ahead			
	Smoothing Constant(s) = 0.05	Smoothing Constant(s) = 0.10	Smoothing Constant(s) = 0.20	Smoothing Constant(s) = 0.30
Simple Moving Average ($N = 8$)	—	—	24.401	—
Double Moving Average ($N = 8$)	—	—	26.667	—
Single Exponential Smoothing	18.926	21.920	23.949	24.743
Double Exponential Smoothing	23.746	25.558	26.244	26.343
Triple Exponential Smoothing	25.657	25.965	26.170	25.653
Winters' Method	27.370	27.464	28.023	28.409

questions

1. Consider the following time-series data from a large hospital.

Month	No. of X-Rays	Month	No. of X-Rays
1	3009	11	3387
2	2641	12	3138
3	2934	13	2908
4	3239	14	3512
5	3490	15	3291
6	2569	16	2804
7	3205	17	3096
8	2561	18	3106
9	3047	19	3195
10	2607	20	3605

a. Plot these data on a piece of graph paper.

b. Apply double and triple exponential smoothing to the data when α = 0.20 and make a forecast for $T = 1$ month into the future. (The computer program in Chapter 5 could be used to check your solution.)

    c.   Calculate the MAD and MSE for each technique and decide which is the more accurate for this set of data.

    d.   What moving average period does this smoothing constant approximate?

2.   List and describe each of the four meaningful components of a time-series.

3.   When we apply techniques such as moving averages and exponential smoothing to a set of data, what are we really trying to accomplish by "smoothing" time-dependent data?

4.   What is the basic trade-off being made in exponential smoothing when a large value of α is used as opposed to a small value of α?

5.   When would Winters' method of exponential smoothing be used instead of triple exponential smoothing?

6.   Give a simple procedure for obtaining a_{est}, b_{est} and c_{est} in developing initial estimates of $S_0^{[1]}$, $S_0^{[2]}$, and $S_0^{[3]}$ for triple exponential smoothing.

7.   What basic assumption underlies all of the techniques covered in Chapter 5?

8.   Compare the advantages and disadvantages of using simple moving averages, double exponential smoothing and Winters' method for each of these situations:

    a.   The historical data are erratic but their average value over time is fairly constant.

    b.   The data have a slight upward trend and they do not fluctuate widely about the trend line.

    c.   The data exhibit an upward trend with seasonal variations being quite pronounced.

chapter 6 . . . the use of subjective information in forecasting

introduction

The quantitative forecasting methods discussed in Chapters 4 and 5 are underpinned by the premise that the future is an extension of the past. However, the future will contain events that today are poorly understood or completely unanticipated. Hence, the aim of this chapter is to explain and illustrate several techniques for developing subjective (i.e., qualitative) information for purposes of making a forecast. Here we shall be dealing with several techniques that to varying degrees are founded on the concept of subjective probability.

As we shall see, the assumption that the future will behave as the past is not a necessary prerequisite to application of methods based on subjectively-derived data. Techniques discussed in Chapter 6 rely on judgment and opinion and are often termed *qualitative* forecasting methods.

Forecasts carefully derived from judgment can provide a coherent structure for evaluating contemplated actions, for "red-flagging" other actions that should be considered or avoided, and for placing bounds on what might be reasonably expected in a world characterized by constant change. With these observations in mind, this chapter focuses on three such structures that have been widely utilized to develop forecasts in situations where subjective information is a principal input to the forecasting problem:

1. The Delphi method,

2. Subjective probability methods (including their use in conjunction with Bayes' Law), and

3. The cross-impact method.

In the following sections, these techniques are presented as systematic methodologies for eliciting subjective data essential to predicting the behavior of some uncertain quantity. After the technique is described, an example problem and/or a reprinted article is provided to facilitate the reader's understanding of an application of the technique.

the delphi method

Most decision makers draw upon the advice of experts as they form their judgments. Often the decision situation is highly complex and poorly understood so that no single person can be expected to make an informed decision. The traditional approach to decision making in such cases is to obtain expert opinion through open discussions and to attempt to determine a consensus among the experts. However, results of panel discussions are sometimes unsatisfactory because group opinion is highly influenced by dominant individuals and/or because a majority opinion may be used to create the "bandwagon effect."

The Delphi method, developed during the late 1940s by the Rand Corporation, attempts to overcome these difficulties by forcing experts involved in the forecasting exercise to voice their opinions anonymously and through an intermediary. The intermediary acts as a control center in analyzing responses to each round of opinion gathering and in feeding back opinion to participants in subsequent rounds. Thus, the Delphi technique is a systematic procedure for soliciting and organizing "expert" forecasts about the future through the use of anonymous, iterative responses to a series of questionnaires, and controlled feedback of group opinions. By following such a procedure, it is hoped that the responses will converge on a consensus forecast that turns out to be a good estimator of the true outcome.

Two premises underlie the Delphi method. The first is that persons who are highly knowledgeable (i.e., recognized as "experts") in a particular field make the most plausible forecasts. Secondly, it is believed that the combined knowledge of several persons is at least as good as that of one person.

Typically, the technique is initiated by writing an unambiguous description of the forecasting problem and sending this, along with relevant background information, to each participant in the study. Often the panel of experts is invited to list major areas of concern in their particular speciality as they may relate to the problem being addressed by the study. The first questionnaire sent out might request the opinion of each expert regarding likely dates for the occurrence of an event identified in the problem statement. Because responses to this type of question will normally reveal a spread of opinions, *interquartile* ranges are customarily computed and presented to the experts at the beginning of the second round. (Interquartile ranges identify values in the continuum of responses such that 25 percent of all responses lie in the first interquartile range, 50 percent of the responses fall in the first and second ranges, and so forth.)

In the second round of the Delphi technique, experts are asked to review their response in the first round relative to interquartile ranges from that round. Participants then have the opportunity to revise their estimates in light of the group response. At this point, participants can request that additional information relevant to the forecasting problem be gathered and sent to them.

If an estimate departs appreciably from the group median, the respondent who furnished it is asked to give reasons for his or her position. Frequently, all panelists are urged to conceive statements that challenge or support estimates (other than their own) falling outside the central range of responses. These reasons, along with routine second-round estimates for the entire group, are again analyzed and statistically summarized (usually as interquartile ranges, although other measures capable of showing group convergence or divergence could be used).

In those cases where a third-round questionnaire is felt necessary, participants receive a summary of second-round responses plus a request to reconsider and/or explain their estimate in view of group responses in the second round. They are again asked to reassess their earlier responses and possibly to explain why their estimates do not conform to the majority of group opinion.

Results from application of the Delphi method have been generally satisfactory since in many cases a reasonable consensus is achieved that permits subsequent planning and decision making to occur. Several of the difficulties associated with implementing these results are discussed below by Gordon and Ament.*

A convergence of opinions has been observed in a majority of cases where the Delphi approach has been used. In the few instances in which no convergence toward a relatively narrow interval could be obtained, opinions generally polarized, so that independent schools of thought regarding a particular issue could be discerned. This may have been an indication that the opinions were derived from different sets of data, different interpretations of the same data, or different understanding of the question. In such cases, it is conceivable that more rounds of anonymous debate by questionnaire eventually might have tracked down and eliminated the basic cause of disagreement and thus led to a true consensus. But even if this did not happen or if the process were terminated before it had a chance to happen, the Delphi technique would have served

*T. J. Gordon and R. H. Ament, Forecasts of Some Technological and Scientific Developments and Their Social Consequences *(Middletown, Conn.: The Institute for the Future, 1969).*

the purpose of crystallizing the reasoning process that led to the positions which were taken and, thus, would have helped clarify the issues.

The last sentence in the above quotation aptly summarizes the principal strength of the Delphi forecasting technique, because Delphi was originally intended as a method of producing consensus judgments in inexact fields of inquiry. For this reason, it would be inappropriate to view such judgments as precise descriptions of the future. Other advantages of Delphi are its relatively low cost, versatility in application and minimal time requirements for the panelists. Probably the most promising uses of this technique are the following.

1. It provides a structured means of studying the process of anticipating future events,

2. It serves as a teaching tool that leads people into thinking about the future in more directions and dimensions than they ordinarily would have, and

3. It is an aid to probing into the goals and priorities of members of an organization.

Despite the many promising features of the Delphi technique, there are numerous criticisms that can be made.* The items listed below summarize much of Sackman's evaluation of conventional Delphi studies with respect to their methodology and application. He concludes that Delphi investigations are:

1. Often characterized by crude questionnaire design.

2. Lacking in minimal professional standards for opinion item analyses and pilot testing.

3. Highly vulnerable on the concept of "expert" with unaccountable sampling; and vulnerable in the selection of panelists, expert or otherwise.

4. Virtually oblivious to reliability measurement and scientific validation of findings.

5. Typically generating snap answers to ambiguous questions representing inkblots of the future.

6. Seriously confusing aggregations of raw opinion with systematic prediction.

7. Capitalizing on *forced* consensus based on group suggestion.

8. Giving an exaggerated illusion of precision, and misleading uninformed users of results.

For a detailed treatise, see H. Sackman, "Delphi Assessment: Expert Opinion, Forecasting and Group Process," R-1283-PR (Santa Monica, Calif.: The Rand Corporation, April 1974).

9. Denigrating group and face-to-face discussion, and claiming superiority of anonymous group opinion over competing approaches without supporting proof.

10. Indifferent to and unaware of unrelated techniques and findings in behavioral science in such areas as projective techniques, psychometrics, group problem solving, and experimental design.

It is well for the reader to be cognizant of these shortcomings in the event that a Delphi forecasting study is utilized to do what it was intended for; namely, as a vehicle to help discover and explore vague and unknown future issues that would be otherwise difficult to address. For this purpose, the Delphi technique can be particularly effective and can provide useful inputs to the decision-making process. Hence, particular care must be taken to interpret Delphi as an informal forecasting exercise among questionnaire respondents. In short, Delphi should be used with realization that the results would be more in the nature of a structured brainstorming session as opposed to a highly scientific exercise in prediction.

To illustrate a well designed and executed Delphi study, an article dealing with estimation of future manpower requirements is presented in the following section.

the use of the delphi procedure in manpower forecasting*

ABSTRACT   This article is a case study in the development, implementation and evaluation of the Delphi technique, which systematically makes use of expert judgment in generating manpower forecasts. The study was conducted in a large national retail organization on professional manpower. The results of the Delphi technique are compared with results generated by conventional regression based models and the actual experience of the organization, which serves as the criterion. The study also analyzes the informational elements used by experts during the Delphi procedures and develops a model based on these elements. The usefulness of the Delphi in generating manpower forecasting models is also discussed.

introduction

Manpower planning defined simply as the process of determining how the organization should move from its current manpower position to its

*By George T. Milkovich, Anthony J. Annoni, and Thomas A. Mahoney, "The Use of the Delphi Procedures in Manpower Forecasting," *Management Science*, Vol. 19, No. 4 (December 1972), pp. 381-388. Reprinted by permission of the publisher.

future desired manpower encompasses most elements of manpower management. . . . Most manpower forecasting models currently in use [19], [21], [22], [24] rely upon historical relationships among parameters and upon the expectation that these historical relationships and changes in them will persist into the future. While manpower specialists in organizations recognize that future conditions may be unique, few systematic procedures for incorporating future uncertain states of nature have been developed, implemented or tested regarding manpower resource decisions. We report a case study of the application and evaluation of the Delphi technique which systematically uses expert judgment in generating a manpower forecast.

The Delphi technique . . . is designed to obtain the most reliable consensus of opinion of a group of experts [7], [8], [9], [10], [11], [12], [17]. Essentially, the Delphi is a series of intensive interrogations of each individual expert (by a series of questionnaires) concerning some primary question interspersed with controlled feedback. The procedures are designed to avoid direct confrontation of the experts with one another.

The interaction among the experts is accomplished through an intermediary who gathers the data requests of the experts and summarizes them along with the experts' answers to the primary question. This mode of controlled interaction among the experts is a deliberate attempt to avoid the disadvantages associated with more conventional uses of experts such as in round table discussions or direct confrontation of opposing views. The developers of the Delphi argue the procedures are more conducive to independent thought and allow more gradual formulation to a considered opinion [7]. In addition to an answer to the problem, the interrogation of the experts is designed to call out the parameters each expert considers relevant to the problem, and the kinds of information he feels would enable him to arrive at a confident answer to the question.

Typically, the answer to the primary question is a numerical quantity (in this study the number of employees required). It is expected that the individual expert's estimates will tend to converge as the experiment continues even if the estimates expressed initially are widely divergent.

The literature on the Delphi reports either the answers to specific problems generated by its use or results of laboratory experiments investigating the effects that varying its procedures had on the estimates generated. Studies concerned with its usefulness relative to other techniques or its use for manpower planning problems are rare [5], [6].

The purpose of this study was to investigate the usefulness of the Delphi procedures in projecting manpower requirements. Usefulness of the procedures is considered on two dimensions. One is the accuracy of the results generated by the Delphi versus conventional regression models compared to the actual employment decisions made by the organization.

The other is to investigate the information elements and implicit models used by the experts in an attempt to formulate an improved forecasting model.

A low profit margin national retail firm agreed to furnish both data and managerial employees who comprised the panel of experts for this study. The firm's expected demand for buyers was selected as the primary question. This decision was based on the firm's contention that a buyer represents the single most critical skill in their organization and the fact that the firm had been unable to generate reliable forecasts of this crucial skill using conventional methods.

A relatively informal method of generating forecasts of employment of buyers had been employed. The manager in charge of all buying activities prepared an annual forecast of employment after consultation with buyers and managers of functions affecting buying activity, e.g. store expansion. This annual forecast was supplied to the personnel function for recruiting purposes and was adjusted and revised during the year as necessary. Past experience has indicated that frequent revision was necessary for recruiting to meet desired staffing levels.

Procedurally, this study used both regression based models and the Delphi procedure to estimate the number of buyers the firm will need "one year from now". The number of buyers actually employed by the firm "one year later" was subsequently recorded without the results of either approach influencing the firm's decisions. Comparisons of the projections generated by the Delphi and conventional models with the firm's actual employment decisions served as the criterion for analyzing the relative accuracy of the Delphi method.

While it is recognized that the actual employment decision by the firm for a one-year period may not represent optimal behavior, it is considered the best available proxy of the firm's "true demand" for buyers.

description of the experiment*

The Delphi forecasting approach was conducted with a panel of seven experts who were company managers. They were selected on three criteria: their direct or indirect involvement in the firm's informal method of generating forecasts, their willingness to participate, and their availability for the duration of the study. Altogether, five questionnaires submitted at approximately eight-day intervals were used to interrogate key personnel involved in determining the firm's employment behavior regarding buyers.

*For extensive discussion of the Delphi procedures, see Dalkey, Norman C., Delphi, P-3704, RAND Corporation, Santa Monica, Calif., October 1967, and The Delphi Method: An Experimental Study of Group Opinion, RM-5888-PR, RAND Corporation, Santa Monica, Calif., June 1969, 79 pp.

In Questionnaire #1, panel members were presented with a statement of a problem and a brief description of the company. Each panel member was asked to indicate what specific information he felt would be needed to solve the problem (to accurately forecast company demand for buyers one year hence), and to indicate how that information would be used, once made available. Individual information sheets were prepared for each panel member, including only that information which the panel member had specifically requested. These information sheets were returned as part of Questionnaire #2.

In Questionnaire #2, each panel member was asked to formulate the best estimate possible based on the information he had received, to indicate how he had "combined" the information to yield that estimate, and was invited to request additional information which would enable him to "refine" his estimate. Once again, individual information sheets were prepared for each panel member consisting of the information requested via Questionnaire #2. These information sheets were returned, along with the interquartile range of initial estimates, as part of Questionnaire #3.

In Questionnaire #3, panel members were asked to formulate an estimate based on all information in their possession, and to indicate how the additional information received had either confirmed the previous estimate or, alternatively, indicated the need for a revised estimate.

For Questionnaire #4, summary information sheets were compiled, which included all information requested by panel members in previous rounds. These sheets were distributed, along with the interquartile range of previous estimates, to all panel members. In Questionnaire #4, panel members were once again asked to formulate estimates, and to indicate how additional information either confirmed the previous estimate or indicated the need for a revised estimate.

In Questionnaire #5, the only information disseminated was the interquartile range of previous round estimates. Panel members were asked, based on all information at their disposal, to formulate a final estimate, and to indicate how that estimate had been made.

results

information requested

The experts were asked to utilize only that information which was furnished to them and their "general experience" in merchandising. Any additional information not requested but used to generate the estimated demand was to be reported. Information requested was furnished, if available, on subsequent rounds. Individual panel members received only that information which they explicitly requested during the first three rounds.

In the fourth round, a summary of all information requested by all experts was disseminated to each expert.

A total of 39 different elements of information was requested with only the ten items in Table 1 requested by two or more experts. Not surprisingly, the data concerning product demand, sales outlets, and buyer productivity were requested by all seven experts. Table 1 reveals that the requests were highest for historical data on the number of retail units, the number of buyers employed, the average sales volume per buyer and the projected sales volume and store expansion plans. While there was considerable commonality over the basic parameters, the majority of the information items requested were unique to a single expert. Under interrogation, the experts revealed that this unique information entered into their judgments about the anticipated rates of change in sales volume and buyer productivity. The sheer volume of requests was the greatest in the first two rounds, and no new information was requested after the third round.

table 1 . . . information requests

Elements	Round					Total
	1	2	3	4	5	
Projected Gross Sales Volume	7					7
No. of Buyers over Past Periods	7					7
Automation Plans for Buyers Decisions	4	1				5
Buyers Productivity Index	4	3				7
No. of Retail Units over Past Periods	4	2	1			7
No. of Retail Units Planned	2	3	1			6
Average Retail Unit Volume	2		1			3
Gross Sales over Past Periods	2	1	1			4
Average Turnover in Past Periods	1	1				2
Total	**33**	**11**	**4**	**0**	**0**	

convergence

The anticipated convergence of the experts' projections is shown in Table 2. . . . The range of estimates decreased from 23 to 11, while the median number of buyers projected increased from 35 in Round 2 to 38 in Round 5. The greatest incidence of change in the projection occurred in Round 3 when 4 out of 7 experts changed their estimates. The interquartile range of the experts' estimates was first fed back to all the experts at the beginning of Round 3. The summary of all the total information elements requested by all experts was included for the first time in Round 4 with little impact apparent on the projections (only 2 out of 7 experts changed their projections).

table 2 . . . projected demand for buyers by round

Round	Experts								No. of Change	Range
	A	B	C	D	E	F	G	Mdn		
2	55	35	33	35	55	33	32	35	—	23
3	45	35	41	35	41	34	32	35	4	13
4	45	38	41	35	41	34	34	38	2	11
5	45	38	41	35	45	34	34	38	1	11
No. of Changes	1	1	1	0	2	1	1		7	

Each expert's reasons for any change in a projection are recorded in Table 3. The principal reasons given are long-range expansion and growth plans of the firm, and the anticipated effects of automating the reordering system upon buyer productivity.

accuracy

Prior to this study, the firm had been investigating the use of linear regression equations and other models to forecast their demand for buyers. The results of these models had never been incorporated into the organization's planning systems due primarily to the lack of confidence in the projection generated.

Table 4 compares the results of these regression equation results with the projection generated through the Delphi procedures and com-

table 3 . . . reasons for projection changes

Expert	Projection in Rounds		Reason Given for Change
	2	3	
A	55	45	• automating reorder decisions deviated too much from interquartile range
C	33	41	• expansion data
E	55	41	• automating reorder decisions
F	33	34	• projected new outlet construction
	Rounds		
	3	4	
B	35	38	• projected number of new stores
G	32	34	• expansion data
	Rounds		
	4	5	
E	41	45	• long-range growth greater than originally anticipated

table 4 . . . forecasts yielded by alternative methods

Method	Point	Range
Actual firm behavior[1]	37	—
Delphi	38	34-45
Regression[2]		
Projected number of retail outlets ($t + 1$)	43.11	38.08-48.13
Current gross retail sales	45.99	41.64-50.34
Current number of retail outlets	49.40	50.20-53.60

Note:
[1] *Actual firm behavior includes one unfilled vacancy.*

[2] *Using projected number of retail outlets yielded the closest forecast when compared to actual firm behavior. Current gross retail sales explained the greatest proportion of variance in the employment level of buyers, and current number of retail outlets yielded results with the smallest standard error of estimation.*

pared them to the firm's actual experience for the period under consideration. The three regression equations chosen had the smallest standard errors of estimation, the largest coefficients of determination and the closest point and interval estimate when compared to the firm's actual behavior. The forecast generated by the systematical albeit clinical Delphi procedures is closer to the firm's "true demand for buyers" than any of the more conventionally generated projections. In fact, none of the three regression equation interval estimates even includes the firm's actual decision of 37 buyers.

In addition to the accuracy of the procedure, the usefulness of the Delphi was also investigated by further analyzing the experts' information requests and judgments in an attempt to formulate a forecasting model that incorporates elements used by the experts.

Under interrogation by questionnaire, all the experts indicated they made use of current sales volume and a simple index of buyer productivity. The differences in the experts' actual projections resulted from their judgments concerning the anticipated rates of growth of both sales and productivity.

The experts who considered that automating buyers reorder decisions would increase productivity tended to be most accurate when compared to the firm's actual behavior . . . .

remarks

The clinical judgments of experts systematically collected generated results closer to the firm's actual behavior than conventional models in this case. Admittedly, the regression equations were very naive; however, given the state of the art reflected in various surveys of the literature and of company practices, they are representative. The greatest utility of the

Delphi procedure seems to lie in its hypothesis or model-generating powers. While models and hypotheses can be developed from several alternative sources, the Delphi procedure does represent an established method of soliciting the decision processes and implicit models of experts, managers and administrators. Further, the information needs revealed by the process can provide a useful source of elements for a manpower information system necessary for effective manpower planning.

Obviously, there are a number of shortcomings in the procedures. While they are discussed extensively elsewhere [7], [8], [9], [10], [11], [12], a few of the crucial ones are:

(1) Role of the Intermediary. Standard feedback takes the form of answers to an expert's inquiry for data, summaries of all inquiries and interquartile ranges of the estimates. The summaries of all inquiries are brief and do not include the richness of interpretation each expert brings to bear on the problem. This is the price paid for not allowing the experts to interact directly.

(2) Independent Expert Responses. Experts are initially instructed not to discuss the experiments with others; however, in practice, it is difficult to prevent discussion of these issues.

(3) Number of Rounds. Five rounds seemed to be the typical number used in reported experiments. However, in our case, most of the convergence and most of the data requests occurred in the early rounds leaving the usefulness of later rounds open to question.

(4) Changes of Estimates. Five out of the seven experts changed their estimate only once, while one did not change his initial estimate at all. From the reported experiments in nonlaboratory settings, this is a low frequency of change. It may be attributed to the short range (one year) of the forecast, and more changes in successively approximating the "true" answer might occur in a long-range problem with greater uncertainty.

At the minimum the Delphi appears to be highly useful in generating preliminary insights into highly unstructured or underdeveloped subject areas such as manpower planning. Further, a carefully developed consensus of managers' opinions may be acceptable when direct empirical data are unreliable or unavailable.

references

1. Adelson, M., Alkin, M., Carey, C. and Helmer, O., "The Educational Innovation Study," *American Behavioral Scientist*, Vol. 10, No. 7 (March 1967), pp. 8-12, 21-27.

2. Brown, Bernice B., *Delphi Process: A Methodology Used for the Elicitation of Opinion of Experts*, P-3925, RAND Corporation, Santa Monica, Calif., September 1968.

3. _____ and Helmer, Olaf, *Improving the Reliability of Estimates Obtained from a Consensus of Experts*, P-2986, RAND Corporation, Santa Monica, Calif., 18 pp.

4. _____ , Cochran, S. and Dalkey, N., *The Delphi Method II: Structure of Experiments*, Rm-5957-PR, RAND Corporation, Santa Monica, Calif., June 1969, 131 pp.

5. Campbell, Robert, "A Methodological Study of the Utilization of Experts in Business Forecasting," Unpublished Ph.D. dissertation, UCLA, 1966.

6. _____ and Hitchin, David, "The Delphi Technique: Implementation in the Corporate Environment," *Management Services* (November-December 1968), pp. 37-42.

7. Dalkey, Norman C., *Delphi*, P-3704, RAND Corporation, Santa Monica, Calif., October 1967.

8. _____ , *The Delphi Method: An Experimental Study of Group Opinion*, RM-5888-PR, RAND Corporation, Santa Monica, Calif., June 1969, 79 pp.

9. _____ , *Experiments in Group Prediction*, P-3820, RAND Corporation, Santa Monica, Calif., March 1968, 13 pp.

10. _____ , Brown, B. and Cochran, S., *The Delphi Method III: Use of Self-Ratings to Improve Group Estimates*, RM-6115-PR, RAND Corporation, Santa Monica, Calif., November 1969, 21 pp.

11. _____ , _____ and _____ , *The Delphi Method IV: Effect of Percentile Feedback and Feed-in of Relevant Facts*, RM-6118-PR, RAND Corporation, Santa Monica, Calif., March 1970, 39 pp.

12. _____ and Helmer, O., "An Experimental Application of the Delphi Method to the Use of Experts," *Management Science*, Vol. 9, No. 3 (April 1963), pp. 458-467.

13. Gordon, T. J. and Helmer, Olaf, *Report on a Long-Range Forecasting Study*, P-2982, RAND Corporation, Santa Monica, Calif., September 1954, 45 pp.

14. Helmer, Olaf, *Analysis of the Future: The Delphi Method*, P-3558, RAND Corporation, Santa Monica, Calif., March 1967, 11 pp.

15. _____ , *Convergence of Expert Consensus through Feedback*, P-2973, RAND Corporation, Santa Monica, Calif., September 1964.

16. _____ , *Social Technology*, P-3063, RAND Corporation, Santa Monica, Calif., February 1965.

17. _____ , *Systematic Use of Experts*, P-3721, RAND Corporation, Santa Monica, Calif., November 1967.

18. _____ and Rescher, Nicholas, "On the Epistemology of the Inexact Sciences," *Management Science*, Vol. 6, No. 1 (1959).

19. Heneman, Herbert G., Jr. and Seltzer, George, *Manpower Planning and Forecasting in the Firm: An Exploratory Probe*, Industrial Relations Center, University of Minnesota, March 1968.

20. Kaplan, A., Skogstad, A. and Girshick, M. A., "The Prediction of Social and Technological Events," *Public Opinion Quarterly* (Spring 1950), pp. 93-110.

21. Keaveny, Timothy J., *Manpower Planning: A Research Bibliography*, Bulletin 45 (Industrial Relations Center, University of Minnesota), University of Minnesota Press, Minneapolis, October 1966, 37 pp.

22. Lewis, C. G., *Manpower Planning: A Bibliography*, American Elsevier Publishing Co., Inc., New York, 1969.

23. North, Harper Q. and Pyke, Donald L., "Technology the Chicken— Corporate Goals the Egg," in Bright, James R. (editor), *Technological Forecasting for Industry and Government*, Prentice-Hall, Englewood Cliffs, New Jersey, 1968.

24. Wikstrom, Walter S., *Manpower Planning: Evolving Systems*, The Conference Board, Inc., New York, 1971.

subjective probability methods

Our purpose in this section is to illustrate how to elicit subjective probabilities and use them in various types of forecasting problems. We begin first with a brief review of subjective probabilities and then discuss different forecasting situations in which subjective probabilities are a key input.

In most forecasting studies some degree of reliance is placed on information available from one or more experts. Estimates of experts are often given as single numbers or perhaps as a range of numbers. Additional information, however, could be gathered regarding the probability of the single "best" estimate's occurring or the probability of several outcomes included in a range of estimates. A method for generating subjective probabilities of an uncertain quantity is demonstrated in this section. Integrating the resultant probability distribution into the decision-making process is an important part of the example presented later.

subjective probability

There are two important schools of thought regarding the interpretation of probabilities: the *objective* school and the *subjective* school.

The objective school adheres to the notion that probability is the relative frequency of some event when an experiment containing that event, as one of its sample outcomes, is repeated a large number of times. This school of thought maintains that probabilities are applicable only to those situations in which an experiment can be repeated many times under identical conditions. Unfortunately, in numerous cases this interpretation of probability is not realistic. Events are often evaluated under circumstances that cannot be treated as a replicable experiment. As an example, consider the weatherman's prediction that the probability of rain tomorrow is 60 percent. Or, how does a business executive indicate his view of the probability that profits will go up by 10 percent next year after a corporate merger occurs this year?

Even though most statistical theory in the last half century or so is based on the objective interpretation of probability, there is a second school of thought that is gaining widespread acceptance. It is discussed below.

The subjective, or personalistic, interpretation of probability was pioneered by L. J. Savage, R. Schlaifer, and H. Raiffa. This school of thought contends that probability is a measure of one's personal belief in a particular outcome of an "experiment." Thus, statements such as "the chances are 7 to 3 that a certain candidate will be elected President of the United States" are reasonable and acceptable. The probability of this event is subjective because various individuals would normally assign different numbers to the odds in favor of (or against) the event.

Subjective probabilities must satisfy the basic axioms of probability theory:

$$0 \leqslant P\,(E_i) \leqslant 1$$

and

$$\sum_i P\,(E_i) = 1$$

where E_i $(i = 1,2,$———$)$ is an event in the sample space of the "experiment." However, a question can be raised concerning what logical basis there is for assigning subjective probabilities to events that will occur only once or a few times at most.

Considerable attention was given to this question by Savage who proved through various experiments and logical arguments that a person's degree of belief can be measured numerically.* (The curious reader is referred to Savage's book cited below.) It should be noted that Savage's theory does not mean that all "consistent" individuals must act in the same manner. Consequently, two persons faced with the same evidence can assign different probabilities to the event in question. A principal advantage to interpreting

---

*L. J. Savage, The Foundation of Statistics (New York: John Wiley and Sons, Inc., 1954), pp. 27-68.

probabilities in this fashion is that a rational approach to studying events that have not occurred yet can be developed.

A formal mechanism for incorporating subjective probabilities into statistical decision analysis is made available through Bayes' Law. In Appendix D there is a discussion of Bayes' Law and its application to a special type of forecasting problem which involves the evaluation of low probability—high consequence events. This situation is typified by an event such as the collapse of a large dam. The development and use of subjective probabilities are vital inputs to the solution procedure for this problem.

A number of methods have been suggested for the assessment of subjective probabilities. In the example that follows, we have chosen to use a method in which probabilities of selected outcomes of an event being forecasted are directly estimated through application of a questionnaire. This method is demonstrated because it is easily understood by the respondent (who is usually not a statistician) and because it has been found to be a valid means of obtaining subjective probabilities.* Hence, in the problem below we demonstrate how subjective probabilities can be obtained that accurately reflect an individual's intuition and prior degree of belief in the future event under consideration.

an example problem—forecasting the unemployment rate

In this problem the State Department of Welfare is attempting to estimate the unemployment rate several months in advance. Officials of the department are attempting to staff their claims processing offices so that they are not grossly understaffed or overstaffed. Unemployment rates are not usually highly erratic from month to month, but Department of Welfare officials have set a goal that they forecast within ±1 percentage point around the true unemployment rate for any given month. For example, if the true unemployment rate turns out to be 6.8%, the forecast should lie in the interval, 5.8% to 7.8%. Officials believe that if forecasts are off by more than ±1 percentage point, the department will be criticized for being "grossly overstaffed and wasteful with the taxpayers' money" or "understaffed and causing great inconvenience and delay to needy citizens of the state."

Here we shall use subjective probabilities to obtain forecasts of a statewide unemployment rate. It should be noted, for example, that this procedure can easily be modified to forecast a company's dollar volume of sales during the next quarter. Often one of the quantitative forecasting techniques of Chapter 3 or 4 is initially used to obtain "baseline" forecasts that in turn are used as input information to the procedure illustrated in this section.

*Winkler, R. L., "The Assessment of Prior Distributions in Bayesian Analysis," American Statistical Association Journal, Vol. 62, No. 319 (1967), p. 776-800.

The problem under consideration involves the development of subjective probabilities for the state's unemployment rate in some future month. This unemployment rate is regarded as a random variable. By obtaining probabilities for various outcomes of the random variable, we should be able to measure explicitly the uncertainty that is present in the quantity being forecasted.

Suppose we have been asked to make our forecast for October 1975 and it is *now* July 1975. Unemployment rates in the state have been collected for the past 30 months, and they are shown in Table 6-1. These data are plotted

table 6-1 . . . thirty months of state
unemployment rates

Month and Year	Unemployment Rate as a Percentage
January 1973	3.3
February 1973	2.8
March 1973	2.9
April 1973	3.0
May 1973	2.9
June 1973	3.0
July 1973	3.4
August 1973	3.1
September 1973	3.0
October 1973	2.9
November 1973	3.0
December 1973	3.1
January 1974	3.5
February 1974	3.4
March 1974	3.3
April 1974	3.4
May 1974	3.5
June 1974	3.5
July 1974	4.6
August 1974	4.0
September 1974	4.0
October 1974	4.4
November 1974	4.9
December 1974	6.3
January 1975	8.3
February 1975	8.3
March 1975	9.6
April 1975	8.8
May 1975	8.3
June 1975	9.4

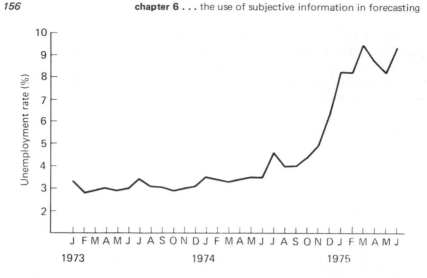

figure 6-1 . . . a graphical summary of data regarding unemployment rate

in Figure 6-1, from which the step increase in unemployment rate that occurs around January 1975 can clearly be seen.

To assess subjectively the probabilities of possible outcomes for the unemployment rate in October 1975, a questionnaire was developed in which selected values of the random variable could be directly evaluated. *The questionnaire is presented here just as it would be administered to an official of the department.* Notice that the illustration of a cumulative distribution function is given in terms of sales tax revenues instead of the unemployment rate. This was done to avoid the possibility of biasing responses to the study. Instructions for the questionnaire and its "answer sheet" constitute the following section.

A QUESTIONNAIRE FOR ELICITING SUBJECTIVE PROBABILITIES   The purpose of this questionnaire is to obtain information that can be used to predict the state unemployment rate in the month of October 1975. We shall attempt to do this by assessing subjective probabilities of this development based on your beliefs concerning future trends in the unemployment rate.

This exercise involves the concept of probability, but it is not necessary for you to have previous familiarity with probabilistic concepts. Two requirements for probabilities must be satisfied as you respond to the questionnaire:

1.   The probability of any one outcome in a total population of outcomes has a value less than or equal to 1, and greater than or equal to 0.

2.   The probabilities of all possible outcomes in the population must sum to one (1.0).

To illustrate these concepts through an analogy, consider the state's monthly sales tax revenues *three months from now*. This quantity is clearly a random variable. If a person said that the value will be between $700,000 and $750,000, he is saying that his best estimate of tax revenues lies in the interval $700,000–$750,000. However, it is possible for the actual value three months from now to be in an interval greater than or less than this interval.

A plot of outcomes for a random variable versus its corresponding probabilities is called a probability mass function (PMF). Figure 6-2 illustrates a probability mass function for sales tax revenues three months from now. Notice that all probabilities are nonnegative and sum to one. This figure also indicates that the most probable sales tax revenue is $700,000 and that it is impossible to experience revenues equalling $800,000.

This same situation can also be considered in terms of a cumulative distribution function (CDF) which is often more useful than a PMF. Here we consider the probability of future sales tax revenues being *less than or equal* a specific dollar amount (i.e., the cumulative probability of a given dollar amount).

In Figure 6-3 the cumulative distribution function for the situation shown in Figure 6-2 has been drawn. The CDF indicates that the probability of sales tax revenues being less than or equal $750,000 is 1.0 (i.e., it is certain the revenues will not exceed $750,000). There is a 60% probability that sales tax revenues will be less than or equal $650,000, which is equivalent to saying that there is a 40% chance that revenues will be greater than this amount. The

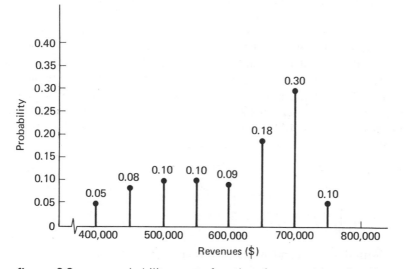

figure 6-2 . . . a probability mass function for monthly sales tax revenues

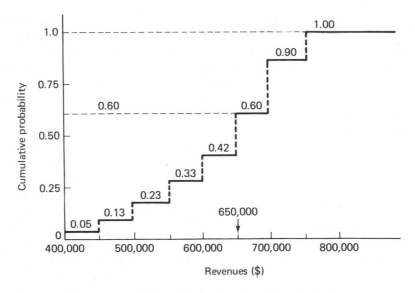

figure 6-3 . . . a cumulative distribution function of sales tax revenues

cumulative probability of a revenue in Figure 6-3 is read from the horizontal
solid line just to the right of the dotted "jump" in probability that occurs
over the revenue amount.

Now that the idea of PMFs and CDFs has been established, a series of
questions is presented whereby it will be possible to determine *subjective*
probabilities for the random variable of interest—the unemployment rate in
October 1975.

Answers to the questions that are presented below permit a cumulative
distribution function (CDF) to be evaluated for a future rate of unemployment in the state. To facilitate your understanding of each question, the following scale is presented to clarify the location of your response on a continuum of cumulative probabilities ranging from 1% to 99%. (Note that each
point on the scale represents approximately 12.5% of the total sample space
for this random variable. The task is now to specify numerical values for
points B, F, E, etc. so that this percentage is valid.)

Cumulative probability

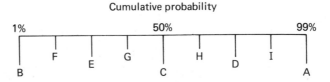

With this scale in mind, please answer these questions:

A. What do you consider to be the *largest possible* value that
the state's unemployment rate in October 1975 can have?

The largest possible value is defined such that you feel there are 99 chances out of 100 that the true unemployment rate will be less than or equal this value. _____

B. What do you consider to be the *smallest possible* value that the unemployment rate can have? The smallest possible value is defined such that there is only 1 chance in 100 that the true unemployment rate will be less than this value. _____

C. Can you determine a value of the unemployment rate in the range resulting from your answers to "A" and "B" such that there is a 50-50 chance that the "true" value will be above or below this value? Note this value in the space provided. It is called the median of your probability distribution. _____

D. For the range between the median value (C) and the largest possible value (A), what value in the range splits the area into two segments of equal probability? _____

E. For the range between the lowest possible value (B) and the median value (C), what value in this range would divide it into two sections of equal probability, i.e., 25% in each? _____

From your responses to (D) and (E) above, divide each of these smaller ranges into two intervals such that each interval contains equal probabilities. Record the value where this would occur. (Refer to the scale above.)

F. (B) to (E) Low value to mid-median _____

G. (E) to (C) Mid-median to median _____

H. (C) to (D) Median to mid-median of high value _____

I. (D) to (A) Mid-median of high value to largest value _____

COLLECTION AND ANALYSIS OF DATA   The 30 months of historical data (see Table 6-1) and the preceding questionnaire were presented to twelve high ranking officials in the Department of Welfare. After a personal interview with each individual where questions regarding the questionnaire could be answered, participants completed the questionnaire and "constructed" their own CDF for October's unemployment rate.

Responses to each question (itemized above) are summarized in Table 6-2. To develop a single CDF for the entire group, the twelve assessments of each of the nine points (A through I) comprising the CDF were averaged. The desired forecast of unemployment rate in October 1975 was chosen to be the *median* of the resultant CDF (i.e., the point that divides the CDF into two equal parts). From Table 6-2 it is seen that the median estimate of unemployment rate in October 1975 is 8.43% (point C).

table 6-2 . . . summary of responses to the questionnaire (percentages) and calculation of average point values

Raw Data:	Point along x-axis of the CDF								
	B	F	E	G	C	H	D	I	A
Respondent 1	6.0	6.25	6.50	6.75	7.0	7.25	7.50	7.75	8.0
Respondent 2	6.0	6.40	6.50	7.00	8.3	8.40	8.50	9.40	9.5
Respondent 3	8.0	8.13	8.25	8.38	8.5	8.63	8.75	8.88	9.0
Respondent 4	6.0	6.70	7.50	8.00	8.0	8.60	8.30	8.80	9.0
Respondent 5	5.0	5.50	6.00	6.50	7.5	8.00	8.25	8.50	9.0
Respondent 6	8.0	8.23	8.45	8.68	8.9	9.13	9.35	9.58	9.8
Respondent 7	7.8	8.00	8.20	8.50	8.8	9.00	9.30	9.40	9.6
Respondent 8	8.0	8.20	8.40	8.60	8.8	9.00	9.20	9.40	9.6
Respondent 9	7.2	7.80	8.26	8.40	8.6	8.80	9.20	9.60	10.0
Respondent 10	6.0	6.68	8.25	8.38	8.5	8.63	8.75	9.33	10.0
Respondent 11	9.2	9.25	9.30	9.35	9.4	9.45	9.50	9.70	9.8
Respondent 12	6.5	6.80	7.20	8.10	8.8	9.00	9.10	9.30	9.5
Point:	B	F	E	G	C	H	D	I	A
Average value	6.98	7.33	7.73	8.05	8.43	8.49	8.81	9.14	9.40
Cumulative probability	1.0%	12.5%	25.0%	37.5%	50.0%	62.5%	75.0%	87.5%	99.0%

Notice that the entire CDF was developed in our questionnaire rather than estimates only of the median. This was done for one primary reason. From the entire CDF we can furnish additional information about the random variable being considered such as "according to the respondents, there are about 3 chances out of 4 that the true unemployment rate will be less than 8.8% in October 1975." In summary, much useful information about the uncertain quantity can be obtained when we take the trouble to develop our entire CDF.

In Figure 6-4 we have drawn the cumulative distribution function based on averaged estimates presented in Table 6-2. A continuous approximation is also shown to facilitate interpretation of probability statements that we wish to make.

Recall that the Welfare Department wanted to be within ±1 percentage point of the unemployment rate in its forecasts. Because 8.43% represents our median estimate of the unemployment rate in October, we could easily determine the probability that this forecast, according to our subjective assessments, falls in the interval 7.43% to 9.43%. Referring to Figure 6-4, this probability is 0.99 - 0.125 = 0.865. The 86.5% "credible interval" for this particular problem is indicated in Figure 6-4. Thus, our subjectively-assessed CDF provides some assurance that if department staffing is based on an 8.43% unemployment rate, our goal will be satisfied. In other words the experts believe there are about 87 chances out of 100 that the actual unemployment rate will lie between 7.43% to 9.43%, which gives us satisfactory confidence in our decision to staff for 8.43%.

If the actual unemployment rate turns out to be 7.6%, for example, our forecasting efforts will have led to a "good" staffing decision. However, a sudden drop in unemployment to a 5.5% would leave the department overstaffed and subject to criticism. Because our forecast was medium-term in nature (four months), we would not expect to experience drastic changes in the unemployment rate. As the forecasting period was extended, say to twelve months, we might then anticipate larger differences between the actual rate and our forecasted rate.

A monthly forecasting system for this general type of problem would be easy to establish. We could use subjective probabilities to prepare forecasts four months ahead, for instance, to assist with manpower planning in the department. If we were forecasting next quarter's corporate sales, the information could be useful in scheduling production, determining inventory policies and purchasing raw materials.

Let us now suppose that the subjective probability procedure described above has already been in effect for one year. We are curious about how we might "calibrate" forecasts to improve on our forecasting accuracy. Starting with the October forecast that we developed previously, suppose that forecasted and actual unemployment rates have been those shown in Table 6-3.

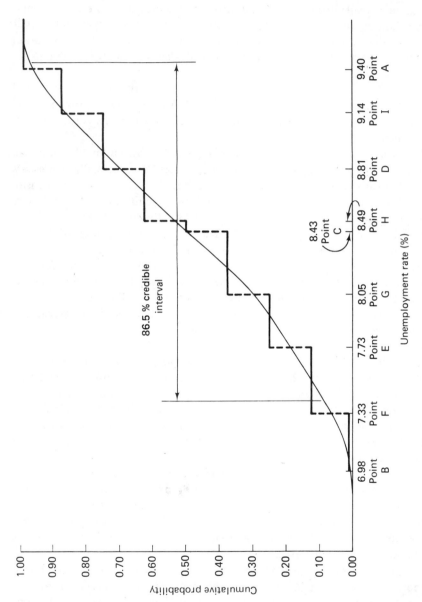

figure 6-4 ... the cumulative distribution function for the unemployment rate

table 6-3 . . . summary of one year's experience with
the unemployment rate forecasting system

Month, i	Forecast, F_i	Actual, A_i	Forecasting Error, F_i-A_i	$\lvert F_i-A_i \rvert$
October	8.4%	7.6%	+0.8%	0.8%
November	8.1%	7.9%	+0.2%	0.2%
December	8.5%	8.6%	-0.1%	0.1%
January	6.8%	7.2%	-0.4%	0.4%
February	6.9%	7.0%	-0.1%	0.1%
March	6.4%	6.2%	+0.2%	0.2%
April	6.8%	6.2%	+0.6%	0.6%
May	5.6%	7.8%	-2.2%	2.2%
June	5.9%	8.2%	-2.3%	2.3%
July	6.3%	7.4%	-1.1%	1.1%
August	7.1%	7.7%	-0.8%	0.8%
September	8.2%	8.6%	-0.4%	0.4%

Remember that these forecasts have been prepared four months ahead of
when we observe the actual unemployment rate.

Our purpose here is to demonstrate how the accuracy, consistency, and
bias of forecasts resulting from subjective probabilities can be determined and
used to improve the quality of further forecasting efforts. We begin by first
computing the forecasting error in month i, which is defined to be the forecast, F_i, minus the actual unemployment rate, A_i. This has been done in
Table 6-3.

In calibrating our forecasts, we make use of the following straightforward
relationships (n is the number of forecasts for which we can compute F_i-A_i):

$$\text{Mean absolute deviation (MAD)} = \frac{\sum\limits_{i=1}^{n} \lvert F_i-A_i \rvert}{n} \quad \text{(measures accuracy)}$$

$$\text{Systematic error} = E_S = \frac{\sum\limits_{i=1}^{n} (F_i-A_i)}{n} \quad \text{(measures bias)}$$

Correction for systematic error = CSE = $A_i + E_S$

Mean deviation about correction for systematic error =

$$MD_{CSE} = \frac{\sum\limits_{i=1}^{n} \lvert F_i-CSE \rvert}{n} \quad \text{(a measure of consistency after bias has been removed)}$$

These expressions permit us to determine the accuracy, bias and consistency of our forecasting system. If two (or more) forecasting schemes had

been in use during the past year, we would be able to compare them in terms of the above expressions and choose the better one. In general, bias is more acceptable than inconsistency because we can correct our forecasts for the bias effect. We strive for a small-valued MD_{CSE} since it is quite difficult to correct for inconsistent forecasts short of adopting a new forecasting system.

Each of the above quantities is calculated below for the twelve months of unemployment data:

Month	CSE
October	7.13%
November	7.43%
December	8.13%
January	6.73%
February	6.53%
March	5.73%
April	5.73%
May	7.33%
June	7.73%
July	6.93%
August	7.23%
September	8.13%

$$MAD = \frac{9.2\%}{12} = 0.77\%$$

$$E_S = \frac{-5.6\%}{12} = -0.47\%$$

$$MD_{CSE} = \frac{8.88\%}{12} = 0.74\%$$

Our MD_{CSE} is roughly 10% of the average actual unemployment rate. This indicates that our forecasting procedure has been fairly consistent over the past twelve months.

Based on the systematic error, our monthly forecasts on the average are about 0.5% too low. If our consistency (as measured by MD_{CSE}) is acceptable, future forecasts that we make with the subjective probability procedure can probably be improved by adjusting them upwards by 0.5%. Every few months we would recalibrate our forecasts by computing the bias, E_S, and checking the acceptability of MD_{CSE}. It should be clear that the above procedure for calibrating a forecasting system could be applied to numerous types of data.

the cross-impact method

In a previous section we discussed how the Delphi technique can be utilized to collect and analyze expert opinion. However, a potential shortcoming of Delphi (as well as many other forecasting techniques) is that interrelationships among events shaping the future are difficult to consider explicitly. Here we shall refer to these interrelationships as *cross impacts*, and the purpose of this section is to describe and demonstrate a forecasting technique that is capable of dealing with cross impacts in preparing forecasts.

We have included the cross-impact method in this chapter because subjective probabilities must be obtained as part of the procedure. When dependencies are suspected among future events, the probability that a potential development will actually occur is influenced by the occurrence or nonoccurrence of related developments. The cross-impact method allows us to estimate each development's probability of occurrence based on interrelationships that exist between events included in the analysis.

This technique was first reported in 1968 by T. J. Gordon and H. Hayward. They described the type of problem for which cross-impact analysis is suitable as follows.*

Consider a set of developments forecast to have occurred prior to some year in the future with varying levels of probability. If these developments are designated $D_1, D_2, ---, D_m, ---, D_n$ with associated probabilities $P_1, P_2, ---, P_m, ---, P_n$ then the question can be posed: If $P_m = 100\%$, (i.e., D_m happens), how do $P_1, P_2, ---, P_n$ change? If there is a cross-impact, then the probability of the individual items will vary positively or negatively with the occurrence or nonoccurrence of the other items.

In this section we shall consider a set of interdependent events related to a carefully defined problem. For example, the problem of interest might involve the evaluation of alternative U.S. energy policies that could be implemented during the next 15 years. After a list of potential developments related to the problem has been prepared, the cross-impact method of analysis can be employed to adjust the expected probability of each development on the basis of suspected interrelationships among events.

Concerning the above problem, suppose for the sake of simplicity that there are three potential developments of interest. Their description and estimated probability of occurrence within 15 years are:

Development, D_n	Probability, P_n
D_1 = Use of coal in various forms to replace demand for oil in all but vehicular applications.	0.8
D_2 = Reduction of domestic oil prices.	0.4
D_3 = Tightening of Federal air-quality and water-quality standards.	0.3

To display the basic interrelationships among these events, a cross-impact matrix is next developed:

*T. J. Gordon, and H. Hayward, "Initial Experiments with the Cross-Impact Method of Forecasting," Futures, Vol. 1, No. 2 (December 1968), p. 101.

If this event were to occur:	Probability of Occurrence	The effect on this event, D_n, would be		
		D_1	D_2	D_3
D_1	0.8	—	↑	↑
D_2	0.4	↓	—	—
D_3	0.3	↓	↓	—

The "up" arrows (↑) indicate positive cross impacts, or in other words, an "enhancing" linkage. An enhancing linkage is one where the occurrence of one development improves or "enhances" the probability of occurrence of a second development. For example, consider the impact of D_1 on D_3. If coal replaces oil as a fuel source within 15 years (excluding vehicular applications), the tightening of Federal air- and water-quality standards will be encouraged because coal is generally regarded as the dirtier fuel. (Several assumptions underlie this statement, but to keep the illustration uncluttered they are not listed here.)

"Down" arrows (↓) indicate negative cross impacts or, in other words, an "inhibiting" linkage. An inhibiting linkage is one where the occurrence of one development diminishes or "inhibits" the probability of occurrence of a second development. If D_3 occurs with certainty, the result would be to discourage, or inhibit, D_1. Another example of an inhibiting linkage is the impact of D_2 on D_1. In this case the reduction of domestic oil prices with probability 1.0 serves to reduce the likelihood that coal would replace oil as a primary fuel source within the next 15 years.

A small horizontal line in the matrix indicates no impact or an "unrelated" linkage which is one where the occurrence of one development has absolutely no effect on the occurrence of a second specific development. Usually the linkage direction (i.e., enhancing, inhibiting, or neither) of the cross impacts is determined by expert judgment through a structured approach such as the Delphi method.

After a matrix showing general directions of interactions among events has been developed, we proceed to "fine tune" our description of the interrelationships. This is accomplished by estimating the *strength* of the relationship between each pair of events (i.e., how strongly does the occurrence of one development affect the probability that another event will occur?).

Because strength concerns the relative effect of one development on the probability of another development, two events are strongly linked if the occurrence of the first produces a large change in the probability of occurrence of the second event. Similarly, two events are weakly linked if the occurrence of the first event produces only a small change in the probability of occurrence of the second event.

How then, are the above concepts applied to determine the change in the probability of D_n if D_m occurs? If P_n is the probability of D_n before the occurrence of D_m and P_n' is the probability of D_n after the occurrence of D_m, Gordon and Hayward have developed the following relationship:

$$P_n' = P_n + KS \cdot P_n \ (P_n - 1) \qquad \text{(Equation 1)}$$

where:

P_n = the probability of occurrence of event D_n by time t prior to the occurrence of event D_m.

P_n' = the probability of occurrence of event D_n sometime after the occurrence of event D_m.

K = -1 or +1 depending on whether the occurrence of D_m enhances or inhibits the occurrence of D_n. K is -1 for the enhancing linkage and +1 for the inhibiting linkage.*

S = a number between 0 and 1, a larger number representing a stronger effect of D_m on D_n (zero designating unrelated events).

Gordon and Hayward are, however, uncertain of the accuracy of the P' versus P relationship presented in Equation 1 and suggest that other relationships should be tested. Typical plots of Equation 1, shown in Figure 6-5, reflect the notion that the relationship between P_n and P_n is nonlinear and that this nonlinearity is affected by the magnitude of P_n.

To demonstrate a completed cross-impact matrix and the use of Equation 1 in computing modified probabilities for each development, we now return to the example problem given earlier on page 165. After describing this problem to several energy experts, they are requested to indicate the direction and strength of cross impacts in the matrix by specifying one of the seven numbers (1-7) shown on the left below:

Nature of Cross Impact	Corresponding Value of KS
1. No impact	0
2. Minor inhibiting impact	+0.5
3. Minor enhancing impact	-0.5
4. Strong inhibiting impact	+0.8
5. Strong enhancing impact	-0.8
6. Very strong inhibiting impact	+1.0
7. Very strong enhancing impact	-1.0

*K is -1 for the enhancing linkage, contrary to the intuitive notion that it should be +1. This can be seen by expanding (Equation 1):

$$P_n' = P_n + KS \cdot P_n^2 - KS \cdot P_n$$

Since $0 \leqslant P_n \leqslant 1$; $P_n^2 \leqslant P_n$. If $K = +1$ the sum of the last two terms above will be negative. When $K = -1$, the sum of these two terms will be positive. Therefore if $K = +1$, P_n' will be less than or equal P_n which indicates an inhibiting interrelationship. When $K = -1$, P_n' will be greater than or equal P_n which indicates an enhancing linkage.

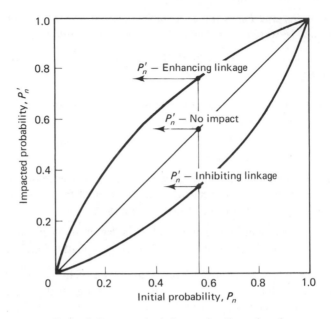

figure 6-5 . . . typical shapes for Equation 1

Expert opinions regarding the nature of cross impacts for this problem are next converted to corresponding values of KS. A Delphi study, for example, could be used to obtain a concensus of KS values (if two divergent sets of opinions were obtained, two separate analyses could be conducted). Probably the most frequent response (i.e., the mode) would be utilized to represent the group's consensus opinion. Upon completing this task, let us suppose the cross-input matrix has these cell entries:

If this event were to occur:	Probability of Occurrence (%)	The effect on this event, D_n, would be		
		D_1	D_2	D_3
D_1	80	0	-0.5	-0.8
D_2	40	+0.5	0	0
D_3	30	+1.0	+0.5	0

Based on Equation 1 the calculation of revised probabilities for each event proceeds in this manner:

A.   One of the N events in the cross-impact matrix is randomly selected.

B.   A random number from 00 to 99 is then generated and this number is compared with the initial probability (P_n) of the event selected in Step A above. If the random number is greater than or equal to the initial probability (P_n) of the selected event, the event did *not* occur. If the random number is less than the initial probability, the event occurred. For example, suppose we have events D_1, D_2, and D_3. Event D_3 is randomly chosen (Step A above) and has an initial probability (P_3) of 30. Now a random number is generated (Step B) and suppose it happens to be 55. Since 55 is greater than the initial probability of event D_3, event D_3 did not occur.

C. (1) If the selected event did not occur, the initial probabilities for the remaining events are considered to be unchanged.

(2) If the selected event did occur, the initial probabilities of all developments affected by D_3 are adjusted according to Equation 1 (or some other mathematical relationship).

D. Now one of the remaining events not yet tested is randomly selected. We proceed to Step B again where a random number is compared with P_n (or P_n' if the initial probability has been already modified). It should be apparent that the random order of event selection will affect the determination of P_n' for the N events in the matrix. However, with a large number of trials this effect will be negligible.

E. The process continues to be repeated until all N events have been tested for occurrence. At this point each event has either a "yes" or "no" reflecting its occurrence or nonoccurrence. This concludes one "trial." The probabilities are now reset to their initial values and we move to Step F.

F. Steps A through E are repeated a *large* number of times (e.g., 1,000 or more trials) and the cumulative number of occurrences for each development is kept. This number, when divided by the total number of trials, provides an estimate of the modified probability for each event that reflects all interrelationships in the matrix.

From Step F the modified probability for each event can be calculated when all trials have been completed. These probabilities are then analyzed with respect to size and direction of shifts from original values and the areas where these shifts were most pronounced.

For the problem being considered, five trials have been conducted to illustrate how Equation 1 was used in Steps A through F. Table 6-4 shows how the computational procedure is performed. In each trial, D_m (m represents either event 1, 2, or 3) is randomly chosen and tested for occurrence or nonoccurrence. For example in trial number 1, D_1 was the first randomly chosen event. The random number selected to test the occurrence of D_1 was 34. Because 34 is less than the initial probability of D_1 (80), this event occurred and P_2' and P_3' are calculated with Equation 1. Remaining events in a particular trial are also randomly chosen and tested for occurrence or nonoccurrence according to their modified (or original) probabilities. Individual calculations for the first trial are on page 171. The second trial is then con-

table 6-4 . . . five trial outcomes in computing P_n' for a cross-impact matrix

Trial Number	D_m	Random Number	D_1 O*	D_1 N/O**	D_2 O*	D_2 N/O**	D_3 O*	D_3 N/O**	$KS_{(1,1)}$	$KS_{(1,2)}$	$KS_{(1,3)}$	$KS_{(2,1)}$
1	1	34	X						0	-0.5	-0.8	
	3	24					X					
	2	23			X							+0.5
2	3	38						X				
	1	64	X						0	-0.5	-0.8	
	2	36			X							+0.5
3	1	35	X						0	-0.5	-0.8	
	3	68						X				
	2	90				X						
4	1	35	X						0	-0.5	-0.8	
	3	22					X					
	2	50				X						
5	2	13			X							+0.5
	3	36						X				
	1	91		X								
Total Number of Occurrences			4		3		2					

*O—occurrence
**N/O—nonoccurrence

Revised probabilities: $P_1' = 4/5 = 0.8$

$P_2' = 3/5 = 0.6$

$P_3' = 2/5 = 0.4$

$KS_{(2,2)}$	$KS_{(2,3)}$	$KS_{(3,1)}$	$KS_{(3,2)}$	$KS_{(3,3)}$	P_1	P_2	P_3	P_1'	P_2'	P_3'
					0.8	0.4	0.3	0.8	0.52	0.468
		+1.0	+0.5	0	0.8	0.52	0.468	0.64	0.3952	0.468
0	0				0.64	0.3952	0.468	0.5248	0.3952	0.468
					0.8	0.4	0.3	0.8	0.4	0.3
					0.8	0.4	0.3	0.8	0.52	0.468
0	0				0.8	0.52	0.468	0.72	0.52	0.468
					0.8	0.4	0.3	0.8	0.52	0.468
					0.8	0.52	0.468	0.8	0.52	0.468
					0.8	0.52	0.468	0.8	0.52	0.468
					0.8	0.4	0.3	0.8	0.52	0.468
	+1.0		+0.5	0	0.8	0.52	0.468	0.64	0.3952	0.468
					0.64	0.3952	0.468	0.64	0.3952	0.468
0	0				0.8	0.4	0.3	0.72	0.4	0.3
					0.72	0.4	0.3	0.72	0.4	0.3
					0.72	0.4	0.3	0.72	0.4	0.3

individual calculations for P_n' in trial no. 1 of table 6-4

$$P_n' = P_n + KS \cdot P_n(P_n-1)$$

Trial No. 1

D_1 occurs:

$P_1' = 0.800$

$P_2' = 0.4 + 0.4 \, (-0.6) \, (-0.5) = 0.520$

$P_3' = 0.3 + 0.3 \, (-0.7) \, (-0.8) = 0.468$

D_3 occurs:
(Use adjusted probabilities
from above where appropriate)

$P_3' = 0.468$

$P_1' = 0.8 + 0.8 \, (-0.2) \, (1.0) = 0.640$

$P_2' = 0.520 + 0.520 \, (-0.480) \, (+0.5) = 0.3952$

D_2 occurs:
(Use adjusted probabilities
from above where appropriate)

$P_2' = 0.3952$

$P_1' = 0.640 + 0.640 \, (-0.360) \, (+0.5) = 0.5248$

$P_3' = 0.468 + 0.468 \, (-0.532) \, (0) = 0.468$

171

ducted, and the occurrences of the various events are recorded as shown in Table 6-4.

After only five trials, little can be concluded regarding our illustrative problem. The revised probability of D_2 and D_3 increased over their original values. But when ten trials are computed for this problem, it was found that $P_1' = 0.9$, $P_2' = 0.7$ and $P_3' = 0.2$. This is an indication that many more trials are required to get improved estimates of the revised probabilities. In summary, this problem has demonstrated how the cross-impact method works; no physical interpretation can be given to our results because of the limited number of trials.

Ideally, the procedure described in Steps A through F should be repeated 1,000 times or so. To do this, a digital computer could be used to evaluate quickly the modified probabilities of events being considered in the cross-impact analysis.

Some of the advantages of the cross-impact method are: (1) its ability to take interactions among events into consideration and (2) its systematic organization of data regarding a large number of possible outcomes into an easy to analyze form. One of the primary drawbacks of the method concerns its rather arbitrary scheme of transforming initial probabilities into modified probabilities through Equation 1. Also, the definition of cross-impact factors is sometimes not specific enough to avoid ambiguous interpretation. These shortcomings can be remedied to some degree by the analyst as the problem being investigated is carefully defined.

Additional insight into the application of cross-impact analysis is made available by the article that follows. Strengths and weaknesses of the method are described in more detail by the author.

an application of the cross impact method*

ABSTRACT   By experimenting with forecasting techniques, potential users can broaden their time horizons and improve their understanding of possible future outcomes. This paper describes the aims, structure and results of a seminar on public administration conducted at Bruges, Belgium in 1969. The primary techniques used were the Delphi method and the cross-impact matrix technique.

introduction

Forecasting is an essential part of any decision to proceed with an action program. Any decision to commit resources assumes that the outcome will have some useful lifetime. This is equally true for the purchase of a

*By Selwyn Enzer, "A Case Study Using Forecasting as a Decision-Making Aid," *Futures* (December 1970), pp. 341-362. Reprinted by permission of the publisher.

meal, a car, or a home. Although the time period involved and the importance of the decision vary greatly in such cases, most of us feel sufficiently confident to make decisions in these situations without excessive difficulty. However, are we as confident in business or national decisions? In today's industrial organizations, for example, decisions often are not expected to return a dividend for a decade, or longer. National decisions may also have long time lags and international implications. How do we make such decisions, which may have lifetimes approaching 20 years or more, in our highly dynamic society? We now make them with a lot of thought, questionable assurance, and great difficulty. To increase our confidence and ease our difficulty are the tasks of futures research.

Modern forecasting bears slight resemblance to fortune telling; it more closely resembles science fiction writing, coupled with probabilistic analysis. In other words, a modern forecaster is not a prophet. He is an analyst who can assist a planner in organizing his thoughts and evaluating them to produce and arrange the alternatives they suggest.

The implications of such analyses can be likened to a ship's guidance system, which displays where a vessel will be if the controls and external forces remain in a given state. A dynamic guidance system of this type acknowledges that nothing can be done to change the ship's present position, only where it will be at some time in the future. Of course, if the current or the ship's controls were to change, in the period being simulated by the guidance system, the ship's future position would also be altered. This analogy characterises what a forecaster tries to evaluate. However, for society, the present position, control system, and external forces are more difficult to define and, hence, forecast.

As in the case of a ship's guidance system, the course must be determined and factors affecting changes in that course must be anticipated. The latitude of the control system must also be understood. With these variables quantified, a probabilistic analysis of future positions is possible. Finally, these outcomes must be displayed in some manner which permits us to appreciate their consequences. These steps suggest that a forecast should:

- Anticipate what occurrences are possible and assess their probabilities.

- Assess the interactions (cross impacts) among these occurrences.

- Identify the occurrences that can be controlled and the extent of such control.

- Evaluate alternative future possibilities, considering varying degrees of intervention that are within our power to control.

- Convert these outcomes into displays that provide us with an assessment of the impact of the possible future.

The importance of such an analysis is a function of the magnitude of the program being considered and the time lag between the decision to proceed and the end of the useful lifetime (or the outcome) of that decision. For any given activity we may be unable to keep in mind and analyse all of the relevant changes likely to affect the outcome. This is particularly true when the activity involves:

- Complex programs in terms of the number and diversity of people and skills involved or affected.
- Long development times.
- Long useful lifetimes.
- Rapidly changing social and technological environments.

Clearly, our society is facing many choices that involves all of these factors.

the demonstration: procedure and results

The demonstration was designed to enhance the insights that can be obtained from informed judgement. The entire demonstration involved the following eight separate activities:

- Identification of events which were possible by 1980 and would be important to the future of Europe if they occurred.
- Selection of ten of these events for inclusion in the demonstration (this limitation was imposed solely for practical reasons dictated by the magnitude of the effort that could be undertaken in two days).
- Estimation of the initial likelihood of occurrence of the ten selected events by 1980.
- Estimation of the cross impacts among these ten events (that is, a description of the effect on the likelihood of occurrence of one event produced by the occurrence of another event).
- Identification of those events where society's intervention could change the likelihood of occurrence, and assessment of the desirable direction of such interventions (to enhance or inhibit the occurrence).
- Probabilistic evaluation of outcomes considering the initial likelihoods of occurrence and the cross impacts among the ten events, with and without interventions by society.
- Probabilistic determination of five possible futures.
- Subjective assessments of the five possible futures in terms of a limited set of social indicators.

The task of selecting the most important events evoked considerable discussion regarding appropriate criteria for such a decision. Because even in an actual analysis practical considerations often necessitate limiting the scope of the effort, this question is of more than just passing interest.

In a futures analysis all candidate developments which satisfy two criteria should be included. First, the development must be important to the subject being evaluated, in the sense that the event should have some impact on an action or a decision that is being contemplated. Second, only those important developments whose outcome is uncertain (that is, those that may occur as opposed to those that almost certainly will or will not occur) should be included in the set being analysed. (The certain events form part of the background information which is to be used in evaluating the likelihood of occurrence of these uncertain events.)

Because the present activity was a demonstration of analytic techniques and employed a highly limited set of developments, it was also desirable for the items to be causally related to each other in some way. In other words, if the ten selected developments had been so dissimilar that the occurrence of one had no significant effect on any of the remaining nine, the value of the set, as a demonstration device, would have been decreased.

A large number of suggested events were considered, and a vote was taken to select the ten to be used in this study. The events selected and their original identification numbers are listed in Figure 1.

The group was asked to estimate the initial or individual likelihoods of occurrence of the ten selected developments by the year 1980. Here again, the criteria for making such judgements are quite vague and can present some difficulties. These difficulties may take two forms. The first involves the very concept of "initial" or "individual" likelihood of occurrence. Clearly, developments such as were being considered in the demonstration do not occur in a social vacuum. And in estimating the likelihood of occurrence of a particular development, one typically sees it in the context of a total environment. At this point all that can be said about the procedure is that the occurrence should be considered in an environment which might have evolved normally from present circumstances. As mentioned earlier, those events which are felt to be virtually certain (either to occur or not to occur) should be included as part of the description of this environment.

The second difficulty occurs in interpreting the numerical values that are given as part of such judgements. Social change is not a repeatable process like tossing a coin or testing a model, and is generally not thought of in these terms. Although social developments can be expressed probabilistically, the mental process that is or should be used in making such judgements is presently unknown, and the meaning of these judgements is far from clear.

Estimate of probability of occurrence of the ten most important developments
Write your estimate of the likelihood of occurrence of each development during
the 1970-80 decade using a scale of 0 to 100

Ten most important developments	Likelihood of occurrence by 1980 (Scale; 0-100)

1. British entry into the Common Market
3. Peaceful reunification of Germany
4. Worldwide open trade with Communist bloc nations
6. Formulation of federations of European nations (consisting of groups of present nations)
27. Introduction of an international monetary system (non-gold) guaranteed by international monetary authority
33. Social and economic homogeneity among Common Market nations
35. Major warfare between Russia and Red China
37. Closer relations between European countries and the USA in international enterprise and research fields resulting in stronger ties with the USA than with each other
39. Four-fold increase in aid (with regard to 1969) to underdeveloped countries by East and West
42. Ten-fold increase in research capabilities (people plus apparatus and techniques) in Europe and the USA

---

figure 1 . . . format for estimating initial probabilities of occurrence

using the delphi technique to obtain consensus

Because of these difficulties, wide divergence of opinion could be expected among the group as to the quantitative values for the initial likelihood of the occurrences being examined. As a result, a limited version of the Delphi technique was used to enhance the prospects of obtaining a group consensus regarding these values. . . .

The Delphi procedure used in this seminar was conventional except that the anonymity of the members of the group was not preserved—clearly an impossibility since they had already spent several months together. However, the Delphi technique involves two degrees of anonymity, one concerning the identify of the *participants* and the other concerning the identity of the *inputs*, that is, knowing which participant made what contribution. This latter consideration—anonymity of the inputs—seems to be the more important of the two, and was maintained in the demonstration for all written inputs.

The reasons for dissensus, however, were discussed openly. To have maintained anonymity in this phase of the Delphi would have necessitated eliciting and processing written inputs. This would have required more personnel and time than were actually available on this occasion. Although the lack of anonymity in discussing the reasons for disagreement appeared to be a significant detriment to communication at the conference, it may not have affected the outcome, since deep-rooted polarity of opinion often exists regarding issues of the type being discussed. But it did compromise the technique, in that many reasons that might otherwise have been elicited were not presented. Thus, while the participants' reassessments were based, in part, on reasons that emerged in the discussion, the spread of quantitative opinion that resulted often revealed a greater degree of dissensus than the discussion suggested.

The first round of the Delphi analysis used the form presented in Figure 1. While the group had little difficulty in making the required estimates, the spread of opinions was quite large. This spread was tabulated and the group was presented with the median and the upper and lower quartile values. Before the group was asked to re-estimate the likelihoods of occurrence, reasons for extreme positions were elicited, as was mentioned earlier. These discussions exposed several areas of misunderstanding regarding the phrasing of the prospective developments. As a result, some of the statements were re-written. For example, Item 35 was originally written, "Long-term warfare between Russia and Red China". Some members of the group considered this event quite unlikely, even though they felt that the possibility of a major conflict between these nations was considerably higher. The problem was the words 'long-term', for the feeling was that such a confrontation would be over relatively quickly. Because the group felt the magnitude of this event (if it were to occur) would be more important than its duration, the wording was changed to that given in Figure 1.

Similarly, several candidate developments proved confusing because they seemed too inclusive. For example, Item 4, "World-wide open trade with Communist bloc nations", presented difficulties in that some participants interpreted the term 'world-wide' to mean trade with every nation in the world. Here again, the group was more concerned with largely expanded trade involving any nation that was so disposed. In these cases the group was advised to consider the intent of the statement more than its exact wording. Of course, had there been sufficient time, the statements would have been revised or the list of events might have been expanded to include several versions of some of the developments.

Following the discussion, the group re-estimated the likelihood of occurrence for each of the ten developments. The range of opinion in

Ten most important developments	Range of opinions regarding likelihood of occurrence*	
	Round one	Round two
1. British entry into the Common Market	UQ–90	85
	M –79	80
	LQ–60	75
3. Peaceful reunification of Germany	UQ–29	20
	M –11	10
	LQ– 5	5
4. Worldwide open trade with Communist bloc nations	UQ–70	60
	M –50	50
	LQ–26	30
6. Formulation of federations of European nations	UQ–70	60
	M –50	50
	LQ–30	20
27. Introduction of an international monetary system (non-gold) guaranteed by international monetary authority	UQ–79	75
	M –60	60
	LQ–35	50
33. Social economic homogenity among Common Market	UQ–70	70
	M –60	60
	LQ–40	50
35. Major warfare between Russia and Red China	UQ–50	50
	M –25	23
	LQ–10	15
37. Closer relations between European countries and the USA in International enterprise and research fields resulting in stronger ties with the USA than with each other	UQ–70	40
	M –50	50
	LQ–35	30
39. Four-fold increase in aid (with regard to 1969) to underdeveloped countries by East and West	UQ–70	40
	M –40	30
	LQ–25	10
42. Ten-fold increase in research capabilties (people plus apparatus and techniques) in Europe and the USA	UQ–60	50
	M –20	25
	LQ–15	15

*Indicated are the upper quartile (UQ), the median (M), and the lower quartile (LQ) positions for the two rounds of estimation.

figure 2 . . . range of opinions regarding initial likelihoods of occurrence

each of these rounds is presented in Figure 2. The second round median values were used for the probabilistic analyses which followed.

As can be seen from these values, the interquartile ranges narrowed considerably after just one iteration and limited open discussion. On the other hand, the medians—the values actually used in the analysis— exhibited very little change. A complete analysis of this type might well have involved more than two iterations; moreover, all of the reasons behind the estimates would probably have been brought out because the anonymity of all the inputs would have been maintained. The result might not have been a tighter consensus than the one achieved in the demonstration, but the participants would definitely have gained a better insight into the differences of opinion that existed within the group.

assessing inter-relationships between developments

The next task involved an assessment of the interrelationships which the group felt existed among the ten selected developments. For this purpose the matrix form illustrated in Figure 3 was used. In completing this form

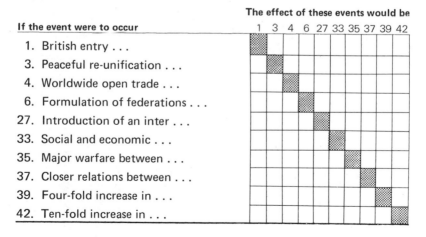

Indicate the effect you would anticipate on the likelihood of occurrence of each of the remaining nine developments if *preceded* by the occurrence of each other development. Use of a positive sign (+) if you feel the effect of the occurrence of the development will be to increase the likelihood of occurrence of the subsequent developments, and a negative sign (–) for the converse. Indicate the strength of the impact numerically according to the following code: 0 = No impact; 1 = Minor impact; 2 = Strong impact; and 3 = Very strong impact.

The effect of these events would be

If the event were to occur	1	3	4	6	27	33	35	37	39	42
1. British entry . . .										
3. Peaceful re-unification . . .										
4. Worldwide open trade . . .										
6. Formulation of federations . . .										
27. Introduction of an inter . . .										
33. Social and economic . . .										
35. Major warfare between . . .										
37. Closer relations between . . .										
39. Four-fold increase in . . .										
42. Ten-fold increase in . . .										

figure 3 . . . cross-impact matrix estimating form

If this event were to occur	**	1	3	4	6	27	33	35	37	39	42
						The effect on these events would be*					
1. British entry	UQ		0	+1	+2	+3	+2	0	+1	+1	+2
	M		0	+1	+1	+2	+1	0	-1	+1	+1
	LQ		-1	+1	-2	+1	-1	0	-1	+1	+1
3. Peaceful re-unification	UQ	+1		+2	+2	+1	+1	0	0	+1	+1
	M	0		+2	0	0	0	0	0	+1	+1
	LQ	-1		+1	-2	0	-1	0	-1	0	0
4. Worldwide open trade	UQ	+1	+2		0	+2	+1	0	0	+2	+1
	M	0	+1		0	+1	0	0	0	+1	+1
	LQ	-1	+1		-1	+1	0	-1	-1	+1	0
6. Formulation of federations	UQ	+2	+1	+1		+3	+3	0	+1	+2	+2
	M	+1	-1	0		+2	+2	0	0	+1	+1
	LQ	-1	-2	-1		+1	+2	0	-2	+1	+1
27. Introduction of an inter	UQ	+2	0	+2	+2		+3	0	+1	+2	+2
	M	+1	0	+1	+1		+2	0	0	+1	+1
	LQ	-1	0	+0	+1		+2	0	-2	+1	+1
33. Social and economic	UQ	+1	0	+1	+3	+2		0	+1	+1	+1
	M	-1	-1	0	+3	+2		0	+1	+1	+1
	LQ	-1	-1	0	+2	+1		0	0	+1	0

The effect on these events would be*

If this event were to occur	1	3	4	6	27	33	35	37	39	42	**
35. Major warfare between . . .	0	+1	+2	+2	0	0		+1	0	+1	UQ
	0	+1	+1	0	0	0		+1	-1	0	M
	0	-2	-2	0	0	0		0	-2	0	LQ
37. Closer relations between . . .	+1	0	+1	+1	+1	+1	0		+1	+2	UQ
	-1	-1	0	-1	+1	-1	0		+1	+1	M
	-2	-2	-1	-2	0	-2	0		0	+1	LQ
39. Four-fold increase in . . .	0	0	-1	+1	+1	0	0	+1		+1	UQ
	0	0	+1	0	+1	0	0	0		0	M
	0	0	0	0	0	0	0	0		0	LQ
42. Ten-fold increase in . . .	+1	0	+1	+2	+1	+2	0	+2	+2		UQ
	+1	0	+1	+1	0	+1	0	+1	+1		M
	0	0	0	0	0	0	0	0	+1		LQ

*A positive sign (+) indicates the effect of the occurrence of the development will be to increase the likelihood of occurrence of the subsequent development, and a negative sign (-) indicates the converse. The strength of the impact is indicated by the following code: 0 = No impact; 1 = Minor impact; 2 = Strong impact; and 3 = Very strong impact.

**UQ = Upper quartile; M = Median; LQ = Lower quartile.

figure 4 . . . range of opinions regarding cross-impact factors each participant was asked to estimate the effect that the occurrence of any one event would have on the likelihood of occurrence of every other event. Because this question is asked for every event, a ten-event matrix requires 90 such estimates.

In completing the matrix, two judgements must be made: Does the occurrence of the event being considered increase or decrease the likelihood of occurrence of another event, and, if so, to what degree? For the purposes of this demonstration, in which the 1970-80 decade was considered as a single interval, the time lag between the occurrence of one event and its impact on the likelihood of another was not considered. Only the sequence of events was explored.

The task of estimating cross-impact relationships was of great interest to the group. One member described it as being highly enlightening because it clarified and often changed his understanding of the importance of these events. In particular, several events which he had thought would have a very marked effect on the others turned out to have little impact when systematically evaluated in the context of the other events.

Figure 4 presents the median values of the cross-impact factors estimated by the group. Also shown are the upper and lower quartile values. As can be seen, the ranges are often quite close. Interestingly, the group's median position regarding the occurrence of Item 35, "Major warfare between Russia and Red China", is not affected by any of the other nine events. Conversely, the occurrence of the war would have some, but relatively little, effect on the other events. It is also interesting to note that Items 39 and 42—"Four-fold increase in aid to under-developed countries by East and West" and "Ten-fold increase in research capacities (people plus apparatus and techniques) in Europe and the USA"—are both enhanced by the occurrence of most of the other events.

It should be noted that the cross-impact of one event on another was estimated only on the assumption that the first event did, in fact, occur. If it did not occur, the cross-impact factor was assumed to be zero. Because the validity of this approach can be easily challenged, it might have been more accurate to have asked the participants to estimate the impact of the non-occurrence of each item on the likelihood of occurrence of the other items, and to analyse the outcomes considering both occurrences and non-occurrences.

Before the cross-impacts were analysed, the group was asked to identify two developments (from the list of ten) which they would like to have society intervene with, to enhance or inhibit their likelihood of occurrence. Such intervention might be in the form of legislation, a decision by some nation or group of nations to promote or inhibit one or more of the developments through the use of resources, or some similar activity.

The answers given to this question are presented in Figure 5, which shows the preferences and the directions of intervention—that is, to increase or decrease the probabilities of occurrence. These results were used to select two pairs of events, Items 6 and 27 and Items 39 and 42, as candidates for intervention in this analysis. Their initial probabilities of occurrence were arbitrarily raised by 20%. The result was to define three separate possible futures for use in the cross-impact analysis, each involving the same events and cross-impact matrix, but varying in the initial probabilities assigned to certain events. The three are presented in

Events	Votes for intervention	
	To increase the probability of occurrence	To decrease the probability of occurrence
1. British entry into the Common Market	4	0
3. Peaceful re-unification of Germany	4	1
4. Worldwide open trade with Communist bloc nations	2	0
6. Formulation of federations of European nations (consisting of groups of present nations)	9	2
27. Introduction of an international monetary system (non-gold) guaranteed by international monetary authority	12	0
33. Social and economic homogeneity among Common Market nations	5	0
35. Major warfare between Russia and Red China	1	0
37. Closer relations between European countries and the USA in international enterprise and research fields resulting in stronger ties with the USA than with each other	0	1
39. Four-fold increase in aid (with regard to 1969) to underdeveloped countries by East and West	13	0
42. Ten-fold increase in research capabilities (people plus apparatus and techniques) in Europe and the USA	7	0

figure 5 . . . selection of candidates for intervention

	Without interventions	With interventions noted*	
Events	Future A; Initial probabilities	Future B; Initial probabilities	Future C; Initial probabilities
1. British entry into the Common Market	0·8	0·8	0·8
3. Peaceful re-unification of Germany	0·1	0·1	0·1
4. Worldwide open trade with Communist bloc nations	0·5	0·5	0·5
6. Formulation of federations of European nations (consisting of groups of present nations)	0·5	**0·7**	0·5
27. Introduction of an international monetary system (non-gold) guaranteed by international monetary authority	0·6	**0·8**	0·6
33. Social and economic homogeneity among Common Market nations	0·6	0·6	0·6
35. Major warfare between Russia and Red China	0·23	0·23	0·23
37. Closer relations between European countries and the USA in international enterprise and research fields resulting in stronger ties with the USA than with each other	0·5	0·5	0·5
39. Four-fold increase in aid (with regard to 1969) to underdeveloped countries by East and West	0·3	0·3	**0·5**
42. Ten-fold increase in research capacities (people plus apparatus and techniques) in Europe and the USA	0·25	0·25	**0·45**

Items in bold had their initial probabilities raised as a result of societal actions.

figure 6 . . . initial probabilities of occurrence for cross-impact analysis

Figure 6, and are listed as possible future outcomes, A, B, and C (a notation used throughout the remainder of this paper.)

The cross-impact analysis used the initial probability and cross-impact estimated to evaluate the final probabilities of occurrence of the ten events. The final probabilities reflect the fact that developments must occur in some sequence (albeit random), and that this sequence will modify the probabilities of occurrence of other events in the set. . . .

Because the cross-impacts are evaluated mathematically, it was necessary to convert the panel's subjective assessment to quantitative values. This was done in the process of deriving the final probabilities in the manner indicated in Figure 7.

The results of this analysis produced the final probabilities presented in Figure 8.

comments on the results

Reviewing the changes indicated in Figure 8, one can see that Items 1, 3, 35, and 37 were most insensitive to the occurrence or non-occurrence of the others in the set. Comparing these changes with the cross-impact factors among these events and the occurrence of the others (the vertical columns in Figure 8), the small changes could be anticipated. As a matter of fact, Item 35, which was not appreciably impacted by any of the other events, should not have changed at all. That is, because the cross-impact factors between each of the other events and Item 35 are predominently zero, its mathematical final probability of occurrence must be close to its initial probability of occurrence.

The strongest changes can be seen in Items 4, 27, 33, and 39, with the remaining two, Items 6 and 42, not far behind. Comparing these changes with the factors shown in Figure 6 it is easily understandable why the probabilities of all of these events rise, since almost all of them contain many positive impacts.

In an over-all comparison, it appears that the social interventions had several very interesting effects. Of course, they raised the probabilities of occurrence of the events affected by the interventions, but more interestingly, they also raised the probabilities of many other events in the set. (The reverse effect was possible, of course, if the events and their cross-impacts had been different.) It is interesting to note that the interventions in Items 6 and 27 appear to have a greater over-all effect than the interventions in Items 39 and 42. While computational inaccuracies may have disguised the magnitude of these differences somewhat, they do represent a real-world possibility. Clearly, the effect of action in one area often has impacts in other areas. In this case, the effect of interventions in Items 6 and 27 seemed to have a strong effect on Items 39 and 42.

The new probability is determined from the relationship: $P_{in} = P_n + P_n(1 - P_n) S_{in}$, where:

P_{in} = Probability of occurrence of event E_n after event E_j has been decided
P_n = Probability of occurrence of event E_n prior to the deciding of event E_j.
S_{in} = Cross-impact of event E_j on event E_n.

The range of S is between −1 and +1. If the preceding event does not occur, then S is assumed to be 0. If the preceding event occurs, the value of S is determined from the interdependencies estimated earlier, according to the following relationship:

Cross-impact factor	Value of S
±1	±0·5
±2	±0·8
±3	±1

Using these relationships and the median values from Figure 4, the values of S are as presented below.

If this event has just occurred	The value of S for computing the new probability of occurrence of these events is									
	1	3	4	6	27	33	35	37	39	42
1. British entry into the Common Market	—	0	+0·5	+0·5	+0·8	+0·5	0	−0·5	+0·5	+0·5
3. Peaceful re-unification of Germany	0	—	+0·8	0	0	0	0	0	+0·5	+0·5
4. Worldwide open trade with Communist bloc nations	0	+0·5	—	0	+0·5	0	0	0	+0·5	+0·5
6. Formulation of federations of European nations (consisting of groups of present nations)	+0·5	−0·5	0	—	+0·8	+0·8	0	0	+0·5	+0·5

The value of S for computing the new probability of occurrence of these events is

If this event has just occurred	1	3	4	6	27	33	35	37	39	42
27. Introduction of an international monetary system (non-gold) guaranteed by international monetary authority	+0·5	0	+0·5	+0·5	—	+0·8	0	+0·5	+0·5	+0·5
33. Social and economic homogeneity among Common Market nations	−0·5	−0·5	0	+1	+0·8	—	0	0	+0·5	+0·5
35. Major warfare between Russia and Red China	0	+0·5	+0·5	0	0	0	—	+0·5	−0·5	0
37. Closer relations between European countries and the USA in international enterprise and research fields resulting in stronger ties with the USA than with each other	−0·5	−0·5	0	−0·5	+0·5	−0·5	0	—	+0·5	+0·5
39. Four-fold increase in aid (with regard to 1969) to under-developed countries by East and West	0	0	+0·5	0	+0·5	0	0	0	—	0
42. Ten-fold increase in research capabilities (people plus apparatus and techniques) in Europe and the USA	+0·5	0	+0·5	+0·5	0	+0·5	0	+0·5	+0·5	—

figure 7 . . . a numeric equivalent of the interdependencies among individual developments

187

Events	Without intervention	With interventions noted	
	Future A; Initial/Final probabilities	Future B; Initial/Final probabilities	Future C; Initial/Final probabilities
1. British entry into the Common Market	0·8/0·8	0·8/0·8	0·8/0·75
3. Peaceful re-unification of Germany	0·1/0·15	0·1/0·1	0·1/0
4. Worldwide open trade with Communist bloc nations	0·5/0·8	0·5/0·85	0·5/0·75
6. Formuation of federations of European nations (consisting of groups of present nations)	0·5/0·7	0·7/0·75	0·5/0·65
27. Introduction of an international monetary system (non-gold) guaranteed by international monetary authority	0·6/0·8	0·8/0·95	0·6/0·9
33. Social and economic homogeneity among Common Market nations	0·6/0·85	0·6/0·85	0·6/0·85
35. Major warfare between Russia and Red China	0·23/0·3	0·23/0·25	0·23/0·2
37. Closer relations between European countries and the USA in international enterprise and research fields resulting in stronger ties with the USA than with each other	0·5/0·5	0·5/0·6	0·5/0·7
39. Four-fold increase in aid (with regard to 1969) to underdeveloped countries by East and West	0·3/0·6	0·3/0·7	0·5/0·75
42. Ten-fold increase in research capacities (people plus apparatus and techniques) in Europe and the USA	0·25/0·35	0·25/0·5	0·45/0·45

figure 8 . . . change in probabilities of occurrence resulting from the cross-impact analysis (final probabilities based on a sample size of 20 runs)

In most real-world situations, decision-makers find that they are limited in resources and that there is more to do than appears practical. In such an environment it is important to determine the total impact of a set of actions. Such insights can identify practical programs that have a more desirable effect than may be intuitively obvious.

Even with the limited set of events employed in this demonstration and after systematically estimating the initial probabilities of occurrence and cross-impacts for these events, the total effect could not be judged. In an actual futures analysis, where more than 100 events may be considered and more than one time interval analysed, such insights are virtually impossible without the benefits of a cross-impact analysis . . . .

conclusions

In summary, we can conclude that the demonstration identified many ways in which the analytic techniques of futures research can affect planning and decision-making. True, there are still many shortcomings with the analytic techniques. However, these same shortcomings exist in the judgemental techniques which are in widespread use in conventional decision-making activities today. As pointed out by one member of the group, the demonstration did not really add any steps to the planning performed in his own organisation. This is perhaps one of the strongest assets that the technique described here possesses. It does not change basic thought processes, *per se*; rather, it uses them and augments their effectiveness by the introduction of systematic analogues which promote order and understanding among complex social relationships. This parallel with the patterns of actual thought is invaluable in subsequently using the results of these analyses in communicating the logic behind planning and decision-making activities.

Thus, one might conclude that tomorrow is the product of the complex interactions of many forces. The goal of forecasting is to be able to anticipate these forces and their mechanisms for interaction, so that society can expand its control over its destiny. And in this regard it may be more important to identify all significant prospects than it is to 'predict' the future accurately . . . .

questions

1. Discuss the principal advantages and disadvantages of the Delphi method of forecasting.
2. During a Delphi study, how can group opinion convergence (or divergence) be evaluated?

3. In your class, attempt to run a Delphi study to determine the price of a gallon of gasoline three years from now. Was group concensus affected by conducting two or three rounds of the procedure?

4. Refer to the article by Milkovich, Annoni, and Mahoney. Explain whether you think the authors draw conclusions from this study that are consistent with the historical intent of the Delphi method.

5. Explain how you might go about developing and using subjective probabilities to predict the total cost of a 2,000-square-foot house in Mobile, Alabama, that is completely dependent on the sun as its energy source.

6. By using the method described in this chapter, attempt to assess a cumulative distribution function for the number of companies in your state that employ more than 200 persons.

7. Explain how cross-impact analysis might be used to evaluate the likelihood that biodegradable cigarette filters will be marketable by 1990.

8. What is an inhibiting linkage in the cross-impact matrix?

9. Discuss the main advantages and disadvantages of cross-impact analysis. What happens if the number of relevant events in the analysis exceeds 10 or so?

chapter 7 . . . technological forecasting

introduction

Technological forecasting is a name given to a myriad of specialized forecasting techniques, and many of these techniques are extensions of established methods such as trend analysis. Forecasting procedures discussed in this chapter are related to those presented in Chapter 6 in that subjectively interpreted information is essential to preparing a forecast. A definition of technological forecasting might go something like this: technological forecasting provides procedures for data collection and analysis to predict future technological developments and the impacts such developments will have on the environment and lifestyles of mankind. These techniques seek to make potential technological developments explicit, but more importantly they require decision-makers to anticipate future developments.

Individuals have undertaken conventional forecasting (i.e., weather, economic conditions) for centuries, but the idea of technological forecasting has emerged because of the "explosion" of technology in the last 50 years. Technological forecasting deals with helping our rapidly changing society anticipate not only new technology itself but also the problems and consequences that may be a product of this technology.

Business and government have long known the importance of anticipating the character, magnitude, and timing of change. Forecasts of sales, production cost, and government spending and budgets, to name a few, are regarded as crucial in planning for the future. While accurate short- and long-range financial analysis and planning are routine for these institutions, forecasting the evolution of the state of the art in manufacturing, improved machine tools, operations, and new products remains vaguely descriptive for the most part. Many managers give little heed to potential progress of their operations, unless it is the expression of fond hopes that the manufacturing engineer will "find a way to improve that mess out in the shop."

Technology forecasting is a method that can be used to estimate the growth and direction of a technology. The goal of technology forecasting *is not* the prediction of conceptual design or hardware, or when a certain knowledge of nature or level of scientific understanding will be achieved. It is the operational parameters that are regarded as important. The anticipated speed of future spacecraft, rather than design of the vehicle, would be an illustration of this distinction. What the tolerance of numerically controlled machines in the future will be is another typical question that technology forecasting attempts to answer. In dealing with operating parameters, the forecast is limited to specific technical units and dimensions.

Many techniques are being developed for technology forecasting. Some are superior to others, depending upon what is to be forecasted. The extremes of these techniques range from mathematical abstraction to verbal descriptive statements. For the most part, technical forecasting *defies* complete capture by the mathematical model, yet a verbal description remains loose, general, and even more uninformative. The technology estimator in operating between these limits attempts to pin his forecast to numerical terms whenever that is possible.

To perform technology forecasting, the estimator must first study the implication of technical history as it pertains to his subject. He or she is forced to consider what has happened in the past and attempt to isolate numerically that which is significant in some quantifiable way. It may be that the accuracy of a numerical measure is imprecise, but the measure is necessary to try. Books that are devoted to developing specific historical patterns and charts for technological estimating are unavailable. In their stead, the estimator must study general technical history books.* Frequently, the technology may be so obscure or new that a written technical history may be unavailable. In this case, the analyst gathers his own history by correspondence, searching, and a general enlightenment about his field.

---

*For example, the reader may wish to refer to the following books:

Melvin Kranzberg and C. W. Pursell, Technology in Western Civilization, *Volumes I and II (New York: Oxford University Press, 1967).*

John W. Oliver, History of American Technology *(New York: The Ronald Press, 1956).*

George Sarton, A History of Science *(Cambridge, Mass.: Harvard University Press, Cambridge, Massachusetts, 1959).*

Charles Singer, (ed), A History of Technology *(London: Clarendon Press, n.d.).*

Abbot P. Usher, A History of Mechanical Invention *(New York: McGraw-Hill Book Company, 1929).*

In short, an important ingredient for good technological forecasting is a thorough understanding of technical history, current developments and future trends that relate to the technical issue under investigation.*

applications of technological forecasting

Technological forecasting techniques can be divided into two broad categories —exploratory and normative. Exploratory forecasts are based on existent technology and provide predictions concerning future developments. Normative forecasting assumes the existence of future technological innovation (predicted with exploratory forecasting) and provides models or methods of achieving these goals.

As mentioned previously, the end result of technological forecasting should be a plan of action for management to follow. An important application of technological forecasting concerns the identification of goals to be met by planning efforts—exploratory techniques can be used in this regard. Based on these goals, normative techniques are then usually employed to determine a means of satisfying them. For example, a new synthetic fiber made from vegetable oil might be identified through exploratory techniques as a desirable product for a company to pursue. The technology required to produce this product commercially could then be explored further with normative techniques.

At present technological forecasting is used mainly in specialized industrial situations by companies with large amounts of resources and data gathering capabilities. Various government agencies are also large users of technological forecasting techniques.** Listed below are typical situations where technological forecasting techniques have been used.

1. Assisting in the planning of research programs with regard to the dollar expenditures, direction, scientific skills needed, and so forth.
2. Guiding engineering programs toward the use of new technology and the adjustment to new technical demands.

*Several of the above comments were taken from Phillip F. Ostwald, "Technology Forecasting Applied to Numerical Control," Journal of Industrial Engineering (October 1971), p. 52-53. Reprinted by special permission of the publisher (the American Institute of Industrial Engineering, Norcross, Georgia).

**For example, in 1972 the Office of Technology Assessment (OTA) was created by the Congress of the United States, and it began operations in January 1974. Its basic function is to help legislative policy-makers anticipate and plan for the consequences of technological changes and to examine the many ways, expected and unexpected, in which technology affects people's lives. The assessment of technology calls for exploration of the physical, biological, economic, social, and political impacts which can result from applications of scientific knowledge. OTA provides Congress independent and timely information about the potential effects and side effects—both beneficial and harmful—of technological applications.

3. Identifying areas where product improvement will be needed and revealing the need for new products.

4. Setting quantitative performance standards for new products, processes, and materials.

5. Helping to establish the timing of new technology.

6. Assisting and identifying the economic potentials and impact of technological progress.

7. Guiding technological planning and its contribution to long-range planning.

8. Helping to identify major opportunities and threats in the technological environment.

9. Identifying the social impact of technological progress on employment, skills, educational needs, and so forth.

10. Identifying possible political developments arising out of technological advances.

description of technological forecasting techniques

Trend extrapolation is often used to make technological forecasts. This technique is based on a historic time-series for a selected technological parameter. It is assumed that the factors influencing historical data are likely to remain constant rather than to change in the future. Usually a single-function parameter such as speed, horsepower, or weight is extrapolated. A good trend extrapolation depends on selection and prediction of key parameters of performance. The trend under study should be capable of quantification in order that it can be portrayed numerically, and an adequate data base should exist on which to base a reliable trend line. An example of trend extrapolation is presented in Figure 7-1. Notice that the *y*-axis is a logarithmic scale.

An advantage of trend extrapolation is that historical data are often readily obtainable. A straight-line or fitted-curve projection of the future is easily understood and used. A drawback to extrapolation stems from the assumption that factors that shaped the past will continue to hold basically unchanged in the future. Trend extrapolation techniques therefore cannot predict unforeseen technology interactions. Unprecedented changes will not be identified by trend extrapolation, nor will the technique indicate the potential of new discoveries.

A technique known as *historical analogy* is a form of trend extrapolation that utilizes simple regression to project values of the parameter of importance. However, as we learned in Chapter 4 and Appendix B, certain problems can arise when regression analysis is used to fit a line to time-series data. Generally speaking, many forecasters have overextended the use of regression in this situation and make statements that cannot be supported by the underlying principles of the technique.

Substitution curve and envelope curve extrapolation rely on advanced trend analysis to fit historical data and project future trends. These two techniques are discussed below and are illustrated further in the article at the end of this chapter.

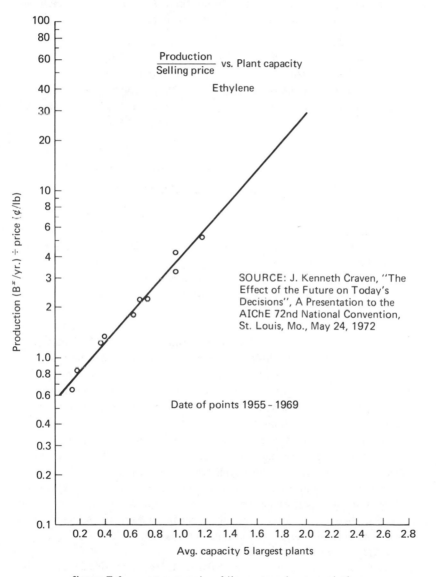

figure 7-1 . . . an example of linear trend extrapolation

The *substitution curve* is based on the belief that a product or technology that exhibits a relative increase in performance over an older (i.e., established or conventional) product or technology will eventually substitute for the one having lesser performance. The relative increase in performance is the important factor in the substitution of one technology for another. A basic assumption with this method is that once the substitution of one technology for another has begun it will irreversibly continue to completion. Listed below are some common examples of the substitution effect:

Old Technology	New Technology
Petroleum lamps	Electric lamps
Horse-drawn carriages	Automobiles
Steam locomotive	Diesel locomotive
Cotton	Synthetic fibers
Leather	Vinyl
Soap	Detergents
Reciprocating engines	Turbojet engines
Hardwood floor	Plastic flooring

The forecast starts with the observation that a new technology is starting to displace an older technology. A measurement term that best defines the fraction of total usage of each technology must be selected, and time-series data are gathered for both technologies. These data are used to establish the initial takeover rate and to predict the year in which takeover will reach 50 percent. A typical substitution effect for two technologies is shown in Figure 7-2.

Envelope curves are based on the inventive process. A succession of different technologies emerges over a period of time to satisfy the demand for improvement of a given capability. The candle, the kerosene lamp, and incandescent bulb and the fluorescent bulb represent the gradual replacement of preceding sources of light. In the area of transportation, the horse, the train, the piston-engine aircraft, and the jet aircraft have gradually replaced each predecessor as man sought more speed. Because any one technique seems to evolve along an S-shaped curve of capability improvement over time, from an overall perspective one sees a succession of these S-shaped performance curves when evolving technologies are plotted against time. By drawing a curve roughly tangent to the peaks of these S-shaped curves, which are plotted on the same performance versus time graph, a roughly exponential curve is described of the overall technological progress in the selected capability. An example of transportation speed versus time is shown in Figure 7-3 to demonstrate an envelope curve.

Envelope curves, like substitution curves, utilize time-series data to make forecasts. Substitution curves forecast the amount of substitution of one technology for another at some future time, while envelope curves forecast

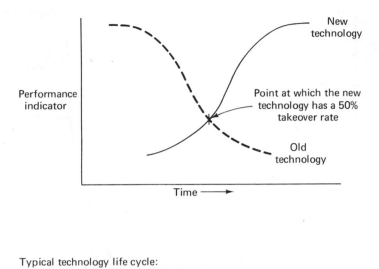

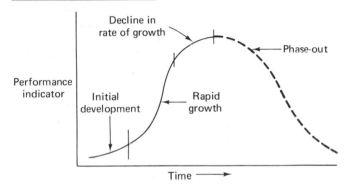

figure 7-2 . . . an example of substitution curves

future performance on the basis of past experience with several different technologies. Both envelope curves and substitution curves are extended models of trend extrapolation. Trend extrapolation makes the implicit assumption that the future is a logical extension of the past. When we extrapolate envelope curves beyond the present, we automatically assume not only continued innovation and improvement, but also a continuation of the rate of invention that has characterized the forecasted system in the past.

Envelope curve forecasting would be useful in those industries experiencing rapid innovation. Electronics and aviation are two such industries. In summary, then, envelope curves represent a general method of predicting the rate of technological innovation in a specific field. Upon estimating the rate of technological innovation, it is possible to determine the effects of alternative systems being considered on performance characteristics believed to be important to the acceptance/feasibility of the technology.

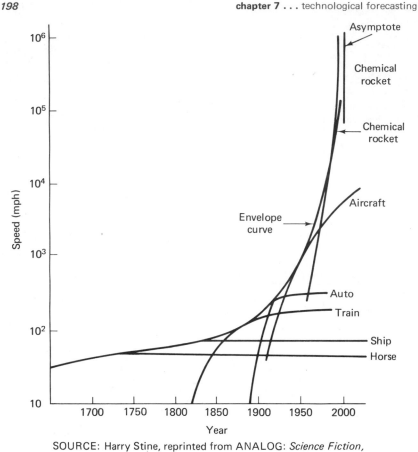

SOURCE: Harry Stine, reprinted from ANALOG: *Science Fiction,*
Science Fact, Conde Nast Publications Inc., 1961.

figure 7-3 . . . an envelope curve for transportation speed

Forecasting by analysis of *precursor events* uses the correlation of performance trends between two innovative technologies. Because technological advance usually follows a pattern of continuous increase, situations frequently occur in which one indicator of technical progress lags another by a given period of time. In this situation the leading indicator is called the *precursive indicator.* It is thus possible to utilize the leading technology to predict the status of the lagging technology over a time period equal to the lag time. A frequently cited example of precursor events is the historical relationship between maximum speed of military aircraft to the maximum speed of commercial aircraft (see Figure 7-4).

In this example, Lenz found that the speed of commercial aircraft followed the speed of military aircraft by six years in the 1920s and eleven years

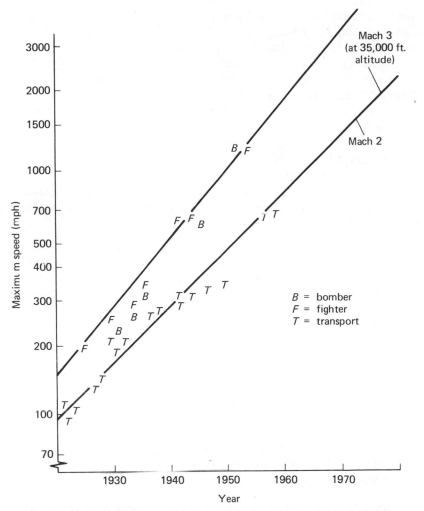

SOURCE: R. C. Lenz, "Technological Forecasting," ASD-TDR-62-414,
Wright-Patterson AFC, Ohio: Air Force Systems Command,
June 1962.

figure 7-4 . . . comparative speed trends of combat and transport aircraft

in the 1950s.* He predicted that commercial aircraft with speeds of Mach 2 may be expected no later than 1970, or, if such aircraft were not introduced at this time, then aircraft with speeds of Mach 3 will be introduced near 1976. The forecast in this situation says, in effect, that there is a logical time

*R. C. Lenz, Jr., "Technological Forecasting," ASD-TDR-63-414, Aeronautical Systems Division, Air Force Systems Command, June 1962.

for the introduction of Mach 2 aircraft but if other forces (for example, economic, social, and political) cause this time to be passed over, then this performance range will also be passed over.

Scenarios are a useful means of developing hypotheses about the future. A scenario is a "dramatic plot" that deals with certain aspects of the future. The plot is based on a current set of conditions and depicts potential actions and events in their likely order of development. For example, a scenario may be directed at anticipating changes in our society brought about by eliminating the production of gasoline-engine automobiles by the year 2000. Or, a scenario might be constructed in which all electrical power is produced with nonnuclear power plants in the year 2010.

A scenario can be based on a direct extrapolation of present conditions or may involve variations formed by adding new conditions to the present environment. Most scenarios exhibit the following attributes:

1. They serve to call attention, sometimes dramatically and persuasively, to the larger range of possibilities that must be considered in the analysis of the future. They are one of the most effective tools in lessening the carry-over thinking that is likely even when it is clear to all that the year 2000 cannot be the same as 1965 or even 1985. Scenarios are one way to force ourselves and others to plunge into the unfamiliar and rapidly changing world of the future.

2. They force the analyst to deal with technological, socioeconomic, and political details and uncertainties that he might easily avoid by restricting himself to only abstract considerations.

3. They help to illuminate interactions among social, economic, cultural, political, and military factors. They do so in a form that permits the comprehension of many such interacting elements at once.

4. They may be used to consider alternative outcomes of actual past and present events.

A practical application of scenario forecasting involved a chemical company that used this technique to prepare for a union strike. If a strike occurred, management personnel would live on the plant site and operate the equipment themselves. This would create many logistical and personnel problems necessitating advanced planning. To prepare for these problems, three different managers were asked to write scenarios, one for a very short strike, one for a medium-length strike and the other for a prolonged strike. Each manager had to develop a contingency plan for his scenario, including detailed manpower staffing plans complete with provisions for all foreseeable difficulties. They were also requested to anticipate the effects if their recommendations were implemented and there was no strike. Top management considered all three scenarios and then developed a coordinated strategy for dealing with a union strike. An interesting footnote is that negotiations were successful and there was no strike. Management believed that union awareness of their preparations was partially responsible for a successful settlement.

Morphological analysis is a method for identifying and counting all possible means to a given end at any level of abstraction. An obvious application is in the analysis of technological opportunities. Morphological analysis first requires that important parameters involved in the problem be identified. Each of these parameters is then considered independently to see how many ways it can be implemented with current technology. All parameters are tabulated in a matrix that contains the number of feasible options for each. This matrix can be carefully evaluated such that many unique and feasible solutions to the problem are obtained. A simplified example of morphological analysis is presented in Table 7-1.

The morphological procedure illustrated in Table 7-1 represents possible solutions for a manual propulsion system for a small boat. In the left-hand column are listed some of the requirements and characteristics of the design, such as input motion, the various input sources for this motion, input devices, output mechanisms, and operator position. The list shown in the left-hand column can be varied in number and type of parameters, depending on the characteristics and requirements given to the design.

Each row lists numerous options for implementing a design parameter. For example, what are the kinds of input motions that could be used to propel a boat? We could consider rotating motion, oscillating motion, linear motion, reciprocating motion, and others. The same procedure is used for each of the other parameter requirements listed in the left-hand column. *If*

table 7-1 . . . a morphological analysis of designing a manual propulsion system for a small boat

Parameters Design Characteristics and Requirements	Ideas Design Alternatives					
Input Motion	Rotating	Oscillating	Linear	Reciprocating	Etc.	
Input Source	One Hand	Two Hands	One Foot	Two Feet	Hand & Foot	Etc.
Input Device	Crank	Turnstile	Pedals	Lever	Treadmill	Etc.
Output	Propeller	Paddle	Paddle Wheel	Fin	Screw	Jet	Etc.
Mechanism	Gears	Chains	Belts	Pump	Linkage	Piston	Etc.
Operator Position	Sitting	Standing	Kneeling	Straddling	Etc.	

SOURCE: L. Harrisberger, *Engineermanship* (Belmont, Calif.: Wadsworth Publishing Company, Inc., 1966).

one idea from each row is combined with one idea from each of the other rows, we have a definition of a manual propulsion system for the boat. For instance, if we combine the ideas marked by asterisks, we obtain a system that is operated by a standing operator who uses both hands to turn a crank mechanism connected by a belt drive to a linkage mechanism that operates a paddle.

The number of solutions to this type of problem can be very large. For example, four rows of ten ideas each produce 10^4 (or 10,000) possible solution concepts. As you might suspect, though, many of these solutions are not feasible in practice. Nevertheless, morphological analysis can be extremely useful because it systematically forces the consideration of unique aspects of the problem.

In the next section, an excellent article by J. P. Martino illustrates how technological forecasting is used in connection with several of the forecasting tools presented in previous chapters.

technological forecasting in the chemical process industries*

ABSTRACT   Advances in the art of technological forecasting have produced a variety of explicit procedures for making credible forecasts. These can significantly improve the quality of decisions that must consider technological change.

what technological forecasting is

A technological forecast can be defined as a prediction of the future characteristics of a useful machine. There are three notable points to this definition.

First, the forecast describes the characteristics of some future machine. This description usually deals with the performance of the machine rather than with the details of how it will work. In other words, the forecaster is not required to invent the machine he forecasts but only to state that a machine with a certain performance will be available. Furthermore, he need not describe the means by which the performance that he is forecasting will be achieved.

Second, the restriction to useful machines is meant to exclude machines intended for luxury or amusement, which are affected more by

*J. P. Martino, "Technological Forecasting for the Chemical Process Industries," Reprinted by special permission from *Chemical Engineering* (December 27, 1971), pp. 54-62. Copyright © 1971 by McGraw-Hill, Inc., New York, New York 10020.

human tastes and fads than by either technological feasibility or economic viability.

Third, the term "machine" is to be interpreted broadly, so as to include tools, techniques and procedures. Biological and behavioral technologies are as much the concern of the technological forecaster as are the more conventional hardware technologies.

When is a technological forecast needed? It is needed whenever a decision must take technological change into account. While decisions are made *in* the present, they are not made *for* the present. The right choice among the options open to a decision-maker will depend upon the conditions that will exist at the time the decision comes to fruition. These may differ from the conditions that exist at the time the decision is made. If the technological conditions that will exist in the future make a difference in the choice of a course of action, the decision-maker needs some estimate or assessment of what those future conditions will be. This estimate or assessment is precisely what is meant by a technological forecast.

At this point, the . . . decision-maker may well ask, "But haven't I been doing that all along?" He might well protest that of course he takes future technological conditions into account when he makes his decisions. Any assertion to the contrary is tantamount to saying he has not been doing his job right.

With this, the technological forecaster would hasten to agree. He might even recite what has come to be almost a cliche in the forecasting field, "There is no such thing as not forecasting."

Suppose the decision-maker has a choice among several options. For each option, there is some possible future in which that option would be better than all the others. Therefore, the choice he actually makes has implicit within it a forecast of future conditions.

what is new in forecasting

Then why the sudden interest in technological forecasting, when it actually has been going on for years? There are two new things responsible for the current excitement over it. The first is the explicit recognition of the need for forecasts; the second, the improved methods for making forecasts.

In the past, decision-makers were often not consciously aware that they were incorporating a forecast of future technological conditions into their decisions. The forecast, although inescapably a part of their decision, was completely implicit within that decision.

This has changed. Decision-makers are coming to recognize that a forecast is an essential part of a decision, and also that the forecast must be explicit, so that it can be examined and challenged, just as any other estimates or assumptions that go into a decision must be examined and challenged.

The second new feature is the use of rational methods for making forecasts. In the past, even if a decision-maker wanted an explicit forecast, he could arrive at it only by "asking an expert." The expert in the technology in question would give his subjective, intuitive estimate of what the technology might achieve by some specified date. However, this forecast could then be evaluated only by comparing it with a forecast of another expert. If the two experts disagreed, there was no way of determining which expert was more "expert," and therefore more likely to be right.

This problem has to a large extent been eliminated. A wide range of explicit forecasting procedures has been developed. And a forecast prepared by means of any one of these procedures can be reviewed by anyone familiar with the methods of forecasting. He can check to see whether each step in the procedure was carried out correctly, whether the facts upon which the forecast is based are actually correct, and whether the assumptions made are reasonable. Furthermore, these methods can be tested scientifically in a variety of situations to assess their validity.

What are these new methods, and how can they be used? This article does not attempt to explain forecasting methods in detail. A number of books are available that give detailed expositions of the modern, rational methods of technological forecasting.[1,2,3] Instead, some of these methods are illustrated in a variety of decision situations typical of those commonly faced by the . . . decision-maker.

some decision situations

Virtually every decision made in the [chemical process industries (CPI)] is involved with considerations of technological change. Now, we will look at some fairly common decision situations, identify the information about the future technology needed to make those decisions, and in each case look at one method that can help provide the information needed.

total market size

How big will the total market for some chemical or class of chemicals be at some particular time in the future? The answer to this question is needed for any decision affecting plant capacity, sales goals, or the market share to be sought.

One way of forecasting total market size is known as trend extrapolation. In this method, the forecaster obtains data on market size for past years and attempts to identify a pattern of growth in the data. He usually settles for a trend rather than look for a more complex pattern. A forecast then is made by extrapolating this pattern into the future.

Fig. 1 shows a forecast of future U.S. production of ethylene. (This was prepared by the planning staff of Monsanto Co.[4]) An exponential trend was fitted to the historical data and projected into the future. This trend appears as a straight line when plotted on semi-logarithmic coordinates.

This forecasting method is straightforward and readily adaptable to visual presentation. However, it is based on the assumption that whatever forces acted to produce the trend will also extend it. As long as this assumption is valid, trend extrapolation is a successful forecasting method. If it is wrong, however, a trend forecast can be seriously in error. For instance, if ethylene were to be displaced by another chemical for some product, this would invalidate the forecast. The beginning of such replacement should be a warning to the forecaster. This technique can also be used to forecast other technological characteristics besides market size, but the same precaution applies.

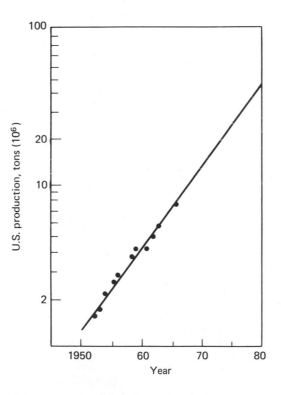

figure 1 . . . extrapolation forecasts ethylene production

sales growth of a new product

When a new product is brought on the market, decisions must be made about the construction of new plants, the provision of adequate supplies of raw materials, and the setting of sales and marketing goals. These decisions will depend upon estimates of the rate at which sales will increase and new production will be needed.

Because there will be no historical data that can serve as a basis for trend extrapolation, some other method must be used for generating a forecast. In such cases, there may be no alternative but to turn to subjective methods based on expert opinion. However, even here there have been changes. Subjective methods are not as subjective as they once were. There are major differences between current and past methods for making subjective forecasts.

One is to rely on a group of experts instead of only one. This has several advantages. A group has more information available to it than does any individual. A group also can consider more factors and more points of view. Finally, an individual may have biases of which he is himself unaware, whereas if the group is properly chosen, there is a fair likelihood that the biases of its members will tend to cancel one another.

However, most decision-makers, aware of the pitfalls of committee action, are often reluctant to depend on committees. Here again, there have been some changes. Scientific studies of small-group interactions have produced methods that gain the advantages of group action while minimizing or eliminating some of the disadvantages. Many of these methods have been applied to the task of eliciting a forecast from a group of experts.

One of the most popular is known as the Delphi [method discussed in Chapter 6] . . . .

Celanese Corp. used a Delphi panel to forecast the growth in sales of a new yarn.[5] The panel was composed of members from research, mar-

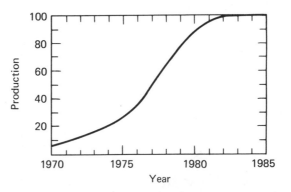

figure 2 . . . individual predicts new yarn's sales growth

keting, sales and top management. A member from one department was able to take into account factors that were not likely to be considered by members from other departments.

One thing estimated by the panel was the likelihood that production of the new yarn would exceed certain levels by various dates in the future. Fig. 2 shows a typical estimate made by a single panel member. He felt that production of the new yarn was virtually certain to reach the specified level by 1981 (a probability of occurrence of 100%).

The estimates of all members of the panel were combined, as in Fig. 3. The circles show the median estimates for 1970, 1975, 1980 and 1985. The shaded area includes the "interquartile range" (middle half) of the panel's estimates. This composite estimate was then presented in the next questionnaire, along with the written comments of panel members as to why they believed other panel members were either too optimistic or too pessimistic. Each member then decided whether to revise his previous estimates on the basis of the opinions and arguments of the other panelists. The final result was a graph similar to Fig. 3, which indicated not only the median panel estimate but the degree of spread or uncertainty in that estimate.

Delphi is only one of a family of "scientifically subjective" methods that can be used for technological forecasting when other methods will not work. These methods can be used not only when data are lacking but also when it is known that the conditions that produced a trend are undergoing changes that would make extrapolation useless. They can also be used when external, nontechnological factors are dominant, and when ethical or moral considerations must be taken into account. Thus, even though explicit forecasting methods are desirable when these are available, there will always be a need for subjectively prepared forecasts. Delphi and similar methods help to increase the validity of these forecasts.

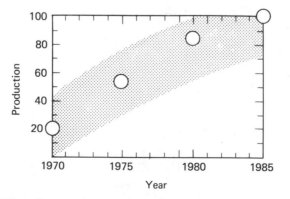

figure 3 . . . estimates of panel members are combined

product replacement

In some cases, a new product is almost a direct substitute for some older product (e.g., margarine for butter, nylon for silk, detergents for soap). It is important to be able to estimate the rate at which a new product will take over an entire market. This estimate is needed not only to plan for the production and sales of a new product but also for phasing out the old one.

Such replacement often obeys a definite mathematical law.[6] If f denotes the fraction of the market captured by the new product, the ratio $f/(1 - f)$ appears to grow exponentially. A typical example of this behavior is seen in Fig. 4, which shows the substitution of detergents for soap in both the U.S. and Japan. Note that the slope of the trend is virtually the same in both cases, although the replacement occurred in countries with different cultures and about a decade apart.

The slope of the trend is characterized by a "takeover time," defined as the time for the new product to grow from 10% to 90% of the market (i.e., from $f = 0.1$ to $f = 0.9$). The takeover time for detergents to replace soap was 8.75 years in the U.S. marketplace and 8.25 years in Japan's.

This method is used in essentially the same way as trend extrapolation. Data on the market share of the old and new products are obtained

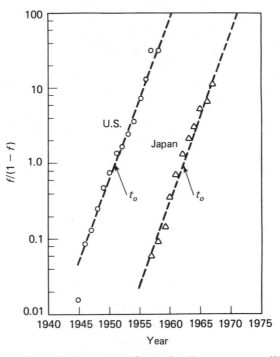

figure 4 . . . displacement of soap by detergent was alike

for a period of several months or years (for example, until the new product has captured 15% to 20% of the market). The ratio of the market share of the new product to that of the old product is plotted, and the trend extrapolated. Takeover time can then be obtained from the slope of the trend.

This method makes the same assumptions as trend extrapolation. It can be used only so long as the conditions that initiated the trend continue it.

selecting capacity for a new plant

When a new chemical plant is to be constructed, a decision must be made as to its size or capacity. Advances in the technology of a particular process often allow a new plant to be built with greater capacity than that of existing ones. This increase in scale usually results in a reduction in unit production cost. Once one firm has such a larger and more economical plant under construction or onstream, its competitors must follow suit. Thus, it is important to be able to estimate when technology will be ready for a larger plant, and what its capacity should be.

For a number of basic chemicals (such as ethylene, benzene and synthetic ammonia), there is a fairly constant ratio between total production and the capacity of the largest single plant.[7] (This same type of relationship has also been observed in a number of other technologies, including oil tankers and electric generators, and so appears to be fairly general.) Fig. 5 illustrates it in the production of synthetic ammonia in the U.S. Between 1953 and 1967, the capacity of the largest single ammonia plant in the U.S. averaged about one-thirtieth of the total U.S. production of synthetic ammonia.[8]

This step-growth forecasting technique can be of considerable help in making decisions about the timing and capacity of new chemical

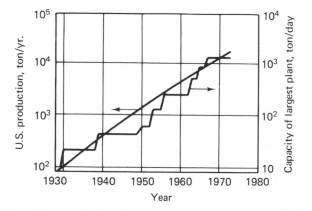

figure 5 . . . ratio shows between production and capacity

plants. If, in the history of the production of a specific chemical, there has been a consistent pattern in the intervals between the introduction of larger-capacity plants, and a consistent pattern in the ratio of these plant capacities to total production, the decision-maker would be well advised to anticipate the possibility that this pattern would repeat itself.

decisions affected by production costs

Some decisions will be affected by costs of production—in particular, decisions about whether or not to enter a certain market, because these costs will have a bearing on whether the market will be profitable. In some cases, advances in technology will reduce production or unit capital costs for a particular type of installation. In these cases, a technological forecast can be helpful in making the decision of whether or not to enter a specific market.

As one instance of this type of decision, the United Kingdom Atomic Energy Authority carried out an analysis to determine whether it would be profitable for one or more British firms to attempt to export desalting plants to underdeveloped countries.

One part of the study, of course, was a market forecast of the future world need for potable water extracted from seawater, brackish water, etc. In addition, the analysis included a technological forecast of the capital costs of desalting plants. The forecast of demand for water was then converted into a forecast of the total sales of desalting plants worldwide, by year. Multiplying the number of plants required by the forecast of capital cost gave the monetary value of the total world market for desalting plants. The British share of this world market was estimated by conventional operations-research techniques, and total sales were discounted back to the present to determine whether the research and development investment in desalting processes would be recovered and a net profit realized. . . .

setting research and development goals

When a project is undertaken to improve an old or develop a new product, it is necessary to set performance goals. If the product that comes out of a project has too low a performance level, it will be a commercial failure. So the goals set for a project must result in a product that will be competitive with what other firms will have on the market, or will have ready for the market at the time the project is completed. If, on the other hand, goals are set too high, the project may attain them only after a longer time and at a higher cost than what were originally anticipated; or the project may become a failure, never reaching its goals. A technological forecast can be of considerable value in helping to set research and development goals that will be high enough to be competitive but low enough to be technically feasible.

A Goodyear Tire and Rubber Co. forecast of future needs and performance of automobile tires, which was prepared to serve as a guide to company planning, provides an excellent example of the use of several techniques to predict different types of outcomes, each of significance for research and development.[10]

One part of this forecast (Fig. 6) shows the performance of automobile tires in terms of mileage before wearing out. The reduction in mileage for the bias tire, occurring after about 1953, is misleading in terms of an assessment of tire technology. The tire tread actually improved, in terms of treadwear rating, but conditions of service became so much more severe (higher automobile horsepower, greater speeds, power steering and brakes, etc) that tire mileage dropped.

There was again an increase in actual tire mileage in the late 1960s, when the belted tire was introduced. Presumably the performance of this tire will also be described by the S-shaped growth curve that the bias tire exhibited. So, the forecaster has chosen to project the envelope of the S-curves. This forecasting method is commonly used for technologies that historically have had a succession of different technical approaches to performing the same function. The performance of each technical ap-

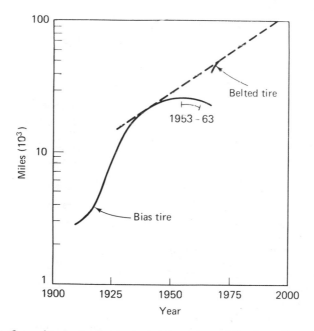

figure 6 . . . forecaster projects future automobile tire mileage from the envelope of the S-curves

proach follows an S-curve, and overall performance is forecast by projecting the envelope of the S-curves. In this case, a tire mileage of 100,000 is
forecast for some time in the 1990s.

Another part of the Goodyear forecast (Fig. 7) illustrates a set of
predictions regarding tires prepared by the Delphi Procedure. In this case,
the committee included experts from tire companies, companies supplying raw materials to the tire industry, consultants to the industry, and
specialists with trade and technical journals.

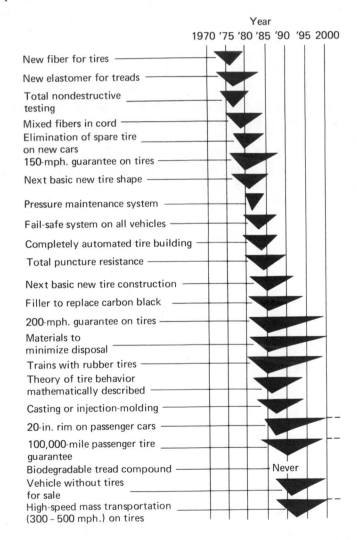

figure 7 . . . realizations of the above events by the indicated dates
are better than 50/50 probable

This Delphi sequence was carried out entirely by mail. The committee members made estimates for each of the specific events shown, and these estimates were refined through several rounds of iteration. The final results are shown. The bottom points of the shaded triangles indicate the median estimates for each event, while the points at the sides indicate the lower and upper quartiles. It is worth noting the similarity between the forecast the Delphi committee made for the 100,000-mile tire, and that of Fig. 6, which was obtained independently. Concurrence between forecasts obtained by different methods, such as this case, increases confidence in the validity of results.

So far, none of the decision situations or forecasting methods we have discussed involved developments representing a complete break with the past. It is developments of this nature that can catch several companies, or even an entire industry, by surprise. We will now take up this type of situation.

predicting the unpredictable

The technological forecaster is often challenged with the question, "How can you predict a technological breakthrough?" Or, alternatively, he may be challenged with, "How can your forecasting methods, which are only based on the past, anticipate something like the DDT ban or the opposition to phosphates?"

These are legitimate questions. Their implication is that there are certain things that are inherently unpredictable, and so beyond the art of the technological forecaster. If the inherently unpredictable consists of a significant fraction—or, worse yet, most—of the factors the forecaster is asked to predict, his art would be nearly useless. It is tautologically true, of course, that no one can predict the unpredictable. So, we must ask: How much of the future is really unpredictable, and how much is merely surprising because those who should have predicted it failed to do so?

If asked to name a technological breakthrough, the average person will likely mention one of the following: the jet engine, the atomic bomb, the laser or the transistor. These are probably the most spectacular technological advances of the past three or four decades. Furthermore, in each case, the advance caught a great many people by surprise, including those in the industries most affected. Hardly anyone in the military anticipated the atomic bomb; hardly anyone in the airplane-engine business anticipated the jet engine; hardly any of the organizations that now make or use the laser anticipated it. These seem to be prime examples of breakthroughs that may be regarded as having been largely unpredictable.

Nevertheless, every one of these advances, as well as a great many more, can be traced back through three or four decades of precursory events that, seen in retrospect, should have given a fairly clear indication of where technology was going and what might have been anticipated.

It might, of course, be pointed out that hindsight is always blessed with 20-20 vision, and that when these precursors were unfolding, they really were of no help to decision-makers. This objection has some merit. During the first half of the Twentieth Century, technical decision-makers were not as aware as now of the processes of technological growth. They did not then have as much experience as we do with the succession of technical approaches that produced advances in a specific technology, neither did they have as much experience with the transition of basic research to technological application. So, one major reason they failed to recognize precursors was that they were not aware of the possibility of so doing.

There are a number of signals that can be watched. The output from basic research laboratories is one. A new reaction or chemical, a better understanding of some phenomenon—all may point to a new product, or a new way of making an old one. Another is inventions, whether patented or not, that "don't quite work" because an important element is missing or the supporting technology is inadequate. The transistor, for instance, was patented at least twice during the 1930s, but the devices described in the patents did not work because chemicals of the required "impurity" were not available. Yet-other signals are inventions or discoveries whose performances are now too low to be competitive but which might be improved.

This looking for signals has been termed "monitoring the environment" by J. R. Bright, who has been a leader in developing the technique.[2] Basic to it is that appropriate sources must be monitored continuously to identify signals.

However, no single signal ever gives a complete picture of the future. So an essential feature of the process is the search for signals that confirm or deny earlier ones. Suppose, for instance, a product has been invented whose performance is too low to be competitive (as was true of the jet engine in the early 1930s). It would then be necessary to ask what would have to be changed to make it competitive—improvements in materials, theoretical understanding, supporting technology? The answers would indicate other sources that should be monitored for signals.

Suppose this product needs to be constructed of better material. We should then watch for the appearance of such a material. If it appeared, this would be a confirming signal additionally warning of a breakthrough. Each confirming signal could indicate others to look for, so that a chain of precursors could be traced to the breakthrough.

"Monitoring the environment" is not limited to forecasting strictly technological events. It can be of even greater value in identifying events that originate outside an industry but that will have a major impact on it. Such events are often of an economic, political or social nature.

In a nation as large as the U.S., such events do not happen overnight. There are almost always precursors indicating changes. For instance, the DDT ban was not a bolt out of the blue. At least as early as the publication of Rachel Carson's "Silent Spring," there was indication that a segment of the population was unhappy with DDT. Although this one signal was not proof a change was coming, it should have been a warning to watch for confirming signals. Was this book followed by similar books and articles? Did newspapers begin to play up fish kills? Did conservation groups begin to make demands for restrictions on DDT? Did politicians begin to take notice of this shift in public opinion?

All these signals, and more, would have been caught by a forecaster or decision-maker who was "monitoring the environment."[11] He might not have been able to predict exactly when a ban would come, but should have been able to anticipate significant restrictions.

Similarly, the current concern about the overall environment did not develop overnight. A forecaster might not have predicted that phosphates specifically would be a target, but he could have predicted that the dumping of industrial wastes would become an issue.

Technological forecasters do not claim that monitoring will eliminate all surprises. There will continue to be details that will remain unpredictable, such as the opposition to phosphates rather than to some other chemical. Nevertheless, systematic monitoring for signals can go a long way towards eliminating surprises.

using the forecast

The technical decision-maker will on some occasions prepare his own forecasts. At other times, he will depend on forecasts readied by professional technological forecasters. In either case, the fact that his information about the future can only be based on inferences from the past will affect the way in which he uses a forecast for decision-making.

questions to ask

When the decision-maker is presented with a forecast, he should ask questions about it, the answers to which will determine whether or not he uses the forecast at all. If he prepares his own forecast, he should ask himself the same questions:

1. What information does this forecast provide? That is, with regard to the decision to be made, what portion of the decision information is provided by the forecast? Is the forecast really relevant to the decision?

What information is not provided by the forecast and must be sought elsewhere?

If the forecast is relevant to the decision, there are other questions to ask:

2. How was the forecast made? That is, what method was used? What logical structure was employed to draw inferences about the future from the data? Is the method appropriate for this particular situation? Has it been adequately tested on similar situations and found valid?

If the forecast is acceptable to this point, the following should be asked:

3. Are the data accurate? If the data are presented explicitly, the sources should be reviewed. Are these sources the best available? Are they complete? Were significant sources overlooked? If the forecast was prepared by subjective methods, the questions should be directed at the experts who participated in it. Are they likely to be well informed about the past and present situations in their field? Do they have any known biases?

4. Are the assumptions valid? In the absence of data, every forecast will depend on some assumptions. These may involve future events, or the actions of others who will have an influence on the outcome. The assumptions should be identified and their validity assessed—are they soundly based, consistent with data available, and adequately tested?

If a forecast is satisfactory, in terms of the answers to these questions, it can be used in a decision, governed by certain considerations.

how much credence to give a forecast

If a forecast is based on an appropriate method, accurate data and valid assumptions, and the decision-maker is satisfied it cannot be improved significantly, how much credence should he give it?

Every forecast, no matter how well it is prepared, will to some extent be in error. Therefore, the decision-maker cannot give it complete credence. Even if it is the best possible forecast, he still needs to assess just how good.

Some insight into this problem can be gained from Fig. 1. Even if a decision-maker feels that a projection of a trend constitutes the best possible forecast of ethylene production, he still has a problem. The data points did not all fall on the trend line but were scattered about it. So it is unlikely that future events will fall on the projected trend line. In fact, the more scatter in the past, the more there is likely to be in the future, so the decision-maker should put even less credence in the accuracy of the trend line.

The same considerations apply to forecasts made by other methods. The more scatter or uncertainty in the data, or the greater inaccuracy a forecasting method has shown in the past, the less credence should be given to it. By thus assessing a forecast, the decision-maker can determine how much uncertainty was resolved by the forecast, and how much still remains for him to take into account in his decision.

when to reject a forecast

A forecast may have been acceptable when it was first prepared, but may later have to be rejected and done again. The decision-maker must be able to determine when a forecast should be rejected.

Suppose, for example, that a forecast of the sort shown in Fig. 1 had been accepted when it was prepared, but that a subsequent event falls far from the trend line (further than can be explained by scatter in the data). This may be a signal of a change requiring the revision of the forecast. If a succession of events show a consistent deviation from the trend (either all above or all below it) instead of random scattering, this also would be an indication of a change requiring revision.

This would also hold true for forecasts made by other methods. A single gross deviation, or a pattern of consistent deviations, would indicate a need for revision. In addition, a marked change in the conditions affecting the technology being forecast, such as a change in research and development expenditures or the appearance of a competing product, should call for revision.

No forecast remains valid indefinitely. For instance, a trend extrapolation should not extend further into the future than one-third to one-half the span of years covered by the data base. When this period has run out, the forecast should be done again even if it has proven highly accurate—if for no other reason than that subsequent events represent data that should be taken into account.

Much the same considerations apply to forecasts prepared by other methods. They should be reworked when their time span expires, and often even before then. In the military services, two years has been found to represent a reasonable cycle for updating a forecast. More-frequent revisions often result in little substantive change, less frequent revisions in obsolescence. Although the . . . decision-maker may find this cycle inappropriate for the technologies of concern to him, it may serve him as a satisfactory rule of thumb until his experience dictates a change.

references

1. Ayres, R. U., "Technological Forecasting and Long-Range Planning," McGraw-Hill, New York, 1969.

2. Bright, J. R. (ed). "Technological Forecasting for Industry and Government." Prentice-Hall, Englewood Cliffs, N.J., 1968.

3. Martino, J. P., "Technological Forecasting for Decisionmaking," American Elsevier, New York (to be published).

4. Barach, J. L., Twery, R. J., Forecasting Techniques in R&D Planning, *Chem. Eng. Prog.*, **6**, 6, June 1970, pp. 15-19.

5. Craver, J. K., Planning for Profitable Growth, paper presented at Commercial Development Assn. meeting, Chicago, Ill., Oct. 12, 1970.

6. Fisher, J. C., Pry, R. H., A Simple Substitution Model of Technological Change, *Technological Forecasting and Social Change*, **3**, 1, 1971, pp. 75-88.

7. Simmonds, W. H. C., Stepwise Expansion and Profitability, *Chemistry in Canada*, Sept. 1969, pp. 16-18.

8. Simmonds, W. H. C., The Canada-U.S. Scale Problem, *Chemistry in Canada*, Oct. 1969. pp. 39-41.

9. Hunt, H., Forecasting the Need for Research and Development, *Futures*, Sept. 1969, pp. 392-390.

10. Kovac, F. J., Technological Forecasting—Tires, *Chemical Technology*, **1**, Jan. 1971, pp. 18-23.

11. Martino, J. P., Examples of Technological Trend Forecasting for Research and Development Planning, *Technological Forecasting and Social Change*, **2**, 3/4, 1971, pp. 247-260.

questions

1. Try to think of some products that are presently in the early stages of a substitution curve effect. List them and try to estimate when the newer product will take more than half the market.

2. How could an envelope curve be used to forecast future innovations in the "convenience foods" industry? What performance characteristics do you believe are important here?

3. Develop a scenario for the year 2000 assuming that railroads in this country are no longer an economically competitive means of moving freight. Repeat your scenario assuming that coal is the only fossil fuel available in 2000 A.D. and that railroads are the *primary* means of hauling freight.

4. Which technological forecasting technique(s) might be useful in deciding whether to introduce a new product that is a synthetic fiber made from vegetable oil? Gather data from the library to support the application of this technique(s).

5. What technological forecasting techniques would be useful if the United States reopened the question of whether to market a supersonic trans-

port aircraft? Repeat, except suppose that the Maritime Administration wants a forecast of need for nuclear-powered cargo vessels in the year 2015. How would you proceed with your analysis? Explain how cross-impact analysis could be useful in making this analysis.

6. List the main advantages and disadvantages of trend extrapolation. Do the same for morphological analysis.

7. After reading Martino's article, attempt to describe how technological forecasting techniques could be used to estimate the nature and timing of technological breakthroughs in the building trades industry (or in some other industry). How could techniques described in Chapter 6 be used to advantage?

8. Assuming our per capita energy consumption *must* decline slowly over the next few decades, describe how techniques discussed in Chapter 7 can be utilized to forecast technological innovations that may occur as a result of this decline.

chapter 8 . . . advanced forecasting techniques

introduction

The techniques described to this point have been fundamental in nature. Sufficient information has been presented for the reader to apply them to real problems and to comprehend intuitively their performance. The objective of this chapter is to introduce, in general terms, some of the more advanced techniques that appear in the forecasting literature. They are not used as commonly as the basic procedures discussed in previous chapters because they are not as easy to comprehend, require more calculations, and tend to be rather expensive to apply.

adaptive filtering

To use adaptive filtering, the forecaster must first decide on the number of previous data points, n, to use in developing each forecast. If the data are seasonal, usually one year's data are used (either $n = 12$ if monthly, or $n = 4$ if quarterly). Then a weight, w_i, $i = 1, 2, \ldots, n$, is assigned to each data point. Usually all $w_i = 1/n$ initially, so the result is at first the same as a simple moving average. Adaptive filtering is unique because these weighting factors are revised with each new observation, according to the following equation:

$$w_i' = w_i + 2\alpha ex \qquad (8\text{-}1)$$

where

w_i' is the revised weight $(1 \leqslant i \leqslant n)$
w_i is the previous weight
α is the smoothing constant, which is referred to as the *learning constant*
     in adaptive filtering
e is the previous forecast error (forecast - actual)
x is the most recent observation

The forecast is obtained by multiplying the w_i values by the previous n data points and summing as shown below:

$$\text{Forecast} = w_n x_t + w_{n-1} x_{t-1} + w_{n-2} x_{t-2} + --- + w_1 x_{t-n+1} \quad (8\text{-}2)$$

The main advantage of adaptive filtering is that the weights are automatically adjusted to deal with changing data patterns. Adaptive filtering has been successfully applied to many different basic data patterns. The main disadvantage is that the procedure is extremely sensitive to the choice of an α value. If α is too small, the model will not react to changes in data patterns, as would be expected with basic exponential smoothing models. If α is too large, however, the model will overreact to such an extent that the weights will never correct themselves and assume reasonable values. Because of this characteristic, it is important to have a substantial amount of data to use in initially developing this model (roughly $5n$ or more points).

A value of α should first be chosen and the procedure then applied to available data, assuming initially that $w_i = 1/n$. The w_i values that result from the first application can be applied to the subsequent data. This process is repeated until the w_i values become relatively stable. The forecaster can also experiment with different α values to locate one that gives the minimum MSE. This "fine tuning" of the model is necessary to obtain the best results and can easily require more effort than subsequent application of the model. Because of the volume of calculations required to successfully define the model, a computer is recommended for practical application of adaptive filtering.

Adaptive filtering has been frequently applied to seasonal data with success. Winters' method should give comparable or superior results with seasonal data, however, and is generally easier to understand and apply. Even though adaptive filtering is considered here to be an advanced procedure, it is not nearly as complex or sophisticated as is the Box-Jenkins method, which is described in the next section.

Adaptive smoothing is a forecasting technique similar to adaptive filtering in that the weighting applied to historical data is revised automatically during the application as new data are obtained. That is, adaptive smoothing is basically an exponential smoothing technique capable of updating the smoothing constant in view of changing data patterns so that the mean square error is minimized.

the box-jenkins method

The Box-Jenkins method is complex, mathematically sophisticated, and expensive; but in many situations, it can be the most accurate technique for forecasting with time-series data. It is best used where there are only a few time-series relationships important enough to justify the expense. Several years of data are necessary to apply the Box-Jenkins method. At least 50 data points are required, and more will be needed if the data have a seasonal effect. Because of its complexity, computer facilities are necessary for its application. There are numerous consultants with a Box-Jenkins computer "package" and technical assistance for hire. Attempts are being made to modify this technique so that calculations can be simplified and computer costs reduced. Like all time-series mathematical methods, the Box-Jenkins method should not be considered a long-range forecasting tool. The following is a discussion of the general mechanics of this technique and is intended to be a general introduction only.*

Forecasters recommending the Box-Jenkins technique emphasize that it can function with complex data patterns and that the forecaster does not have to describe initially these data patterns. The Box-Jenkins model systematically eliminates inappropriate models until the most suitable one is left for the data being considered. A three-step procedure of identification, estimation, and diagnostic checking is used to arrive at a specific model. This procedure requires that the forecaster have a sound mathematical background and access to computer facilities. Because autocorrelation is an integral part of the Box-Jenkins method, it will be explained very briefly here. Then general features of the method are presented.

Autocorrelation can be explained best through an example. Raw data are presented in column (2) of Table 8-1. In column (3), the same data are given, but one time-unit out of phase with the data in column (2). That is, the first point in column (3) is the second point in column (2), and so on. A correlation coefficient (refer back to Chapter 4) calculated for these two columns of data is the *autocorrelation coefficient* for the data with a time lag of 1. Column (4) presents the data with a time lag of 2. The correlation coefficient calculated for columns (2) and (4) is the autocorrelation coefficient for a time lag of 2. With seasonal data, an autocorrelation coefficient for a time lag of 12 with monthly data reveals the strength of the seasonality. By considering time lags of 1, 2, 3, 4, . . . and plotting the results, as in Figure 8-1, the autocorrelation in the data can be defined. The data of Figure 8-1 exhibit some characteristic that causes a moderately strong relationship between observations which have been lagged by six periods. These occurrences

A detailed discussion may be found in George E. Box and Gwilym Jenkins, Time Series Analysis, Forecasting and Control, *rev. ed. (San Francisco: Holden-Day, Inc., 1976).*

are taken into account in the Box-Jenkins procedure. Usually the autocorrelation coefficient for a one-period lag is high, indicating the presence of serial correlation which is discussed in Appendix B. If all autocorrelation coefficients were low, this would indicate random data.

After applying a forecasting technique, the error terms, e_i (e_i = forecast$_i$ - actual$_i$), can be analyzed by using autocorrelation analysis in exactly the same manner as the raw data were analyzed in Figure 8-1. An example plot of autocorrelation coefficients for e_i values is given in Figure 8-2. This indicates that forecast errors with time lags of 1, 4, and 9 are related. The presence of autocorrelation in the e_i values indicates there is information in the raw data that was not utilized in making the forecast. A forecasting technique that makes the best use of available data should have random error terms.

The Box-Jenkins method has three basic building blocks, which are termed *autoregressive, moving average*, and *mixed*. In the autoregressive relationship, an equation such as the following is used to develop a forecast based on a linear, weighted sum of previous data:

$$y^* = \phi_1 y_{t-1} + \phi_2 y_{t-2} + --- + \phi_p y_{t-p} + e_t \qquad (8\text{-}3)$$

where y^* is the forecast
  y_i ($i = 1, 2, \ldots, p$) is the observed value at time i
  ϕ_i is the weighting coefficient for the pth previous period
  e_t is the expected forecast error at time t

The weights and the e_t values are determined by using multiple regression analysis, hence the name autoregressive.

table 8-1 . . . illustration of lagged time-series data for computing autocorrelation coefficients

(1) Period t	(2) y_t	(3) y_{t+1}	(4) y_{t+2}
1	10	11	13
2	11	13	15
3	13	15	14
4	15	14	12
5	14	12	13
6	12	13	15
7	13	15	16
8	15	16	17
9	16	17	15
10	17	15	16
11	15	16	—
12	16	—	—

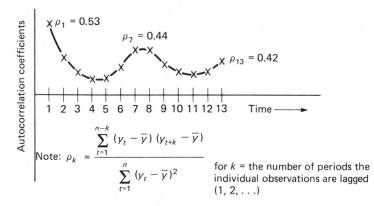

figure 8-1 . . . autocorrelation coefficients for data

The second relationship is that of a moving average in which the forecast is a function of previous forecast errors.

$$y^* = e_t - \theta_1 e_{t-1} - \theta_2 e_{t-2} - \ldots - \theta_q e_{t-q}$$

where y^* is the forecast

e_{t-i} $(i = 1, 2, \ldots, q)$ is the forecast error at time t

θ_i $(i = 1, 2, \ldots, q)$ is a weighting coefficient for the qth previous period, which is calculated by a nonlinear least-squares method

The third relationship is a combination of the first two, referred to as the mixed autoregressive moving-average model.

In applying the Box-Jenkins method, the analyst must examine a basic autocorrelation plot such as that of Figure 8-1 and decide which time lags

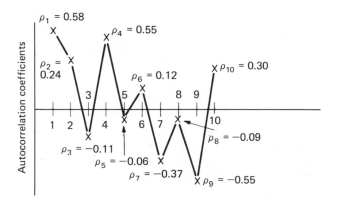

figure 8-2 . . . autocorrelation coefficients for forecast error

should be considered in the model. A computer program is then used to calculate the coefficients for the equations listed above. The results of applying
these equations to available data can be diagnosed to determine if the error
terms are random and normally distributed. If they are not, the basic model is
modified (inclusion of additional terms and/or a different relationship). Then
the above procedure is repeated until a satisfactory model has been developed.

econometric models

Econometric models are an attempt to express, in mathematical equations,
the intricate and complex relationships among factors influencing the economy (such as interest rates, inventory levels, unemployment, etc.). The aim of
the model is to measure the impact of one economic variable on another so as
to forecast future developments. In this manner economists attempt to forecast the effects of changes in national monetary and/or fiscal policy.*

The difficulty in developing a set of equations to describe the economy is
that there are hundreds or thousands of variables involved and most of them
are interrelated. In developing the model it is necessary, but often difficult, to
avoid a vicious circle in which everything depends on everything else. A
description of some of these variables and their interrelationships is given in
the article in Appendix A, "A Manager's Primer on Forecasting."

To simplify the problem of dealing with these interrelationships, variables are classified as *endogenous* or *exogenous*. Endogenous variables are
determined within the system and include such factors as income, employment, and interest. Exogenous variables are those determined by forces external to the system such as noneconomic institutions and the physical limitations of nature. Available data and estimates of exogenous forces are used
to analyze the effects on the endogenous variables.

Econometric forecasting is truly unique because of the special mathematical procedures that have been developed to deal with hundreds or thousands of interrelated quantities. Application of these procedures requires
individuals with mathematical sophistication and computer facilities because
mathematical developments have become increasingly complex. However, developments in computer science have resulted in the trend toward models
that consider more variables and are more mathematically rigorous.

Because of the expense involved in econometric models, only the federal
government and a few large companies have employed them. A company that
wishes to develop its own econometric model must obtain the services of individuals with expertise in this area and be prepared to spend $100,000 or more
for the model. Several months are necessary to develop and refine the model,

---

An excellent coverage of this topic is given in Michael K. Evans, Macroeconomic
Activity: Theory, Forecasting, and Control *(New York: Harper & Row Publishers,
Inc., 1969).*

and it must be continually updated to reflect changes in the economy. In addition, other individuals having insight into current economic conditions and developments must *guide* the econometric models as changes in the economy are evaluated.

One characteristic of our economy that facilitates the use of econometric models is that changes seldom occur instantaneously. After the federal government makes a change in fiscal or monetary policy, it usually takes from 6 to 12 months for the full effect to be felt throughout the economy. With an econometric model and expert judgment to guide the model, the effects of such changes can often be forecasted months in advance. There have been significant improvements in the models, and there is no doubt that further research and development can be justified. Unfortunately, these models have not been generally successful in predicting turning points in the economy. In periods of increased instability and uncertainty in our economy, even the leading economists seldom agree on which action the government should take to improve the situation. In summary, it is not reasonable to expect present econometric models to provide all the answers to complex and often little understood problems of national scope.

input-output tables

An input-output table is a detailed record of the flow of production within an economy. It is a matrix presentation showing the production of each major segment of the economy and the consumer of that production. Realistic input-output tables developed by the government and large companies may contain relationships for hundreds of industries.* A simple example for a hypothetical four-industry economy is given in Table 8-2.

Input-output tables can be used for control and as tracking devices. As a control device, input-output tables would be most commonly used in highly regulated economies such as the USSR. For example, if some innovation resulted in increased demand for electronics devices in the automobile industry, the government could determine what increased production from other industries would be necessary to increase the production of electronics devices. The possibility of diverting electronics devices from other industries would then be examined, and overall effects on the general economy could be estimated. If the United States became involved in a prolonged major war, national input-output tables would be an invaluable control tool for allocating resources.

In a free economy, input-output tables are more useful as a tracking device for signalling when basic market conditions have changed. For example, when new plastics and alloys are being developed, the input-output table

---

For detailed information, refer to W. Leontief, Input-Output Economics *(New York: Oxford University Press, 1966).*

table 8-2 . . . a hypothetical input-output table (all
units in billions of dollars)

From This Industry	To This Industry				Consuming Sector	Total
	Steel	Glass	Electronics	Automobile		
Steel	2	1	1	100	2	106
Glass	2	1	4	25	10	42
Electronics	4	2	10	12	10	48
Automobile	2	2	2	2	100	108

would be valuable to the steel industry in determining the effects on the economy and anticipating the future demand for steel. The input-output table would be valuable to a company planning to produce a new, different product in a large market that involves many industrial sectors.

Input-output tables are an expensive, long-range forecasting tool. A company interested in developing its own tables should be willing to invest in the neighborhood of $100,000. Approximately 10 to 15 years of previous data should be collected, and at least six months of preparation time would be required. The final result provides a picture of developments in the general economy over the last several years and should be useful in evaluating and estimating developments for the next five or so years.

The major drawbacks to input-output tables stem from the sheer volume of data required. In a constantly changing technological economy, models must be updated continuously if they are to be meaningful. Because of the time required to gather data and incorporate them into the model, the table may not reflect current conditions. Because there are limitations on the size of the tables, some industries must be omitted or grouped in a common category. Many input-output tables in use do not generally agree on which industries to include and how to categorize them. These differences often result in disparate results from one set of tables to another. The quality of the forecasts is very sensitive to the capabilities of the technical and marketing personnel who manipulate the tables and interpret their results.

Many U.S. companies now have developed their own input-output tables. More companies will probably use them in the future since experts are expected to find ways of developing smaller models reflecting the economic relations of interest to particular companies. There should also be efforts to combine econometric models with input-output tables to give more stable, accurate forecasts.

forecasting in the future

The people of the United States have always expected the future to be better than the past. Abundant, relatively inexpensive natural resources have provided a basis for a continually improving standard of living. But now our population is stabilizing, and resources, particularly energy, are no longer going to be inexpensive. If our standard of living increases in the future as it has in the past, industry and government are going to have to manage better and make more careful use of our natural resources.

Forecasting must also improve. New techniques must be developed and existing techniques must be refined. More importantly there must be a widespread, conscientious application of the basic techniques. A young agricultural agent who was unsuccessful in selling new chemicals to an old farmer received the reply, "Son, I don't need these new chemicals, I'm not farming half as well as I know how to now." When industry and government "farm" as well as they know how to, there will be improved data collection methods, planned forecasting programs, and more use of the quantitative and qualitative techniques described in this book.

questions

1. What forecasting procedures are competitive with adaptive filtering?

2. Give an example of a situation where the Box-Jenkins method is applicable.

3. If foreign conditions resulted in an immediate doubling of the price of oil, how would existing econometric models and input-output tables be affected? How could they be used?

4. Give examples of industries that you would expect to have their own input-output tables.

5. Develop a scenario for the future of forecasting in medium-sized companies.

appendix a . . . a manager's primer on forecasting*

ABSTRACT   Forecasting economic trends and business behavior is an essential prelude to making forecasts of conditions
which a company or a company's industry faces. With or without the aid of market experts or professional economists, managers must reach decisions based on expectations of the future.
Here are explanations of many of the important leading, coincident, and lagging indicators to help the manager relate economics to the pragmatic business world.

introduction

The concern for accurate and expedient business economic information
has grown enormously in the past decade. No doubt it will accelerate
with even greater impetus in the future as business becomes ever more influenced by national and world economic currents.

Obviously, forecasting economic and general business behavior is an
essential prelude to predicting future conditions in a company's industry
and in the company itself. If the data are sufficiently relevant and the
forecast sufficiently realistic, a company is in a good position to prepare
for eventualities. If a highly leveraged company, for example, pinpoints a
downturn in the economy soon enough, it can avoid a drastic reduction
in cash flow and the high interest payments of a company in debt bond-
age.

*By Robert S. Sobek, "A Manager's Primer on Forecasting," *Harvard
Business Review*, May-June 1973, p. 6 ff.; Reprinted by permission of
the publisher, © 1973 by the President and Fellows of Harvard College;
all rights reserved.

In an effort to aid businessmen, I have assembled an abbreviated list describing 21 leading, coincident, and lagging indicators which are discussed often in the various media. My aim is to give an overview of these economic barometers, a brief description of their significance, and how they relate to some particular industries. I have also drawn up some guidelines for putting together a diffusion index, whose purpose is to summarize the business indicators used.

Most of the indicators described are contained in a list of statistical series which the National Bureau of Economic Research assessed as the most useful indicators, out of many hundreds examined, for forecasting and measuring cyclical changes in business activity. Some other barometers not contained in that list I have included in this presentation because of their use by some leading economists.

It should be borne in mind that in nearly all circumstances that make up U.S. industrial enterprise, it is next to impossible to apply economic statistics to any particular situation. Rational and well-founded decisions, with respect to turning points in business cycles, can be made only after logical evaluation of past and current events relevant to the company's circumstances.

leading indicators

The purpose of leading indicators is to forecast the turning points of business cycles as well as assess the magnitude of rising or declining economic activity. Of the many such barometers, I have selected eight that are either the most significant or the most useful to the business forecaster.

fiscal policy

This involves the use of government purchases and taxation to regulate fluctuations in national income, employment, and prices. There are two types of fiscal policy, automatic and discretionary.

The former does not require conscious decisions on the part of public officials because of the inherent stabilizers that inhibit declines in national income and employment. Changes in tax receipts, savings, unemployment insurance, and parity programs (price subsidies to farmers and the like) are the four primary automatic stabilizers. For example, when economic activity is sliding, tax receipts form a smaller percentage of national income. This relative increase in disposable income stimulates investment and consumer spending.

The other form of fiscal policy, discretionary policy, consists of intervention by government bodies in the form of various public expenditures, transfer programs, tax rates, and budget surpluses and deficits.

The federal budget, the largest component of fiscal policy, rises and falls directly with the level of U.S. military spending. Prime contract awards and procurement outlays are two particulars yielding advance notice of the impact of government purchases on the economy.

Federal spending should be followed only for its long-term trend and not its absolute value or month-to-month changes. Since sales of government assets are deducted from federal expenditures rather than added to receipts as in standard accounting practice, the economic impact is often understated and consequently unreliable from month to month.

Although social programs have recently been a large contributor to the federal budget, their impact is minor compared with military requirements. Today, about three fourths of the budget is directly or indirectly devoted to national defense (such as veterans' benefits and interest on the national debt).

Trends in fiscal policy greatly affect both private and governmental employment. In fact, a comprehenisve econometric model of the economy developed by the Chase Manhattan Bank shows that corporate tax cuts and increased defense spending would be less effective in raising employment and incomes and have a briefer effect on economic growth than a tax credit of the same fiscal magnitude.

monetary policy

Action taken by the Federal Reserve Board in its attempts to stabilize economic growth by controlling credit, and thereby the money supply in the marketplace, is termed monetary policy. The FRB's function is to help the federal government achieve its goals by providing sufficient bank reserves to finance growth without significant inflation, to strengthen credit, and to encourage economic recovery in recessions by reducing the cost of money. In controlling the nation's money through credit regulation, the FRB uses four principal tools: open-market operations, changes in the discount rate, variations in bank reserve requirements, and persuasion.

Open-market operation is the most effective tool of monetary policy. By buying or selling government securities to member commercial banks, the FRB increases or reduces their reserves. Since banks must maintain a percentage of their demand deposits as reserves held by the "Fed," its open-market activity affects the amount of money the banks can lend and also indirectly influences interest rates.

Frequently these days, economists refer to the money supply in two ways: M_1 (currency plus demand deposits held by the public) and M_2 (M_1 plus commercial bank savings and time deposits other than large certificates of deposit). Recent studies state that a 6% to 8% annual expansion of M_1 and a 7% to 12% rise in M_2 should be maintained for consistent growth in an anti-inflationary program. To allow for the distorting effect of the Fed's Regulation Q, which sets the maximum interest rates that banks may pay on desposits, the business forecaster should monitor M_1 and M_2 to obtain a satisfactory measure of monetary policy. In situations where M_2 is not pertinent because it contains the variable of consumer-type savings deposits, M_1 is a useful indicator.

Research has established that a close, regular, and predictable relation exists, involving the quantity of money, national income, and prices over a considerable number of years. Milton Friedman, a well-known economist at the University of Chicago, argues that it is control of the nation's stock of money, rather than fiscal policy, that brings about orderly economic growth. Severe and sustained contractions in the rate of money-supply growth—below the recommended minimum of 2% a year—have invariably preceded recessions.

Conversely, Friedman contends, a rapid increase in the supply of money lowers interest rates and stimulates investment. But such heightened activity, in turn, raises income and eventually increases the transaction demand for money. This trend produces generally rising prices, including the price of credit, and leads to spiraling inflation in a chain of action and reaction. Recent decisions by the Fed regarding the supply of money reflect the increasing influence which the Friedman monetary school has had on economic thought.

A rough guide to monetary policy can be found in the FRB's weekly statistics showing the net reserve position of U.S. commercial banks. Comparison of the current four-week statistic for banks' free reserves with those of the preceding four weeks gives evidence of a trend; if the current free reserves are lower, a reduction in the money supply is probably in the offing.

GNP deflator

As the broadest and most comprehensive measure of price behavior in the economy, the GNP deflator relies heavily, but not exclusively, on monthly wholesale and consumer price data. As an index of inflation, the implicit price deflator for the GNP has become more widely accepted by economists than the two price indexes (though the public unfortunately confuses it with "deflation").

Tastes, trends, and styles vary, and these shifts in the composition of demand subsequently alter the deflator. Shown in *Exhibit I* are the components of the GNP deflator. Note how the components for nonresidential structures—as well as federal, state, and local purchases—have changed in character by rising more than 50% above the increase in GNP for the five-year period. This change in composition affects the total GNP deflator, which is the weighted sum of deflators for the components.

exhibit I . . . implicit price deflators for the GNP

(1958 = 100)

Components	1967	1972	Percent increase
Gross national product	117.3	145.9	24.4%
Personal consumption			
expenditures	114.3	137.4	20.2
Durable goods	100.4	112.9	12.5
Nondurable goods	112.9	135.8	20.3
Services	122.1	151.8	24.3
Gross private domestic			
investment			
Fixed investment	115.6	146.1	26.4
Nonresidential	113.5	142.9	25.9
Structures	123.6	184.0	49.0
Producers' durable			
equipment	109.1	127.5	16.8
Residential structures	123.6	154.0	24.6
Nonfarm	123.1	154.1	25.2
Farm	122.6	148.2	20.9
Net export of goods and			
services			
Exports	109.5	129.7	18.4
Imports	104.2	132.6	27.2
Government purchases of goods			
and services	126.8	178.2	40.6
Federal	121.2	171.8	41.7
State and local	133.3	183.1	37.3

These weights are proportionate to each component's share of total GNP for the period under consideration and are not fixed weights—they are adjusted every few years. Primarily because of this weight shifting of the major components of GNP, the deflator is considered an inclusive index of inflation.

A decline in the index does not necessarily indicate an easing of price trends; it may reflect technical factors that boost the rate of advance in one quarter and lower it the next. For instance, the deflator may climb at an unusually high rate in a quarter because of a federal pay raise—or some factor equally stimulating—which adds nothing to real output and only increases outlays. Without these and other technical factors, such as a shift in the composition of spending, the resulting GNP deflator should normally rise at an annual rate of less than 5%.

productivity

This is simply measurement of the amount of goods and services (output) produced in a given labor period (input). A problem for the economy occurs when wage increases rise disproportionately to gains in productivity. Labor, of course, is not solely responsible for productivity changes; trends also reflect technological innovation, scales of production, materials flow, management skills, and numerous other factors that are often unmeasurable.

A comparison between two data series and the GNP deflator in *Exhibit II* shows the recent pattern of productivity gain and the degree of inflation in the economy. Inflation was mild during the middle 1960's but rose significantly after 1965 because of compensation increases which were not offset by improvements in productivity. By charting the behavior of its industry's standing against these three national indexes and then using regression analysis, a company can project the compensation and productivity pattern of the industry. The statistical correlation between the difference in wages and productivity, incidentally, is much higher in the implicit price deflator than in the consumer price index.

exhibit II . . . productivity correlation between worker compensation and output

| Year | Percent change over previous year | | Inflationary increase (or productivity improvement) | Implicit price deflator for GNP |
	Compensation per man-hour	Output per man-hour		
1960	3.9%	1.5%	2.4%	—
1961	3.7	3.4	0.3	—
1962	4.5	4.8	(0.3)	—
1963	3.9	3.6	0.3	—
1964	5.1	3.9	1.2	—
1965	4.0	3.3	0.7	—
1966	6.9	4.0	2.9	3.0%
1967	5.8	2.0	3.8	3.5
1968	7.7	3.0	4.7	5.0
1969	7.2	0.7	6.5	5.8
1970	7.5	0.5	7.0	6.7
1971	6.9	3.6	3.3	4.6
1972*	8.8	6.7	2.1	3.0

Preliminary.

consumer spending

All economists agree that the consumer leads the way to a healthy economy, but the difficulty in guessing whether the consumer will spend, and how, accounts in large part for the wide differences in forecasts for the GNP. Consumer spending and housing starts generate the impetus for most business recoveries; sustained increases in expenditures for such items as autos and appliances eventually lead, of course, to major increases in manufacturers' capital investment.

Consumer outlays are stimulated by higher personal income and lower tax rates, which occur during economic recovery periods. (Conversely, the rate of change in consumption decreases sharply before and during recessions.)

Spending rises whenever consumers' debt-to-income ratio is low and their liquid assets, in the form of savings, are large. As the money supply rises, consumers find they have accumulated larger cash balances than they desire to hold, so they shift excess balances into income-earning assets. This translation results in rising stock market prices and falling interest rates. As financial yields decline, consumers step up consumption of real assets—cars, houses, home furnishings, and refrigerators.

Increases in consumer credit, based on the debt-to-income ratio, of about $900 million, seasonally adjusted, must be examined segmentally for any statistical aberration. (Below that figure, disproportions are not particularly significant.) The expansion of credit must be evenly distributed among auto, personal, and consumer goods loans; otherwise, the whole economy is not being affected.

residential construction

Housing starts move up, down, or sideways months before the broader measures of GNP or industrial production change. In fact, housing has historically moved in cycles counter to the economy. As the *Monthly Economic Letter* of First National City Bank of New York notes: "The dividing line between fundamentally favorable and fundamentally less favorable conditions for new home construction seems to come at an unemployment rate in the neighborhood of 5%. A more comprehensive dividing line is in terms of the so-called GNP gap—the gap between real gross national product and what real GNP would be at a steady 'full employment' pace of around 4% unemployment. Home building, historically, seems to have flourished best when the economy was running at least 3-4% below its full employment potential."[1]

The course of residential construction depends to some extent on developments in the mortgage market. One third of that market, in turn,

[1] *August 1971, p. 5*

depends for financing on the availability of money from sources that also supply the corporate and governmental sectors. (The other two thirds of mortgage money is supplied by savings and loan associations.) When money is tight because of heavy borrowing in other segments of the economy, the mortgage market suffers.

Eventually mortgage commitments are translated into building permits. As permits are translated into completed houses and apartments, home-furnishings sales receive a boost—after a lag of 9 to 12 months—for the obvious reason that new homes must be furnished after they are built.

stock market

Of the leading indicators of general economic activity, stock prices are the only barometer where virtually no time lag exists in compiling the statistics. To be significant, a general rise in stock prices must coincide with comparable, underlying improvement elsewhere in the economy. In the last four expansion periods since 1949, Standard & Poor's index of 500 common stocks has always increased significantly in the first year.

One segment of the stock market to be watched is the short interest, which is the number of shares of stock sold short (that is, borrowed stock sold) and not yet repurchased for return to the lenders. The seller expects a price decline that will enable him to repurchase an equal number of shares later at a lower price, thereby yielding a profit. A significant number of brokers consider a decline in the short interest as bearish because it portends lessening demand for stock.

Some market followers also believe that whenever the percentage of the odd-lot short interest to total odd-lot sales dips below 1% for several months, an approaching bear market is indicated. Although these are technical factors in the market, they have been fairly reliable predictors.

Also, the behavior of bonds is of paramount importance to the equity market. When bond yields rise enough to be competitive with stock returns, bonds siphon investment money away from stocks. The volume of newly issued, high-grade utility bonds is an indicator of the general market trend, since issuance is controlled by experts who follow the market and the economy.

population trends

The generation produced by the post-World War II baby boom has completed schooling and entered the labor market. In a year or two, the median age of the population will reverse its decline.

The young homemakers, better known as the 25-to-34 age bracket, now constitute the major demographic group in the country. Representing about one of every five workers in 1968, this group will have increased by 50% at the end of this decade and will number one of every four workers by 1980. While constituting only 24% of the total U.S. population, this age group controls 42% of the nation's purchasing power based on both total and discretionary income.

Census figures show that the birthrate is continuing to decline, reflecting the wide acceptance of family planning. This trend eventually will affect many industries, beginning with the makers of toys. If the decline in birth continues, reverberations will sound through the economy for decades to come. Companies that specialize in market segments according to age grouping are assigning greater emphasis to population figures and projections.

coincident indicators

Consisting primarily of statistical series of data, coincident indicators reveal what is happening now in various sectors of the economy, and thus serve as aids to reliable predictions about the economy's future course.

gross national product

No doubt the most widely followed yardstick of the country's economic performance is the series that measures the total market value of the nation's output of goods and services, known familiarly as the GNP. It reflects the sum of consumer spending, government purchases, gross business investment, and net exports.

As tabulated, the GNP gives equal weight to luxuries and necessities. A disaster causes it to rise, rather than fall, because a disaster results in stepped-up consumption of goods and services.

There are two ways in which the GNP is expressed, in real terms and in current dollars. The former statistic is based on 1958 dollars, which strips away the effects of inflation by eliminating distortions due to price changes. To stabilize prices and reduce the unemployment rate, real GNP must exceed a 4% annual growth rate. Current GNP, expressed in present purchasing power, should rise about 9%-10% for price stability, with a moderate inflation rate of 5%-6% factored in.

When the GNP values are graphed for a period of time on a monthly or quarterly basis in order to establish a trend line, then compared with charts for consumer spending and residential construction, they can yield considerable insight into business behavior. The GNP betrays a continuous, strong growth trend, so it should be used as a predictor only when other statistical series are taken into account.

corporate profits

As a concept, profit is widely misunderstood and emotionally charged, so it must be approached with precision. The level or trend of corporate profits is used extensively as an indicator of economic activity because it

exhibit III . . . corporate after-tax profits in first
and third quarters of five economic recovery periods
[dollar figures in billions]

Recovery period	Profits in first quarter	Profits in third quarter	Percent gain
1949-1950	$18.1	$27.6	52.4%
1954-1955	20.9	26.5	26.7
1958-1959	20.2	28.0	38.6
1960-1961	24.4	30.1	23.3
1970-1971	39.2	45.8	16.8

is far more vulnerable to business swings than personal income; it declines rapidly in a recession and rises rapidly in a recovery. It is more precise than the broader yardsticks of GNP, industrial production, or unemployment.

During the first year of an economic recovery, profits tend to increase steadily. *Exhibit III* compares two quarters in each of five postwar
upturn periods. In the second year, however, when the recovery has
taken a firm hold, profit margins normally shrink, even though business
is still expanding. An exception is the steel industry, whose largest profit
gains are delayed until the upturn is well under way.

Obviously, profit figures are not generally available until considerably after the fact. Hence great care must be exercised in their usage.
These data should be analyzed in conjunction with other reliable
barometers.

industrial production

This barometer is the Federal Reserve Board's all-embracing index which
measures the output of all factories, mines, and utilities. It is a valuable
indicator because it accounts for a large share, 35%, of the GNP and it is
unaffected by inflation.

Since the industrial sector is one of the most volatile in the economy, this index is very sensitive; it can pinpoint the relative sluggishness
of a recovery, whereas the broader yardstick of real GNP cannot. The
index is extremely useful for developing industry and company forecasts
of changes in demand and sales.

In a healthy economy, production increases at a 4% seasonally adjusted annual rate. Additionally, to increase utilization, production must
grow at a faster rate than expansion in capacity. Unless utilization increases, corporations lack incentive to expand their facilities. An increase
in production, however, does not always signify a rising economy; recovery from strikes may be the cause. To generate a rise of any absolute

value, net plant excess capacity (total excess capacity less new capacity) must shrink.

Big gains in industrial production underlie large productivity gains that normally occur early in recoveries. So, when production rises steeply, hourly output does too. Milton Friedman has recently affirmed his findings that industrial production responds in three to six months to the impact of money-supply changes. This leads to the conclusion that when the money supply is restrained, plant output will decline.

unemployment rate

This indicator, figured as a percentage of the total work force, naturally correlates closely with the amount of unused manufacturing capacity.

A signal that unemployment is rising generally, and a decrease in business activity is impending, is increased joblessness among short-duration workers. Conversely, a rise in the use of temporary employees on business payrolls may be due to a reluctance of employers, feeling the need for more help, to hire permanent personnel until an economic upswing fully establishes itself. So this development can herald expansion of the permanent employees' roles.

Another favorable sign for the economy is an increase in the length of factory workweeks. Often it is viewed as a prelude to stepped-up hiring as a recovery period gathers momentum. However, it can also reflect reluctance of companies to increase payrolls as sales pick up momentarily.

help-wanted advertising

This is a little-noticed, but useful barometer. In comparing trends in industrial production, idle manufacturing capacity, and unemployment with that of help-wanted advertising, the analyst can note whether their behavior coincides. If he can show that each curve begins its respective turn-around at approximately the same time, he can validate turning points in business cycles.

This analysis is reasonable: as corporations see new orders declining and decide that the situation will become a trend, they reduce production, which raises the unemployment level and increases inactive manufacturing capacity.

adjusted credit proxy

A measure for estimating the current status of bank loans and investments, the credit proxy encompasses all deposits at Federal Reserve member banks; it is adjusted to include nondeposit liabilities such as commercial paper issued by the parent or bank affiliate, loan participations and sales, and Eurodollar deposits. Since bank credit more directly affects spending than does money or money-related variables—because it can be identified with outlays in a particular sector—this monetary aggregate is useful for analyzing the quality and distribution of credit.

(It should be noted that the Federal Reserve Board does not directly control this aggregate. Instead, by controlling bank reserves through its monetary policy, it exerts indirect influence.)

The primary measures of bank liquidity are the loan/deposit and liquid asset ratios. Operationally, a decline in the liquid asset ratio indicates that banks have relatively fewer readily marketable earning assets. Furthermore, a decline may show that the FRB is fighting a growth in the money supply by altering market interest rates. Such a restrictive policy can place a damper on consumer buying and housing starts as well as reduce the amount of lendable funds for corporate expansion.

An increase in the loan/deposit ratio reflects the situation when banks become loaned up and their earning assets (loans) increase. The severity of high interest rates and the length of the restrictive policy can be estimated roughly when the proxy is compared with the barometers of prime interest rate and monetary policy.

wholesale price index

As a measure of price movements other than at the retail level, this index helps indicate changes in the purchasing power of the dollar. The data used in compiling this exponent are taken from the primary market—that is, the first commercial transaction of each commodity exclusive of transportation charges. It does not include prices paid or received by wholesalers, jobbers, or distributors. Two categories of classification make up the index: industrial commodities, and farm products and processed foods and feeds.

It is not considered an accurate measure of inflation because it excludes prices for services and is disproportionately weighted with volatile raw material and agricultural commodity prices. But the seasonally adjusted WPI often foreshadows retail price trends because of the link to changes in food prices.

Since farm prices are heavily influenced by conditions outside the economic system (such as weather and blight), they are not central to the inflation problem. On the other hand, the rate of price increases on industrial products is responsive to fluctuations in economic activity. Increases vary between 2% and 4% annually.

A rise in prices of industrial commodities may indicate heavy demand for raw materials, on the logical assumption that companies decide to produce more finished goods because they anticipate increased demand. A rise in a commodity's price, however, may mean no more than stockpiling against future shortages because of, say, an impending strike.

lagging indicators

Although lagging indicators reach their turning points after the turns in economic activity, they help to verify that the trends of leading indicators are indeed predictive of a real economic trend and are not merely the result of statistical aberrations. The laggers are generally used for comparative purposes with data from past years or quarters.

prime rate

Defined as the interest rate charged by banks to their most credit-worthy customers, the prime rate is not, and never has been, the fixed figure that all the formality implies. As money tightens, for example, some companies find that they no longer qualify for the prime rate and must compete in the open market for their funding. Fluctuations in interest rates reflect shifts in the demand and supply of credit caused by changes in business activity and price expectations. A rising cost of capital is but one symptom of impending inflation.

Fluctuations in the prime rate usually follow the dates when corporations make their quarterly federal income tax payments. Then companies borrow heavily to meet their liabilities and bankers usually want to evaluate the intensity of this loan demand before taking corrective action on the prime rate. Banks rally to meet these requests in different ways, depending on the mix of business. West Coast banks depend heavily on consumer deposits for lendable funds, whereas their New York counterparts draw largely on institutional deposits.

This indicator should be followed because any improvement in the economic outlook will likely increase demand for short-term credit, exert upward pressure on interest rates, and produce a relative scarcity of lendable funds. A sustained and pronounced downward trend in the cost of short-term funds to banks, combined with a moderation in loan demand, can provide the impetus for a widespread reduction in the prime rate.

Conversely, a rising rate gives companies more incentive to raise money with sales of bonds rather than through bank borrowing. An increased supply of bonds in the marketplace will depress bond prices, so that outstanding bonds offer higher yields.

commercial paper

This phrase is the money-market designation for a short-term, unsecured promissory note issued by a large corporation and sold to an investor at a specified rate of interest (usually a discount) for a fixed maturity. When purchased by other companies or institutional investors, commercial paper is a major source of short-term funding for U.S. companies. As such, it provides corporations with a means of borrowing from one another and bypassing normal bank channels (a process known as disintermediation).

Fluctuations in the paper rate closely follow conditions in the money markets. Corporate borrowers seek use of the commercial paper market when the rate spread between the prime rate and the paper rate is in the latter's favor. This siphoning of loan demand puts pressure on banks to lower the prime rate which, in turn, lowers the cost of capital for borrowers.

Because of this close relationship between the two rates, the trend of one can be verified by comparison with the other. The coincident movement between them and the GNP series is due to the link between the demand for credit and the level of economic activity.

Because rates of short-term instruments like commercial paper are more directly affected by changes in working capital, they are usually the main source of funds over the business cycle. Long-term rates are influenced only indirectly by economic activity; variations in output influence business expectations with respect to the profitability of new investments, which affects demand for long-term financing to underwrite those investments.

capital expenditures

A period of sustained economic growth is always accompanied by a pronounced rise in capital spending. Despite what many textbooks say, corporate investment tends to occur late in the recovery from a recession because businessmen are cautious; they wait until the economy shows continued strength before committing corporate resources toward expansion.

An increase in capital appropriations by leading manufacturers usually indicates a healthy climate for machine-tool makers and heavy-equipment suppliers. Usually, new appropriations lead actual outlays by six to nine months. Continued rising labor costs, such as we have experienced in recent years, stimulate companies to invest in cost-cutting machinery and upgrade existing facilities. The volatility of manufacturers' appropriations and expenditures presents an argument against attaching too much significance to short-run developments, but when an increase in appropriations is consistent with data on plant and equipment from other sources (e.g., new orders in durable goods industries), this barometer becomes necessary to follow in long-range planning.

A lesson of business-cycle experience is that capital spending typically bottoms out after the trough in general business activity has been reached, and turns up only after a recovery is well under way. So attention should be focused on the categories of new appropriations and producers' capital goods industries which give a clue to capital-spending plans.

inventory/sales ratios

Low inventory/sales ratios and the slow growth in inventory accumulation in 1971 and early 1972 led many analysts to conclude that business was becoming generally pessimistic about the economy. Studies of the long-run behavior of inventories, however, show a decline in this ratio, indicating better management of inventory stocks.

When a pronounced drop occurs in the ratio, strengthening of both production and inventory spending is in the offing. For instance, a lean inventory/sales ratio—below 1.5 months of sales or an absolute ratio of 1.53—indicates that business will have to step up production, raw-material buying, and employment to meet increased demand.

Generally, inventory accumulation stimulates expansion early in an economic recovery period by increasing stocks of finished goods, work in process, and materials. In a trillion-dollar economy such as we have, inventories should normally rise by $7 billion-$10 billion a year.

A slow rate of inventory accumulation produces favorable credit-market conditions because many company treasurers use their idle funds to finance capital expansion, rebuild liquidity, and supply short-term credit markets. This provision of funds to credit markets indirectly lowers short-term interest rates. While a period of inventory accumulation exerts an upward pressure on interest rates, the drain does not place a heavy burden on the financial community because rising sales produce more funds for internal corporate application.

retail sales

Consumers account for about two thirds of this country's economic activity. So their behavior makes this index a good barometer to follow. Since this indicator fluctuates seasonally and is published on a monthly basis, several months' data are needed to pinpoint a trend.

The increased willingness of consumers to finance purchases through bank loans or installment credit may indicate a rise of consumer confidence in the economy. Observation of personal credit statistics can lend credence to a forecast of higher retail sales, when other indicators are pointing upward.

When consumer demand is encouragingly strong for such durable items as cars and color TV sets, coinciding with high levels of housing permits and starts and personal savings, retail sales will no longer lag but lead economic expansion. There is a six- to nine-month lag before the retail sector begins to benefit from a housing boom, which means that gains in retail sales will continue at high levels long after housing starts have fallen.

consumer price index

A measure of alterations in the cost of living, this index deals with the amounts actually charged to consumers for goods and services—including sales and excise taxes—by measuring the weighted changes in prices. It does not, however, indicate where the outlays actually went. Furthermore, it does not purport to measure changes in spending as a result of changes in the standard of living; it indicates changes in spending caused by changes in prices.

Interpretation of this monthly figure is difficult because of distortions in the method of compiling. Some economists, in fact, believe that an upward bias of 1%-2% a year is an inherent defect of the index.

The structure of the CPI has been criticized because it focuses on the cost to a wage earner of a relatively fixed staple of goods and services. The index does not—

. . . add and delete items fast enough,

. . . adjust values of the heavily weighted items that are of lessening importance to the consumer

. . . reflect the effect of new methods of distribution;

. . . take account of the enormous growth in discounting.

Nevertheless, the index is widely used by employers in arriving at a base for escalation clauses in labor contracts. As such, a 2%-3% annual rise in consumer prices is anti-inflationary, whereas anything higher leads to price instability and consequently heftier wage settlements. But not until the CPI and the wholesale price index (a coincident indicator) are moving together can an inflationary or deflationary trend be confirmed.

conclusion

To be of comparative use, statistical data must be examined where applicable on a seasonally adjusted basis. Even then, they are often misleading because of variations in business upturns and downturns and frequent statistical aberrations in our economy. To avoid these difficulties, forecasters prefer, where possible, to use data expressed in real terms—that is, where the effects of inflation have been discounted.

Care must be exercised in following too few or randomly selected economic trends. The list of the Department of Commerce contains 40 leading, 26 coincident, and 12 lagging indicators. Only when a preponderance of a company's relevant indicators are moving in one direction can a rational decision about the future be reached.

Of the numerous methods of summarizing business barometers, the simplest and most widely used is a numerical diffusion index. For each rising indicator at any point in time, a value of 1 is assigned. If some are stationary, they are counted as one half each and added to those that are rising. A falling indicator has a value of zero. The sum is expressed as a percentage of the total number of indicators. The resulting value is called a diffusion index because it shows how widely diffused is a movement among the indicators.

Diffusion indexes above 50% occur usually during expansion cycles, whereas those below that level appear during business contractions. This type of index must always be based on one type of indicator—leading, coincident, or lagging—never a mixture. . . .

Obviously, the diffusion index cannot compensate for the inaccuracies of indicators; it is only a convenient parameter for comparing and analyzing changes in a particular indicator. Forecasting is still an art. The accuracy of business barometers depends on a myriad of factors, such as the content of the forecast, the relevance and availability of data, the accuracy desired, the period of data collection, the value of the indicators to the company, and the time available for analysis.

. . . using a diffusion index

The tabulation in *Table A* represents a convenient arrangement for calculating a diffusion index for the economy. All the indicators are coincident in this example, and all are reported monthly except for the GNP and corporate profits, which are reported quarterly. The terms in which the indicators are expressed (dollars, percent, or compared with a base year) do not matter as long as they are internally consistent from one period to the next.

table A . . . diffusion index calculation

Indicator	Latest figure	Previous figure	Numerical change
Gross national product	783.1	766.5	1
Corporate profits	49.5	48.0	1
Wholesale price index	118.2	117.5	1
Industrial production	112.4	112.1	1
Adjusted credit proxy	33,261.0	33,276.0	0
Help-wanted advertising	93.0	93.0	0.5
Percent unemployment	5.5	5.8	1*
			5.5

This indicator is an inverted series functioning conversely to the others; that is, a decrease in its value registers a positive change.

Dividing 5.5 by the number of indicators used, then multiplying by 100 gives a result of 78.6%. Since this value is well above 50%, it indicates an expansionary movement of the economy.

Indexes based on leading indicators usually shift position before those based on coincident or lagging indicators. To expose cyclical swings in the data, reduce the influence of erratic movements due to statistical aberrations, and account for the difference in significance between a rapidly falling and a slowly declining index, longer time spans of from one to six months can be used. For example, when the span is six months and the last available figure is July, a preliminary entry for May can be obtained by comparing February with July, and an entry for June can be obtained by comparing March with July.

For a comprehensive explanation of the use of the diffusion indexes, including the variable time span, see the article in the 1960 edition of *Research on Indicators of Cyclical Revivals and Recessions*, published annually by the National Bureau of Economic Research (New York).

A company can formulate its own diffusion index by analyzing the economic factors that directly affect it. A valuable aid for relating barometers to particular business cycles is the monthly publication. *Business Conditions Digest* (BCD), issued by the Bureau of Economic Analysis, Department of Commerce. The indicators listed in it have been chosen primarily for their cyclical behavior and usefulness in forecasting short-term fluctuations in economic activity. The BCD classifies them by economic process and cyclical timing.

Statistical weighting factors can be employed in a diffusion index prepared for a specific industry or company. However, this generally involves complex econometric analysis and regression equations for the causal relationships among the indicators and the economic estimates for the industry or company. These calculations are beyond the scope of this primer; see John Johnston's book, *Econometric Methods* (New York, McGraw-Hill, 1963).

Other useful sources for the business forecaster include the *Survey of Current Business*, issued by the Office of Business Economics, Department of Commerce; the *Federal Reserve Bulletin*, published by the Federal Reserve Board; and *Economic Indicators*, prepared by the Council of Economic Advisors and issued by the Joint Economic Committee of Congress.

appendix b . . . tests for
serial correlation
in regression analysis

introduction

In Chapter 4 several assumptions were noted that must be satisfied before we can be reasonably assured of high reliability in results of regression analysis (page 60). Basically these assumptions concerned the error term (residual), by specifying that it must be a normally distributed random variable with a zero mean and constant variance and that autocorrelation must not exist among error terms.*

In many practical uses of regression we are dealing with time-series data, and the task is to prepare a forecast for some future point in time. When regression analysis is applied to such situations, the behavior of the error term often does not satisfy the assumptions noted above and the validity of our analysis is questionable. The main difficulty involves autocorrelation in the error terms. This arises because of serial correlation existent in time-series data, which means that one data point can be used to approximate the following point by adding to it a small predetermined amount (subtraction, multiplication or division could be involved). Hence, the purpose of Appendix B is to present the reader with procedures that can be employed to test for *autocorrelation* in the error terms and *serial correlation* among the data.

Autocorrelation exists when there is interdependence among residuals of the regression equation. Thus, autocorrelation is a term used here to describe serial correlation of the residuals—serial correlation means there is time dependence in the data. Most time series are serially correlated because the values in successive time periods are of similar magnitude.

The concept of serial correlation was introduced in Chapter 4 as a non-random (i.e., a predictable) pattern in time-series data. (Similarly, autocorrelation of error terms is present when there is a predictable association among them.) Specifically serial correlation is the correlation between pairs of equally spaced observations. In a series of observations, $x_1, x_2, x_3, \ldots, x_n$, serial correlation is the correlation between pairs x_i and x_{i+h}, where h is the time lag between the two points. In time-series data h is usually considered to be 1, which indicates correlation between successive observations. Data that are seasonal over a year's period will have serial correlation for $h=1$ and also for $h=12$.

If serial correlation exists, regression will seriously underestimate the true variance and the usual tests of significance discussed in Appendix C are not valid. In this case, the true underlying relationship among variables is not expressed by the regression equation; the forecaster who uses regression when serial correlation is present is misleading himself as to the significance and accuracy of his forecast. With strong serial correlation among data, the forecaster is well advised to resort to the time-series techniques discussed in Chapter 5 in preparing his forecast.

von-neuman ratio test

This statistical test, which was introduced by Von-Neuman in 1941, is used to check for serial correlation in time-series data. The test investigates the ratio of mean square successive differences between pairs of data points to the total variance. The ratio is represented by δ^2/S^2 and, for a series of T observations, $x_1, x_2, \ldots, x_T$, is calculated by:

$$\frac{\delta^2}{S^2} = \frac{\sum\limits_{t=2}^{T} (x_t - x_{t-1})^2/(T-1)}{\sum\limits_{t=1}^{T} (X_t - \overline{X})^2/T}$$

The distribution of this ratio is illustrated in the following diagram, where $(\delta^2/S^2)_0$ is a critical value of the ratio for a certain confidence level. These critical values are given in Table B-2 which is later utilized in an example application of the test.

The mean of this symmetrical distribution is $2T/(T-1)$. If successive x_t values are close to each other, the ratio will be small since the numerator

$$\sum\limits_{t=2}^{T} (x_t - x_{t-1})^2$$

contains small differences that are squared. The ratio will then fall in the left critical region that indicates positive serial correlation. If successive values of

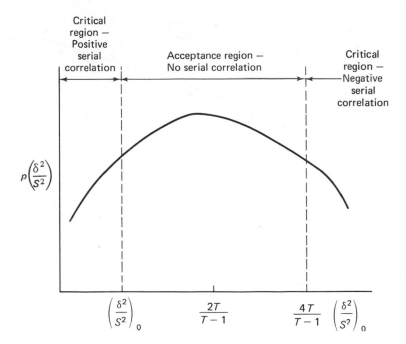

figure B-1 . . . critical regions of the von-neuman ratio test

x_t are unusually far apart, the ratio will be large and will fall in the right critical region that suggests negative serial correlation. If our calculated ratio falls in the mid-region, we conclude that there is no serial correlation. Graphical interpretations of positive and negative serial correlation are shown in Figure B-2.

durbin-watson test

This test examines the residuals of a regression equation, where the residual for period t, R_t, has been defined as follows:

$$R_t = \left(\begin{array}{c} \text{Observed data for} \\ \text{period } t \end{array} \quad - \quad \begin{array}{c} \text{Forecast value for} \\ \text{period } t \end{array} \right)$$

The equation for the Durbin-Watson statistic, d, is

$$d = \frac{\sum\limits_{t=2}^{T} (R_t - R_{t-1})^2}{\sum\limits_{t=1}^{T} (R_t)^2}$$

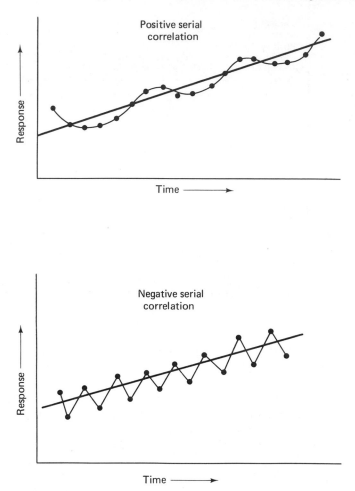

figure B-2 . . . positive and negative serial correlation

The distribution of this statistic is illustrated by Figure B-3, where d_u and d_ϱ are critical values of the statistic for a certain confidence level. These critical values are given in Table B-2, which is utilized in an example problem to follow. From Figure B-3 it can be seen that this symmetric distribution has a mean of 2. If a calculated value of d falls in the left region, $d < d_\varrho$, positive serial correlation is indicated; in the right region, $d > 4 - d_\varrho$, negative serial correlation is present in the residuals; in the mid-region, $d_u < d < 4-d_u$, no serial correlation is likely. If d falls between d_ϱ and d_u or between $4-d_u$ and $4-d_\varrho$, no decision can be reached regarding autocorrelation among residuals.

example problem

A practical example is presented here that illustrates the use of the Von-Neuman Ratio Test and the Durbin-Watson Test to check for serial correlation.

In recent years, forecasters have examined the trade-offs between economic growth and environmental quality and have attempted to predict the future effects of historical trends. One such interesting problem involves forecasting the amount of carbon dioxide (CO_2) in the atmosphere. From Figure B-4 it can be seen that the CO_2 concentration has increased steadily for twelve years. If this trend continues, there will be two pronounced effects. The CO_2 will act as a blanket over the earth, possibly resulting in increased climatic temperatures and subsequent melting of considerable amounts of Arctic ice. The second effect (which is favorable) is a higher rate of photosynthesis.

The purpose of this example is to examine twelve years of data on CO_2 content in the atmosphere, use regression to fit a line through the data, and employ the Von-Neuman Ratio and the Durbin-Watson Tests to check for serial correlation. By using regression, this equation was determined for the data and subsequently drawn in Figure B-4,

$$y = 311.8792 + (0.3818)x$$

where y is the carbon dioxide content and x is the time period. The equation states that the carbon dioxide in the atmosphere increases 0.3818 parts per million (volume) each six months. Figure B-5 is a plot of the residuals that are calculated in Table B-1. By examining Figures B-4 and B-5, the reader should begin to suspect that the data exhibit positive serial correlation. Let us apply

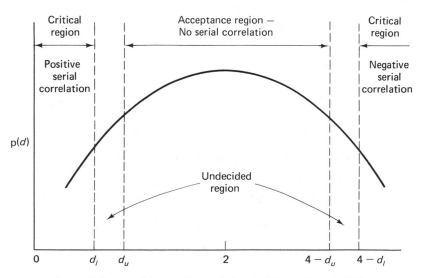

figure B-3 . . . critical regions of the durbin-watson statistic

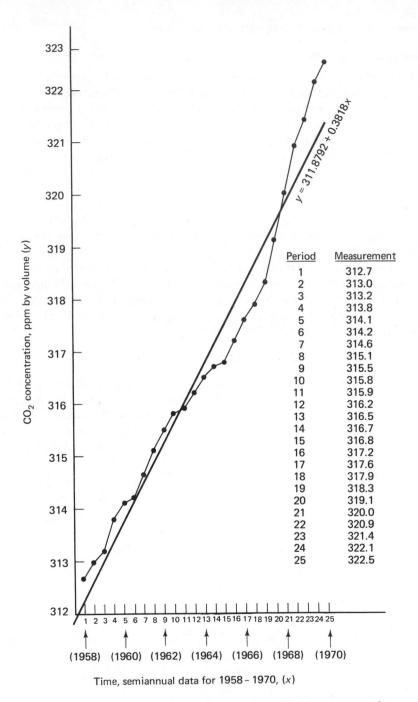

Period	Measurement
1	312.7
2	313.0
3	313.2
4	313.8
5	314.1
6	314.2
7	314.6
8	315.1
9	315.5
10	315.8
11	315.9
12	316.2
13	316.5
14	316.7
15	316.8
16	317.2
17	317.6
18	317.9
19	318.3
20	319.1
21	320.0
22	320.9
23	321.4
24	322.1
25	322.5

$y = 311.8792 + 0.3818x$

CO₂ concentration, ppm by volume (y)

Time, semiannual data for 1958 – 1970, (x)

(1958) (1960) (1962) (1964) (1966) (1968) (1970)

figure B-4 . . . changes of atmospheric carbon dioxide concentration

Period	Residuals	Period	Residuals	Period	Residuals
1	0.4392	10	0.1028	19	−0.8337
2	0.3574	11	−0.1792	20	−0.4155
3	0.1755	12	−0.2610	21	0.1025
4	0.3938	13	−0.3428	22	0.6206
5	0.3120	14	−0.5247	23	0.7388
6	0.0300	15	−0.8064	24	1.0571
7	0.0483	16	−0.7883	25	1.0752
8	0.1665	17	−0.7700		
9	0.1846	18	−0.8521		

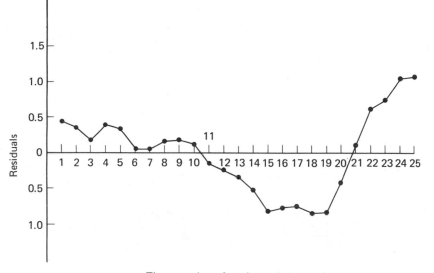

Time, number of semiannual observations

figure B-5 . . . a plot of residuals (simple regression)

the Von-Neuman Ratio Test and Durbin-Watson Test to confirm our suspicions.

VON-NEUMAN TEST   *The null hypothesis H_0:* Each data point is uncorrelated with the succeeding member.

The alternative hypothesis H_a: Each data point is positively correlated with the succeeding member.

Significance value: $\alpha = 0.05$.

table B-1 . . . summary of calculations for serial correlation

Period	X	Estimate $\hat{X}$	R	R^2	$(R_t - R_{t-1})$	$(R_t - R_{t-1})^2$	$(x_t - \bar{x})^2$	$(x_t - x_{t-1})$	$(x_t - x_{t-1})^2$
1	312.7	312.2607	0.4392	0.1929	—	—	17.172736	—	—
2	313.0	312.6426	0.3574	0.1278	-0.0818	0.0067	14.776336	0.3	0.90
3	313.2	313.0244	0.1755	0.0308	-0.1819	0.0351	13.278736	0.2	0.40
4	313.8	313.4063	0.3938	0.1551	0.2183	0.0477	9.265936	0.6	0.36
5	314.1	313.7881	0.3120	0.0974	-0.0818	0.0067	7.529536	0.3	0.09
6	314.2	314.1699	0.0300	0.0009	-0.2820	0.0795	6.990731	0.1	0.01
7	314.6	314.5518	0.0483	0.0023	0.1830	0.0335	5.254180	0.4	0.16
8	315.1	314.9336	0.1665	0.0277	0.1182	0.0354	3.034153	0.5	0.25
9	315.5	315.3154	0.1846	0.0341	0.0181	0.0003	1.806336	0.4	0.16
10	315.8	315.0973	0.1028	0.0106	-0.0818	0.0067	1.089936	0.3	0.09
11	315.9	316.0791	-0.1792	0.0321	-0.2820	0.0795	0.891136	0.1	0.01
12	316.2	316.4609	-0.2610	0.0681	-0.0818	0.0067	0.414736	0.3	0.09
13	316.5	316.8428	-0.3428	0.1175	-0.0818	0.0067	0.118336	0.3	0.09
14	316.7	317.2246	-0.5247	0.2753	-0.1819	0.0031	0.020736	0.2	0.04
15	316.8	317.6064	-0.8064	0.6503	-0.2817	0.0794	0.001936	0.1	0.01
16	317.2	317.9883	-0.7883	0.0215	0.0181	0.0003	0.126736	0.4	0.16
17	317.6	318.3701	-0.7700	0.5929	0.0183	0.0003	0.571536	0.4	0.16
18	317.9	318.7520	-0.8521	0.7260	0.0821	0.0067	1.115136	0.3	0.09
19	318.3	319.1338	-0.8337	0.6951	0.0184	0.0003	2.119936	0.4	0.16
20	319.1	319.5156	-0.4155	0.1727	0.4182	0.1749	5.089536	0.8	0.64
21	320.0	319.8975	0.1025	0.0105	0.5180	0.2683	9.960336	0.9	0.81
22	320.9	320.2793	0.6205	0.3852	0.5180	0.2683	16.451136	0.9	0.81
23	321.4	320.8611	0.7388	0.5458	0.1183	0.0140	20.757136	0.5	0.25
24	322.1	321.0430	1.0571	1.1175	0.3183	0.1013	27.625536	0.7	0.49
25	322.5	321.4248	1.0752	1.1560	0.0181	0.0003	31.990336	0.4	0.16
	7921.1			**7.8450**		**1.2897**	**197.45286**		**5.22**

$$\bar{x} = 316.844$$

Test statistics: (Note that all calculations have been made in Table B-1.)

$$\frac{\delta^2}{S^2} = \frac{\sum\limits_{2}^{25}(x_t - x_{t-1})^2/(T-1)}{\sum\limits_{1}^{25}(x_t - \bar{x})^2/T}$$

$$\sum\limits_{t=1}^{25}(x_t - \bar{x})^2 = 197.4528616$$

$$S^2 = \frac{197.4528616}{25} = 7.898$$

$$\delta^2 = \sum\limits_{t=2}^{25}(x_t - x_{t-1})^2/(T-1) = \frac{5.22}{24} = 0.2175$$

$$\frac{\delta^2}{S^2} = \frac{0.2175}{7.898} = 0.02753$$

From Table B-2, for $T = 25$ and a confidence level of $\alpha = 0.05$, we see that $\delta^2/S^2 = 1.36$. The test becomes:

$$\left(\frac{\delta^2}{S^2}\right).05 = 1.36 > 0.02753$$

Conclusion: We can reject H_0 and accept H_a and claim that positive serial correlation exists in our data.

DURBIN-WATSON TEST   *Null hypothesis, H_0*: The residuals are not serially correlated.
Alternative hypothesis, H_a: the residuals are positive serially correlated.
Significance level: $\alpha = 0.05$.
Test statistic: (Calculations can be found in Table B-1.)

$$d = \frac{\sum\limits_{t=2}^{25}(R_t - R_{t-1})^2}{\sum\limits_{t=1}^{25}(R_t)^2}$$

$$\sum\limits_{t=2}^{25}(R_t - R_{t-1})^2 = 1.2897$$

$$\sum\limits_{t=1}^{25}(R_t)^2 = 7.8450$$

$$d = \frac{1.2897}{7.8450} = 0.1643$$

Critical region: For $\alpha = 0.05$, $K = 1$ (K is the number of coefficients in

table B-2 . . . the distribution of

$$d = \frac{\delta^2}{s^2} = \frac{T-1}{T} \cdot \frac{\delta^2}{S^2} = \frac{\sum_{2}^{T}(R_t - R_{t-1})^2}{\sum_{1}^{T} R_t^2}$$

The probability shown in the second column is the area in the lower tail. K is the number of independent variables in addition to the constant term. *Example:* With 20 observations, and a regression involving three independent variables and a constant term, Hart gives a probability of 5 per cent for a value of d less than 1.30, and Durbin and Watson give a probability of 5 per cent for a value of d between 1.00 and 1.68. The distributions are symmetrical about the point $2T(T-1)$.

Values of d_L and d_U from Durbin and Watson [1951]

Sample Size T	Probability in Lower Tail	Values of $d = \delta^2/S^2$	$K=1$ d_L	$K=1$ d_U	$K=2$ d_L	$K=2$ d_U	$K=3$ d_L	$K=3$ d_U	$K=4$ d_L	$K=4$ d_U	$K=5$ d_L	$K=5$ d_U
15	.01	.89	.81	1.07	.70	1.25	.59	1.46	.49	1.70	.39	1.96
	.025	1.04	.95	1.23	.83	1.40	.71	1.61	.59	1.84	.48	2.09
	.05	1.16	1.08	1.36	.95	1.54	.82	1.75	.69	1.97	.56	2.21
20	.01	1.04	.95	1.15	.86	1.27	.77	1.41	.68	1.57	.60	1.74
	.025	1.18	1.08	1.28	.99	1.41	.89	1.55	.79	1.70	.70	1.87
	.05	1.30	1.20	1.41	1.10	1.54	1.00	1.68	.90	1.83	.79	1.99
25	.01	1.12	1.05	1.21	0.98	1.30	0.90	1.41	0.83	1.52	.75	1.65
	.025	1.26	1.18	1.34	1.10	1.43	1.02	1.54	0.94	1.65	.86	1.77
	.05	1.36	1.29	1.45	1.21	1.55	1.12	1.66	1.04	1.77	.95	1.89

n	level											
30	.01	1.19	1.13	1.26	1.07	1.34	1.01	1.42	0.94	1.51	0.88	1.61
	.025	1.32	1.25	1.38	1.18	1.46	1.12	1.54	1.05	1.63	0.98	1.73
	.05	1.42	1.35	1.49	1.28	1.57	1.21	1.65	1.14	1.74	1.07	1.83
40	.01	1.29	1.25	1.34	1.20	1.40	1.15	1.46	1.10	1.52	1.05	1.58
	.025	1.40	1.35	1.45	1.30	1.51	1.25	1.57	1.20	1.63	1.15	1.69
	.05	1.49	1.44	1.54	1.39	1.60	1.34	1.66	1.29	1.72	1.23	1.79
50	.01	1.36	1.32	1.40	1.28	1.45	1.24	1.49	1.20	1.54	1.16	1.59
	.025	1.46	1.42	1.50	1.38	1.54	1.34	1.59	1.30	1.64	1.26	1.69
	.05	1.54	1.50	1.59	1.46	1.63	1.42	1.67	1.38	1.72	1.34	1.77
60	.01	1.42	1.38	1.45	1.35	1.48	1.32	1.52	1.28	1.56	1.25	1.60
	.025	1.51	1.47	1.54	1.44	1.57	1.40	1.61	1.37	1.65	1.33	1.69
	.05	1.58	1.55	1.62	1.51	1.65	1.48	1.69	1.44	1.73	1.41	1.77
80	.01	—	1.47	1.52	1.44	1.54	1.42	1.57	1.39	1.60	1.36	1.62
	.025	—	1.54	1.59	1.52	1.62	1.49	1.65	1.47	1.67	1.44	1.70
	.05	—	1.61	1.66	1.59	1.69	1.56	1.72	1.53	1.74	1.51	1.77
100	.01	—	1.52	1.56	1.50	1.58	1.48	1.60	1.46	1.63	1.44	1.65
	.025	—	1.59	1.63	1.57	1.65	1.55	1.67	1.53	1.70	1.51	1.72
	.05	—	1.65	1.69	1.63	1.72	1.61	1.74	1.59	1.76	1.57	1.78

SOURCE: Carl F. Christ, *Econometric Models and Methods* (New York: John Wiley and Sons, Inc., 1966), p. 672.

the regression equation that have been estimated, less one. For simple linear regression, $K=1$.)

The value of d_ϱ and d_u are found from Table B-2 to be 1.29 and 1.45, respectively. If $d < 1.29$ reject H_0. If $1.29 < d < 1.45$ we are undecided. If $1.45 < d$ we accept H_0.

Conclusion: Since $d = 0.1643 < 1.29$, we can reject H_0 and state that residuals are positively serially correlated.

From the results of the Von-Neuman Test and the Durbin-Watson Test, we can conclude that the simple regression model is not suitable for our data, and we probably ought to use another forecasting technique.

appendix c . . . statistical tests
for regression methods

The objective of this appendix is (1) to present basic tests that can be used to evaluate the statistical significance of a linear regression equation of the form $y = a + bx$, and (2) to illustrate their use with an example problem. The reader who is interested in theoretical foundations of these tests, or in advanced aspects of multiple linear or nonlinear regression, should refer to a good statistics book. Because most computer programs for regression analysis of data provide calculations of the t-test and F-test statistics, this appendix gives the reader a fundamental understanding of how these statistics should be interpreted and how they are useful in forecasting work.

It is assumed that the basic assumptions of regression, as described in Chapter 4, are satisfied. In all t-tests and F-tests, and "α value" is specified initially. In statistical hypothesis testing, α represents the probability of rejecting the null hypothesis when it is true. An α value of 0.05 is commonly used in practice. This means that there are 5 chances out of 100 of rejecting a statistical hypothesis concerning a parameter of interest when, based on sample evidence available, it should have been accepted. The term α is also used in Chapter 5 to denote a smoothing constant in the exponential smoothing technique. Each separate use of α will be clear to the reader by the nature of the problem under study.

To apply the t-tests and F-tests, the regression equation should be determined and the information shown below obtained. This particular illustration utilizes the data of Table 4-1 that are plotted in Figure 4-4. The information summarized here is taken from Tables 4-1 and 4-2.

$\Sigma x_i y_{ai} = 2{,}626{,}817$ $\Sigma x_i^2 = 1{,}416{,}926$
$\bar{x} = 250.6$
$\bar{y} = 489.4$ $a = 218.5$ (estimated from data)
$n = 20$ $b = 1.081$ (estimated from data)
$\Sigma(y_{ai} - y_i)^2 = 52{,}482.8$

A. Use of the F-test to determine if the regression line represents a statistically significant relationship between the variables.

1. Form the null hypothesis, H_0: the linear relationship is *not* significant (i.e., it does not exist for all practical purposes).

2. Choose an α value and use the F-statistic. Here we let $\alpha = 0.05$.

3. Find the appropriate value of the F-statistic from Table C-1. Because we have $n = 20$ data points, there are $n - 2 = 18$ degrees of freedom (2 degrees of freedom are lost when we made estimates of a and b). The value of the F-statistic for $\alpha = 0.05$, and 18 degrees of freedom is $F_{0.05,\,18,\,1} = 4.41$.

4. Calculate F' from the data, where F' is the test statistic that is calculated from the available data:

$$F' = \frac{b(\Sigma x_i y_{ai} - n\bar{x} \cdot \bar{y})}{\left[\dfrac{\Sigma(y_{ai} - y_i)^2}{n - 2}\right]}$$

$$= \frac{1.081 \, [2{,}626{,}817 - 20(250.6)\,(489.4)]}{\left(\dfrac{52{,}482.8}{18}\right)}$$

$$= 64.49$$

5. Compare F' to $F_{\alpha,n-2,1}$. If F' is greater than $F_{\alpha,n-2,1}$ then reject the null hypothesis. The alternate hypothesis is that a linear relationship between the variables exists. Here $F' = 64.49$, which is greater than $F_{0.05,\,18,1} = 4.41$ so we reject H_0 and conclude that there is a statistically significant relationship between the independent and dependent variable when $\alpha = 0.05$.

B. Use of the t-test to determine if the calculated intercept, a, is equal to some other value a'. Here we will test whether $a' = 0$.

1. The null hypothesis is H_0: $a = a'$. That is, our initial hypothesis is that the true intercept is zero.

2. Choose a value of α and use the t-statistic. Here again we elect to use $\alpha = 0.05$.

3. Find the appropriate value of the t-statistic from Table C-2. There are $n = 20$ data points and $n-2 = 18$ degrees of freedom. By using $\alpha =$

table C-1 . . . percentage points of the *F* distribution

$$F_{\alpha, n-2, 1}$$

$n-2$	.50	.25	.10	α .05	.025	.01	.005
1	1.00	5.83	39.86	161.00	648.00	4052	16211
2	0.667	2.57	8.53	18.50	38.50	98.5	198
3	0.585	2.02	5.54	10.10	17.40	34.1	55.6
4	0.549	1.81	4.54	7.71	12.20	21.2	31.3
5	0.528	1.69	4.06	6.61	10.00	16.3	22.8
6	0.515	1.62	3.78	5.99	8.81	13.7	18.6
7	0.506	1.57	3.59	5.59	8.07	12.2	16.2
8	0.499	1.54	3.46	5.32	7.57	11.3	14.7
9	0.494	1.51	3.36	5.12	7.21	10.6	13.6
10	0.490	1.49	3.29	4.96	6.94	10.0	12.8
11	0.486	1.47	3.23	4.84	6.72	9.65	12.2
12	0.484	1.46	3.18	4.75	6.55	9.33	11.8
13	0.481	1.45	3.14	4.67	6.41	9.07	11.4
14	0.479	1.44	3.10	4.60	6.30	8.86	11.1
15	0.478	1.43	3.07	4.54	6.20	8.68	10.8
16	0.476	1.42	3.05	4.49	6.12	8.53	10.6
17	0.475	1.42	3.03	4.45	6.04	8.40	10.4
18	0.474	1.41	3.01	4.41	5.98	8.29	10.2
19	0.473	1.41	2.99	4.38	5.92	8.18	10.1
20	0.472	1.40	2.97	4.35	5.87	8.10	9.94
21	0.471	1.40	2.96	4.32	5.83	8.02	9.83
22	0.470	1.40	2.95	4.30	5.79	7.95	9.73
23	0.470	1.39	2.94	4.28	5.75	7.88	9.63
24	0.469	1.39	2.93	4.26	5.72	7.82	9.55
25	0.468	1.39	2.92	4.24	5.69	7.77	9.48
26	0.468	1.38	2.91	4.23	5.66	7.72	9.41
27	0.467	1.38	2.90	4.21	5.63	7.68	9.34
28	0.467	1.38	2.89	4.20	5.61	7.64	9.28
29	0.467	1.38	2.89	4.18	5.59	7.60	9.23
30	0.466	1.38	2.88	4.17	5.57	7.56	9.18
40	0.463	1.36	2.84	4.08	5.42	7.31	8.83
60	0.461	1.35	2.79	4.00	5.29	7.08	8.49
120	0.458	1.34	2.75	3.92	5.15	6.85	8.18
∞	0.455	1.32	2.71	3.84	5.02	6.63	7.88

SOURCE: R. Lowell Wine, *Statistics for Scientists and Engineers* (Englewood Cliffs, N.J.: Prentice-Hall, Inc., 1964), Table VII, pp. 632-645.

table C-2 . . . percentage points of the *t* distribution

n–2 \ α	.25	.20	.15	.10
1	1.000	1.376	1.963	3.078
2	.816	1.061	1.386	1.886
3	.765	.978	1.250	1.638
4	.741	.941	1.190	1.533
5	.727	.920	1.156	1.476
6	.718	.906	1.134	1.440
7	.711	.896	1.119	1.415
8	.706	.889	1.108	1.397
9	.703	.883	1.100	1.383
10	.700	.879	1.093	1.372
11	.697	.876	1.088	1.363
12	.695	.873	1.083	1.356
13	.694	.870	1.079	1.350
14	.692	.868	1.076	1.345
15	.691	.866	1.074	1.341
16	.690	.865	1.071	1.337
17	.689	.863	1.069	1.333
18	.688	.862	1.067	1.330
19	.688	.861	1.066	1.328
20	.687	.860	1.064	1.325
21	.686	.859	1.063	1.323
22	.686	.858	1.061	1.321
23	.685	.858	1.060	1.319
24	.685	.857	1.059	1.318
25	.684	.856	1.058	1.316
26	.684	.856	1.058	1.315
27	.684	.855	1.057	1.314
28	.683	.855	1.056	1.313
29	.683	.854	1.055	1.311
30	.683	.854	1.055	1.310
40	.681	.851	1.050	1.303
60	.679	.848	1.046	1.296
120	.677	.845	1.041	1.289
∞	.674	.842	1.036	1.282

SOURCE: R. Lowell Wine, *Statistics for Scientists and Engineers* (Englewood Cliffs, N.J.: Prentice-Hall, Inc., 1964). Table VI, p.631.

.05	.025	.01	.005	.0005
6.314	12.706	31.821	63.657	636.619
2.920	4.303	6.965	9.925	31.598
2.353	3.182	4.541	5.841	12.941
2.132	2.776	3.747	4.604	8.610
2.015	2.571	3.365	4.032	6.859
1.943	2.447	3.143	3.707	5.959
1.895	2.365	2.998	3.499	5.405
1.860	2.306	2.896	3.355	5.041
1.833	2.262	2.821	3.250	4.781
1.812	2.228	2.764	3.169	4.587
1.796	2.201	2.718	3.106	4.437
1.782	2.179	2.681	3.055	4.318
1.771	2.160	2.650	3.012	4.221
1.761	2.145	2.624	2.977	4.140
1.753	2.131	2.602	2.947	4.073
1.746	2.120	2.583	2.921	4.015
1.740	2.110	2.567	2.898	3.965
1.734	2.101	2.552	2.878	3.922
1.729	2.093	2.539	2.861	3.883
1.725	2.086	2.528	2.845	3.850
1.721	2.080	2.518	2.831	3.819
1.717	2.074	2.508	2.819	3.792
1.714	2.069	2.500	2.807	3.767
1.711	2.064	2.492	2.797	3.745
1.708	2.060	2.485	2.787	3.725
1.706	2.056	2.479	2.779	3.707
1.703	2.052	2.473	2.771	3.690
1.701	2.048	2.467	2.763	3.674
1.699	2.045	2.462	2.756	3.659
1.697	2.042	2.457	2.750	3.646
1.684	2.021	2.423	2.704	3.551
1.671	2.000	2.390	2.660	3.460
1.658	1.980	2.358	2.617	3.373
1.645	1.960	2.326	2.576	3.291

0.05 and 18 degrees of freedom, the value of the t-statistic is $t_{0.05,18}$ = 1.734.

4. Calculate t' from the data, where t' is the test statistic that is determined from available data:

$$t' = \frac{a - a'}{\left[\dfrac{\Sigma(y_{ai} - y_i)^2}{n(n-2)}\right]}$$

$$= \frac{218.5 - 0}{\left(\dfrac{52.482.8}{18(20)}\right)} = \frac{218.5}{12.07} = 18.10$$

5. Compare t' to $t_{\alpha,n-2}$. If t' is greater than $t_{\alpha,n-2}$ reject the hypothesis that $a = a'$. The alternate hypothesis that a is significantly different than 0 would then be accepted. Here $t' = 18.10$, which is greater than $t_{0.05,18} = 1.734$ so we reject the null hypothesis that $a = 0$. We have concluded by means of a statistical test that the true intercept of the regression equation is not zero. We are $100(1-\alpha)\%$, or 95%, confident in this statement.

C. Use of the t-test to determine if the calculated slope, b, is statistically significant.

1. Form the null hypothesis that the calculated slope is equal to some other value b'. Here we shall test against whether $b' = 0$. The null hypothesis is, $H_0: b = b'$. Our null hypothesis is that the true slope of the calculated regression equation is equal to zero.

2. Choose a value of α and use the t-statistic. Here we choose a value of α equal to 0.05.

3. Find the correct value of the t-statistic from Table C-2. There are n = 20 data points and $n-2 = 18$ degrees of freedom. By using $\alpha = 0.05$ and 18 degrees of freedom, the value of t-statistic is $t_{0.05,18} =$ 1.734.

4. Calculate t', where t' is the test statistic that is calculated from available data:

$$t' = \frac{b - b'}{\left[\dfrac{(\Sigma(y_{ai} - y_i)^2}{n-2}\right] \Big/ \Sigma x_i^2}$$

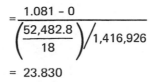

$$= \frac{1.081 - 0}{\left(\dfrac{52{,}482.8}{18}\right) \Big/ 1{,}416{,}926}$$

$$= 23.830$$

5. Compare t' to $t_{\alpha, n-2}$. If t' is greater than $t_{\alpha, n-2}$ then reject the hypothesis that $b = b'$. Here $t' = 23.830$, which is greater than $t_{0.05,18} = 1.734$, so we reject the null hypothesis that $b = 0$. Based on available data, we are 95% confident that the true slope of the regression equation is not zero.

appendix d . . . forecasting high consequence, low probability events

introduction

This appendix deals with the prediction of an event that has a very small probability of occurrence but has potentially devastating consequences if it does take place. Such events might include the core meltdown of a nuclear power reactor, an aircraft crash in a populated area, or the collapse of a large dam that is upstream from a large population center. In the absence of scientific, cause-effect relationships and/or actual data for these highly unlikely (although possible) events, the forecaster must draw upon expert opinion and use whatever means are available for developing his forecast. A Bayesian model for dealing with this situation is demonstrated here.

This general type of problem arises rather often in the public domain where the health and safety of people are involved. For example, the State Department of Transportation might want to estimate when an overpass on a heavily traveled interstate highway might collapse from accumulated internal stresses. This information is essential so that measures can be taken to avoid such an accident without incurring prohibitive losses. In the private sector, an industrial firm may be acutely concerned about how long it will be before one of their railroad tankers filled with chlorine is derailed at an intersection suspected of being dangerous. Clearly, these events are remote in their probability of occurrence but, given that they occur, their consequences endanger human lives and property.

The example problem presented in this section illustrates one method (a Bayesian model) for predicting the time at which low probability, high consequence events might occur. It utilizes the opinions of experts to develop sub-jective probabilities that are useful when attempting to analyze this type of problem. Information resulting from this technique can then be used to deal with the situation by alerting public (or company) officials to the combined judgment of experts regarding the event in question.

There are two aspects of the Bayesian model being demonstrated. One re-quires the development of subjective probabilities and the other aspect in-volves the utilization of Bayes' Law for transforming initial judgments of experts into final estimates of event probabilties. We briefly discussed how to assess subjective probabilities earlier in Chapter 6. Consequently, a short digression into the development and illustration of Bayes' Law is provided at this point before we analyze a low probability-high consequence problem.

bayes' law

Probability has been referred to as the language of uncertainty. By using the concepts of probability, it is possible to measure uncertainty associated with decision situations.

Suppose we have interest in the outcome of an "experiment" that could involve, for example, the amount of rain that falls on a certain city during the coming month or the number of defective items in a sample of 100 items from a particular production process. For such experiments there are num-erous outcomes possible, but we cannot be sure of the exact outcome of the experiment before it is actually observed. For instance, inches of rain next month can take on a value from 0 to a fairly large positive number. At the end of the following month, we will know the outcome of this experiment with certainty.

The number of outcomes of an experiment comprises its sample space, and the number of points in the sample space can be quite large (perhaps infinite), as in the case of the rainfall experiment, or small (finite) as in the production sampling situation. If the occurrence of one of the outcomes in the sample space of an experiment precludes the occurrence of all other points, the outcomes are said to be the *mutually exclusive*. Suppose we draw 100 items from a production process and find 3 defective items. Then for that particular sample it is impossible to discover 10 defective items or 16 de-fective items, etc.

For purposes of this appendix, we have elected to interpret probability in a broad sense by saying that probability is a numerical encoding of the state of knowledge of the person making the assignment. Being able to incorporate new knowledge in our assignments of probability is made possible by Bayes' Law. This law applies to situations where the occurrence of one outcome, de-fined on the sample space for an experiment, causes a change in our state of knowledge concerning one or more other outcomes.

To illustrate, suppose an experiment consists of drawing two balls from a container that has in it six green and four red balls. The probability that the first ball will be red is 4/10. If the first ball is replaced and we draw at random a second time, the probability that the second ball is red is again 4/10. However, *if the first ball is not replaced prior to drawing the second ball*, you can see that the probability of drawing a red ball on the second draw depends on the color of the ball that was observed on the first draw. One of two outcomes can exist and we express their probabilities as follows.

$$P(R_2| R_1) = 3/9 \qquad\qquad (1)$$

$$P(R_2| G_1) = 4/9 \qquad\qquad (2)$$

Here $P(R_2| G_1)$, for example, is read "the probability that we observe a red ball on the second draw, *given* that we drew a green ball on the first draw." Such a probability statement is called a *conditional probability* because the probability of the second outcome is dependent on the first outcome.

As you see, the probabilities of (1) and (2) above are not the same. This simple example shows that care must be taken to identify events that are dependent so that their conditional probabilities can be taken into account. Conditional probabilities such as these exist when there are dependencies among two or more events comprising the sample space of an experiment such as the one described above.

This simple experiment without replacing the balls has four outcomes, one of which *must* occur when two balls are drawn at random. In tree diagram form they are:

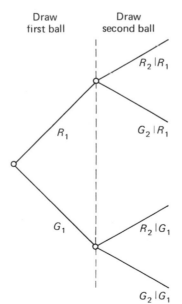

The probabilities of the second set of "branches" in the tree are listed below.

$$P(R_2| R_1) = 3/9 \Big\}$$ ____ Sum is 1
$$P(G_2| R_1) = 6/9$$

$$P(R_2| G_1) = 4/9 \Big\}$$ ____ Sum is 1
$$P(G_2| G_1) = 5/9$$

These conditional probabilities must sum to 1.0 because once the first ball is drawn, it is *certain* that the second ball will be either green or red.

In the above experiment suppose we are interested in determining the probability that a red ball is removed from the urn on the first draw *and* another red ball is obtained on the second draw. Balls are *not replaced* after they are drawn. Here we can write

$$P(R_1 \text{ and } R_2) = P(R_1) \cdot P(R_2| R_1) \tag{3}$$

since the probability of a red ball on the second draw is conditional upon observing a red ball on the first draw. That is, $P(R_1 \text{ and } R_2) = P(R_1) \cdot P(R_2| R_1) = (4/10) \cdot (3/9) = 12/90$.

From (3) above we see that $P(R_1 \text{ and } R_2) = P(R_1) \cdot P(R_2| R_1)$. If we solve this simple expression for $P(R_2| R_1)$, we obtain

$$P(R_2| R_1) = \frac{P(R_1 \text{ and } R_2)}{P(R_1)}$$

We already know that $P(R_1 \text{ and } R_2) = 12/90$ and $P(R_1) = 4/10$. Thus, the conditional probability $P(R_2| R_1)$ could have been determined to be:

$$P(R_2| R_1) = \frac{12/90}{4/10} = 3/9$$

Returning to the tree diagram above, we can now fill in the probabilities of each branch by utilizing the fact that $P(R_2| R_1) \cdot P(R_1) = P(R_1 \text{ and } R_2)$, etc. From this point forward we let $P(R_1 \text{ and } R_2) = P(R_1 \cdot R_2)$, for example, to simplify our notation. The completed tree appears on page 273.

Notice on page 273 that the probabilities of all terminal (right-hand) branches in the tree sum to 1.0. These probabilities are called *joint probabilities*, and they are the product of a conditional probability, i.e., $P(R_2| G_1)$, and in unconditional probability, i.e., $P(G_1)$.

We will return to the tree diagram shortly because it is an excellent way to illustrate graphically the basic concepts of Bayes' Law. First, however, this law is stated in terms of conditional probabilities. We can write that $P(A, B) = P(B, A)$ when the probabilities of observing A and B are not affected by whether event A precedes event B or vice versa. Then it is true that $P(A) \cdot$

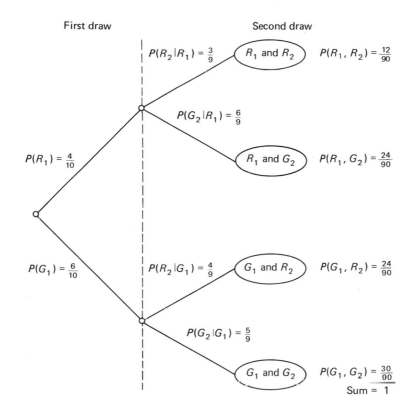

First draw

Second draw

$P(R_1) = \frac{4}{10}$

$P(G_1) = \frac{6}{10}$

$P(R_2|R_1) = \frac{3}{9}$ R_1 and R_2 $P(R_1, R_2) = \frac{12}{90}$

$P(G_2|R_1) = \frac{6}{9}$

R_1 and G_2 $P(R_1, G_2) = \frac{24}{90}$

$P(R_2|G_1) = \frac{4}{9}$ G_1 and R_2 $P(G_1, R_2) = \frac{24}{90}$

$P(G_2|G_1) = \frac{5}{9}$

G_1 and G_2 $P(G_1, G_2) = \frac{30}{90}$

Sum = 1

$P(B|A) = P(B) \cdot P(A|B)$ since we have said $P(A, B) = P(B, A)$. By solving for $P(B|A)$ we see that

$$P(B|A) = \frac{P(A|B) \cdot P(B)}{P(A)} \qquad (4)$$

To complete the statement of Bayes' Law, we must examine the denominator of (4). The term, $P(A)$, can be expanded by considering Figure D-1. Here B_1, B_2, B_3, and B_4 represent events (sets of points) defined on the total sample space, S. Notice that one of these events *must* occur when we perform an experiment involving S. Hence, we can say that B_1, B_2, B_3, and B_4 are mutually exhaustive. If B_2 occurs, for example, as the result of the experiment, the other events (i.e., B_1, B_3, B_4) cannot occur. We can also say that the B_i events ($i = 1,2,3,4$) are mutually exclusive.

By examining Figure D-1, you can see that the probability of occurrence of event A is conditional upon which one of the B_i events has been observed. The probability of event A can therefore be written:

$$P(A) = P(A, B_1) + P(A, B_2)$$
$$+ P(A, B_3) + P(A, B_4)$$

We know that $P(A, B_i) = P(A|B_i)P(B_i)$ from [3] so the above expression becomes:

$$P(A) = P(A|B_1) \cdot P(B_1) + P(A|B_2) \cdot P(B_2)$$
$$+ P(A|B_3) \cdot P(B_3) + P(A|B_4) \cdot P(B_4) \tag{5}$$

If we substitute (5) into the following expression and generalize,

$$P(B_i|A) = \frac{P(A|B_i)P(B_i)}{P(A)}$$

the result shown below is a mathematical statement of Bayes' Law:

$$P(B_i|A) = \frac{P(A|B_i) \cdot P(B_i)}{\sum_{i=1}^{4} P(A|B_i) \cdot P(B_i)} \tag{6}$$

When using Bayes' Law, it is assumed that initial probabilities of events B_1, B_2, B_3 and B_4 have been estimated before the experiment is conducted. These probabilities are called *a priori* probabilities, and they are often based on a subjective assessment made by a group of experts. After a sample outcome, A, is observed in an experiment and the conditional probability of $A|B_i$ is determined, Bayes' Law is applied to revise the *a priori* probabilities in view of this new information. In equation (6) the probabilities $P(A|B_i)$ are termed *likelihoods* and the revised probabilities $P(B_i|A)$ are known as *a posteriori* probabilities. Thus, Bayes' Law permits us to make an inference about the true probability of B_i based on sample information, A.

The tree diagram on page 273 demonstrates Bayes' Law in terms of conditional probabilities and joint probabilities. *Suppose we know that the second ball drawn was green.* How can we determine the probability that the first ball drawn was *red*? In graphical terms (see Figure D-1) we know that the

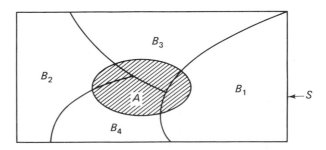

figure D-1 . . . a venn diagram showing event A that is dependent on four other events

second ball was green (i.e., the outcome of A is G_2). There are two B events, namely (1) the first ball was red and (2) the first ball was green. From Bayes' Law we can calculate the desired probability:

$$P(R_1| G_2) = \frac{P(G_2| R_1) \cdot P(R_1)}{P(G_2| R_1) \cdot P(R_1) + P(G_2| G_1) \cdot P(G_1)}$$

$$= \frac{(6/9) \cdot (4/10)}{(6/9) \cdot (4/10) + (5/9) \cdot (6/10)}$$

$$= 12/27$$

In terms of joint probabilities we could write:

$$P(R_1| G_2) = \frac{P(G_2, R_1)}{P(G_2, R_1) + P(G_2, G_1)}$$

$$= \frac{P(G_2, R_1)}{P(G_2)}$$

$$= \frac{24/90}{24/90 + 30/90}$$

$$= 12/27$$

If instead we want to determine the probability that the first ball was green, given that the second ball was green, the following calculation would be made.

$$P(G_1| G_2) = \frac{P(G_2| G_1) \cdot P(G_1)}{P(G_2| G_1) \cdot P(G_1) + P(G_2| R_1) \cdot P(R_1)}$$

$$= 15/27$$

These two probabilities sum to one since the two events, $R_1| G_2$ and $G_1| G_2$, are mutually exclusive and represent the total sample space for this simple "experiment".

A more convenient way to utilize Bayes' Law is to perform the calculations in tabular form. A table such as the one below simplifies an understanding of how Bayes' Law works and provides an easy-to-follow format for determining the posterior probabilities. For the example problem above, the table would be as follows.

1.   Given a green ball on the second draw, what is the probability that the first draw produced a red ball? A green ball?

Event	Prior Probability	Likelihood	Prior Prob. x Likelihood	Posterior Probability
R_1	$P(R_1)=4/10$	$P(G_2| R_1)=6/9$	24/90	$P(R_1| G_2) = 24/90 \div 54/90 = 12/27$
G_1	$P(G_1)=6/10$	$P(G_2| G_1)=5/9$	30/90	$P(G_1| G_2) = 30/90 \div 54/90 = 15/27$
			$P(G_2) = 54/90$	$\Sigma = 1$

Before we are told the second ball was green, the probability that it would turn out to be green is 54/90. In this case we can say that the *predictive probability* of observing a green ball on the second draw is 54/90.

2. Given a red ball on the second draw, what is the probability that the first draw resulted in a red ball? A green ball?

Event	Prior Probability	Likelihood	Prior Prob. x Likelihood	Posterior Probability
R_1	$P(R_1)=4/10$	$P(R_2| R_1)=3/9$	12/90	$P(R_1| R_2) = 12/90 \div 36/90 = 1/3$
G_1	$P(G_1)=6/10$	$P(R_2| G_1)=4/9$	24/90	$P(G_1| R_2) = 24/90 \div 36/90 = 2/3$
			$\Sigma = 36/90$	$\Sigma = 1$

Thus, *before* we are told that the second ball was red, the predictive probability of its being red is 36/90. Once we know for certain that the second ball is red, the probability it was preceded by a red ball on the first draw, for example, is 1/3.

To summarize how Bayes' Law works, we first develop an *a priori* probability for each mutually exclusive event associated with an experiment whose sample space is known. The experiment in Bayesian analysis usually involves the collection of some sort of sample information (e.g., taking a sample of *n* items from a production process and determining the number of defective items). Next, the experiment is conducted and its outcome *A* is noted. The probabilities of $A|B_i$ are determined (i.e., the likelihoods) and utilized to calculate the *a posteriori* probabilities. In many cases the likelihoods are determined with a probability model (binomial, Poisson, etc.) that has been chosen to represent the sampling process. For a more advanced discussion of Bayesian statistics and decision making, the reader is referred to the books below*.

Robert L. Winkler, Introduction to Bayesian Inference and Decision *(New York: Holt, Rinehart and Winston, Inc. 1972)*.
Robert Schlaifer, Analysis of Decisions Under Uncertainty, *(New York: McGraw-Hill Book Company, 1969)*.

an example problem utilizing bayes' law

An example problem is included here to illustrate how Bayes' Law might be used to update probability statements concerning an uncertain event in view of available sample information.

As the quality control inspector for a small manufacturing company, you routinely sample finished items from four production areas and determine whether they are "good" or "bad." You inspect one item per hour from each area, and the items produced in each area are identical. Historical records indicate the following probabilities of a defective item from each area.

Area 1: $P(\text{Defect}) = 0.02$ Area 3: $P(\text{Defect}) = 0.08$

Area 2: $P(\text{Defect}) = 0.05$ Area 4: $P(\text{Defect}) = 0.03$

Suppose you have just collected the four items requiring inspection this hour, and you forgot to mark which area each item came from. After inspecting the items, you discover that one item is defective. What can you infer about which production area it came from? What is the predictive probability that you would find a defective item from any of the four areas this hour?

Since you forgot to mark each item, you decide to state your subjective belief regarding probabilities that the defective item came from each area. After thinking for a moment, you remember that Area 1 was short of raw materials and that Area 4 workers have been dissatisfied with their new supervisor. Suppose you decide that your *a priori* probabilities are:

$P(\text{Area 1}) = 0.25$ $P(\text{Area 3}) = 0.20$

$P(\text{Area 2}) = 0.20$ $P(\text{Area 4}) = 0.35$

Given that you have observed a defective item, your records show the likelihood of finding a defect at each production area. For example, $P(\text{Defect} | \text{Area 1}) = 0.02$ (see above).

The probability that the defect could have come from each production area is determined by applying Bayes' Law:

$$P(\text{Area } i | \text{ Defect}) = \frac{P(\text{Defect} | \text{Area } i) \cdot P(\text{Area } i)}{\sum\limits_{i=1}^{4} P(\text{Defect} | \text{Area } i) \cdot P(\text{Area } i)}$$

$$P(\text{Area 1} | \text{Defect}) = \frac{0.02(0.25)}{0.0415} = 0.12$$

$$P(\text{Area 2} | \text{Defect}) = \frac{0.05(0.20)}{0.0415} = 0.24$$

$$P(\text{Area 3} | \text{Defect}) = \frac{0.08(0.20)}{0.0415} = 0.39$$

$$P(\text{Area 4} | \text{Defect}) = \frac{0.03(0.35)}{0.0415} = 0.25$$

In tabular form, Bayes' Law can be implemented as follows:

Event	Prior Probability	Likelihood	Prior Probability x Likelihood	Posterior Probability
Area 1	0.25	0.02	0.0050	0.12
Area 2	0.20	0.05	0.0100	0.24
Area 3	0.20	0.08	0.0160	0.39
Area 4	0.35	0.03	0.0105	0.25
			0.0415	1.00

It can be seen that the *a priori* probabilities for each area have been modified in view of available information regarding a known defective item from one of the four production areas. The *a posteriori* probabilities indicate that Area 3 is now the most probable source of the defective item. Before knowing the item was defective, the most likely source would have been Area 4. From the above table, the predictive probability of a defective item is seen to be 0.0415. Figure D-2 illustrates the extent to which the prior probabilities have been modified by utilizing the historical likelihood data to determine posterior probabilities.

a procedure for event forecasting based on bayes' law

A Bayesian model can be utilized in connection with the Delphi method to generate probability estimates for the various times at which a high consequence-low probability event might occur. In this manner the uncertainty

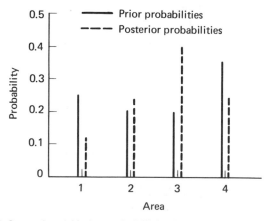

figure D-2 . . . the shift in probabilities by taking historical data into account

associated with outcomes of opinion surveys can be identified and utilized by a decision maker as he develops a forecast.

It is apparent that the exact time of a future event's occurrence is highly uncertain. Consequently, the purpose of the procedure described here is to provide a clearer notion of uncertainty associated with the event being fore-casted. This is accomplished by first using the Delphi method to obtain sub-jective prior probabilities for the event. Next, these probabilities are modi-fied by using judgment and/or past experience regarding the accuracy of Delphi experiments through an application of Bayes' Law. The result is a set of posterior probabilities for the event's time of occurrence. To illustrate the development and application of the procedure, a hypothetical example is presented:

> A large commercial airport is situated near a heavily-populated metropol-itan area. The area also is the center of an industrial complex containing petroleum refineries, numerous chemical plants and a large electrical power station. Flight patterns of arriving and departing aircraft are con-sidered to be potentially dangerous in the event of a control tower error and/or major aircraft malfunction. Plans are now well under way to re-locate the airport, but it is expected to take better than *two years* to have the new facility operational.
>
> Suppose the City Council has asked your advice on whether a large percentage of air traffic to and from the city should be rerouted to an-other safer airport that is almost 70 miles away. Considerable concern about public safety has been expressed by numerous citizen groups. You are actually being requested to evaluate the consequences of a low prob-ability, although quite catastrophic, aircraft collision against the loss of a sizeable source of revenue to the city by virtually closing its airport for two years.
>
> As a key first step in analyzing this problem, you have decided to quantify the probability that there will be a major aircraft collision $\tilde{N}$ months from the present time. A maximum value of $\tilde{N}$ is chosen to be 25 months because the new airport will be operational by that time. To ob-tain these probability estimates, you have selected 10 individuals who are widely acknowledged as being experts on air safety and related matters. With their expert opinions to work with, you now set about determining one of the principal inputs to your evaluation for the city—a probability distribution for months of safe operation of the airport.

After reviewing several forecasting methods available, you elect to use a technique based on the Delphi method and Bayes' Law. The procedural steps of this technique are shown in Figure D-3. There are two Delphi questioning rounds, followed by the application of Bayes' Law. The purpose of Round 1 is to get some general idea of the period of time before an accident takes place. Round 2 is used to develop probabilities for time estimates obtained in Round 1. The results of Round 2 are carefully examined and possibly mod-

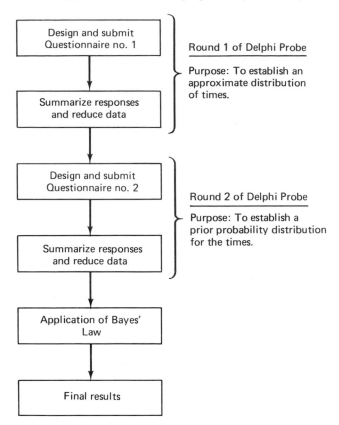

figure D-3 . . . a block diagram of the forecasting procedure

ified with Bayes' Law to arrive at the final (posterior) set of probabilities for the number of months before an accident occurs.

Implementation of the procedure shown in Figure D-3 is described below.

delphi round 1

Through an impartial selection process, ten experts have been chosen to participate in your study. Since the prediction that you desire is highly uncertain, each expert is first asked to bracket the time that will elapse before an accident occurs. You discuss fully in the questionnaire what is being done in the study and why.* Furthermore, you explain that responses should reflect the experts' experience and give consideration to human error, component failures, sabotage, etc. You request that three time estimates be given.

---

*The questionnaire should be formulated very carefully to insure that the respondents will take into account the location and the size of the airport in question, its traffic pattern, its geographic hazards, its characteristic weather conditions, and

The first estimate should represent the experts' appraisal of the *shortest time* before an accident occurs, and the second estimate is the *longest time* in months. The third estimate should represent the experts' current best thinking on the *most likely* number of months until a catastrophe occurs. Each participant is told that the most likely time will be weighted four times as heavily as the other two estimates in the data reduction process.

Table D-1 contains hypothetical results of the Round 1 questionnaire and indicates the average time that each respondent gave.

delphi round 2

The purpose of this round is to develop a set of probabilities for the various times generated in Round 1. Feedback to each of the experts from Round 1 is shown in Figure D-4. In addition, each participant is given his responses to the Round 1 questionnaire so that a basis of comparison is available. After receiving this information, each expert is asked in Round 2 to estimate the odds (chances in 10) in favor of $\widetilde{N}$, the actual number of months before an accident, being either 5, 10, 15, ———, 35, 40 months. Table D-2 shows a typical response (for participant number 1) and the transformation of his odds estimates into probabilities. All ten sets of responses are given in Table D-3. Finally the desired result of Round 2 is provided in Table D-4, i.e., estimated probabilities for $\widetilde{N}$. Also note that the overall average is about 21 months.

table D-1 . . . summary of responses from round 1

Expert No.	Shortest (S)	$\widetilde{N}$ Most Likely (ML)	Longest (L)	Average $\widetilde{N}$ (months)*
1	9	11	25	13.0
2	20	26	35	26.5
3	9	14	24	14.8
4	17	19	22	19.2
5	12	16	25	16.8
6	10	13	26	14.7
7	20	30	40	30.0
8	5	8	19	9.3
9	21	29	36	28.8
10	7	21	28	19.8

$$*Average\ \widetilde{N} = \overline{N} = \frac{S + 4ML + L}{6}$$

---

the caliber of the aircraft monitoring system in use at the airport. Obviously, collision probabilities are not the same for all airports and may not even be similar for any two airports in the country. Consequently, the experts chosen for the survey must have the capability of applying their general knowledge to the situation at the particular airport in question.

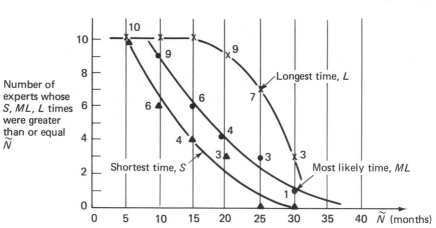

figure D-4 . . . an example of feedback (from round 1) given to each participant in round 2

Because our experts have provided an average estimate of $\widetilde{N}$ that is less than 25 months, the decision would certainly be to close the airport (based only on this information). In fact, the group has concluded there are roughly 78 chances out of 100 (0.784) that an accident will occur in 25 months or less. At this point, the decision maker(s) must satisfy himself regarding the credibility of these group results. If he is unwilling to accept them completely, the next step of the procedure would be undertaken.

table D-2 . . . typical response to round 2

	(Expert No. 1)		
$\widetilde{N}$ (Months)	Odds (Chances in 10)	Raw Probabilities	Normalized Probabilities
5	0	0.000	0.000
10	1	0.100	0.062
15	2	0.200	0.125
20	5	0.500	0.313
25	6	0.600	0.375
30	2	0.200	0.125
35	0	0.000	0.000
40	0	0.000	0.000

Sum = 1.000

Average $\widetilde{N} = \overline{N}$ = 5(0.000) + 10(0.062) + 15(0.125) + ––– + 40(0.000)
= 19.99 months

Mode = 25 months (most likely value of $\widetilde{N}$)

table D-3 . . . summary of responses from round 2

$\widetilde{N}$ (Months)	Odds Given by Expert Number									
	1	2	3	4	5	6	7	8	9	10
5	–	–	–	–	–	–	–	3	–	–
10	1	–	6	5	2	–	–	7	–	5
15	2	4	7	6	4	8	–	6	–	6
20	5	5	6	7	6	6	5	5	5	8
25	6	7	5	5	5	5	6	–	6	7
30	2	6	–	3	4	–	6	–	7	6
35	–	5	–	–	–	–	4	–	6	–
40	–	–	–	–	–	–	3	–	–	–

application of bayes' law

In this problem the accuracy of Round 2 forecasts regarding $\widetilde{N}$ may be a subject of concern as the event under consideration becomes more distant in time. If the decision maker believes this phenomenon should be included in the analysis, Bayes' Law can be applied to results of Round 2. Prior probabilities of $\widetilde{N}$ are given in the last two columns of Table D-4, and they can be revised on the basis of intuition and judgment that the decision maker possesses concerning similar past surveys of expert opinion.

Suppose that you have been requested to challenge the validity of group results by gathering historical data regarding the operation of this and other airports having comparable potential for a serious air disaster. You do this by sorting through available data kept by government agencies relative to (1) numbers and seriousness of known operator errors (aircraft and control tower), (2) component failures of aircraft and ground control equipment, (3) frequencies of bomb threats and hijacking attempts, etc. Additionally, you assemble historical statistical data regarding the accuracy of past Delphi studies in an effort to quantify the uncertainty present in results of such studies.*

After carefully reviewing government data and the reported accuracy of historical Delphi analyses, you next construct a table of "confidence probabilities" relating the likelihood that the group would *estimate* the true value to be N' (in 5 month increments) *when actually* the true value is $\widetilde{N}$. Your appraisal of these likelihoods is shown in Table D-5.

From Table D-5 it can be seen that when the true value of $\widetilde{N}$ is fifteen months, there are 20 chances out of 100 that the experts (as a group) will have *estimated* it to be ten months (i.e., $N' = 10$). Similarly when the true $\widetilde{N}$ is 30 months, which means that a major accident will not occur before the new airport is completed, there are 35 chances out of 100 that it will be esti-

---

*For example, see J. P. Martino, "The Precision of Delphi Estimate," Technological Forecasting *(March 1970), pp. 293-299; and R. H. Ament, "Comparison of Delphi Forecasting Studies in 1964 and 1969," Futures (March 1970), pp. 35-44.*

table D-4 . . . reduced data from round 2

	Probabilities Assigned by Expert Number										Average Probability, $\bar{P}$	Cumulative Probability, $\bar{P}$
$\tilde{N}$ (Months)	1	2	3	4	5	6	7	8	9	10		
5	.000	.000	.000	.000	.000	.000	.000	.143	.000	.000	0.014	0.014
10	.062	.000	.250	.192	.095	.000	.000	.333	.000	.156	0.121	0.135
15	.125	.149	.292	.231	.191	.421	.000	.286	.000	.188	0.201	0.336
20	.313	.185	.250	.270	.286	.316	.209	.238	.209	.250	0.243	0.579
25	.375	.259	.208	.192	.238	.263	.250	.000	.250	.218	0.205	0.784
30	.125	.222	.000	.115	.190	.000	.250	.000	.292	.188	0.136	0.920
35	.000	.185	.000	.000	.000	.000	.166	.000	.250	.000	0.067	0.987
40	.000	.000	.000	.000	.000	.000	.125	.000	.000	.000	0.013	1.000
$\bar{N}$	19.99	25.55	17.08	19.04	21.19	19.21	28.74	13.10	27.94	20.47		

Overall Average = 21.23 months   Mode = 20 months

table D-5 . . . probabilities relating the confidence of round 2 results

| | | The likelihood that we *estimate* the true value to be N' is: N' | | | | | | | |
		5 mo.	10 mo.	15 mo.	20 mo.	25 mo.	30 mo.	35 mo.	40 mo.
When the *true* **time**	5 mos.	0.70	0.20	0.05	0.05	—	—	—	—
	10 mos.	0.30	0.60	0.08	0.02	—	—	—	—
	15 mos.	0.10	0.20	0.60	0.10	—	—	—	—
to an	20 mos.	—	0.10	0.20	0.50	0.15	0.05	—	—
accident	25 mos.	—	—	0.10	0.15	0.50	0.20	0.05	—
is $\tilde{N}$	30 mos.	—	—	—	0.20	0.30	0.35	0.15	—
	35 mos.	—	—	—	—	0.20	0.30	0.30	0.20

mated to be 30 months. It should be emphasized that these likelihoods are an attempt to indicate the accuracy of group estimation of the actual value of $\widetilde{N}$.

Now Bayes' Law can be called upon as a means of modifying the concensus opinion of experts in light of likelihoods displayed in Table D-5. Suppose you decide to use the average estimate of $\widetilde{N}$ as a "best approximation" of actual time until a major catastrophe happens. (In some cases the mode would be a better "best approximation.") From Table D-4 this was 21.23 months, which we shall consider to be 20 months (the nearest 5-month interval). The relevant likelihood probabilities shown below are taken from Table D-5:

$$\text{Prob. } (N' = 20 \mid \widetilde{N} = 5) = 0.05$$

$$\text{Prob. } (N' = 20 \mid \widetilde{N} = 10) = 0.02$$
$$\text{Prob. } (N' = 20 \mid \widetilde{N} = 15) = 0.10$$

$$\text{Prob. } (N' = 20 \mid \widetilde{N} = 20) = 0.50$$
$$\text{Prob. } (N' = 20 \mid \widetilde{N} = 25) = 0.15$$

$$\text{Prob. } (N' = 20 \mid \widetilde{N} = 30) = 0.20$$

Note that these likelihoods do not have to sum to one. Given that $N' = 20$ months is the most realistic estimate available for the airport under consideration, updated posterior probabilities for the true value of $\widetilde{N}$ would be computed with Bayes' Law:

$$P(B_i \mid A) = \frac{P(A \mid B_i) \cdot P(B_i)}{\sum_{i=1}^{6} P(A \mid B_i) \cdot P(B_i)}$$

In the above expression, A is the sample information that $N' = 20$ months and B_i are possible values of $\widetilde{N}$ (i.e., 5, 10, 15, 20, 25, or 30 months). The likelihoods, listed above, are $P(A \mid B_i)$ while $P(B_i)$ are prior probabilities of $\widetilde{N}$ obtained from the panel of experts (refer to Table D-4). Calculations required in applying Bayes' Law can be quickly accomplished as shown in Table D-6. The posterior probabilities of $\widetilde{N}$ are given in Column D of this table.

By considering group opinion to be additional information about $\widetilde{N}$, the use of Bayes' Law is a justifiable approach to revising probabilities of $\widetilde{N}$ in view of the accuracy inherent to the initial probability estimates. From Table D-6 we can easily determine the *posterior* average value of $\widetilde{N}$ to be:

$$5(0.003) + 10(0.012) + 15(0.099) + --- + 30(0.134) = 21.44 \text{ months}$$

In addition the revised probability that $\widetilde{N}$ is *less than or equal to* 25 months is 0.866. As a result of applying Bayes' Law to this problem, the analyst now observes that the estimated probability of experiencing a major accident goes from 0.784 (before Bayes' Law is utilized) to 0.866. Even though the prior average estimate of $\tilde{N}$ agrees closely with the posterior average, the increase in the probability that $\tilde{N}$ is less than or equal 25 months would probably cause the City Council to close the airport immediately. (On the other hand, a decision-making body willing to accept risk in return for extra tax revenues from the airport would perhaps elect to keep the facility open for business.)

The accuracy of this procedure can reasonably be expected to lie somewhere between that of an individual's off-hand guess and perfect knowledge of the actual outcome. A basic advantage of such a forecasting procedure is that it provides a prediction representing the composite thinking of a number of experts.

table D-6 . . . final results of bayesian forecasting procedure

$\tilde{N}$ (Months)	A Prior Probability (from Table D-4)	B Likelihoods (From Table D-5)	C Product A x B	D Posterior Probability C ÷ 0.2027
5	0.014	0.05	0.0007	0.003
10	0.121	0.02	0.0024	0.012
15	0.201	0.10	0.0201	0.099
20	0.243	0.50	0.1215	0.600
25	0.205	0.15	0.0308	0.152
30	0.136	0.20	0.0272	0.134
35	0.067	0	0	0
40	0.013	0	0	0
			0.2027	1.000

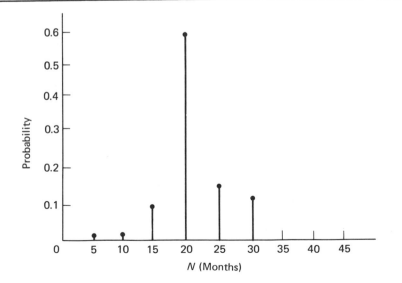

index

Accuracy of forecasting techniques, 29, 32, 36–39, 74, 84, 106, 163, 213, 216, 250
Adaptive filtering, 221
Adaptive smoothing, 222
Adjusted credit proxy, 241
Advanced forecasting techniques, 221, 269
Advantages of exponential smoothing, 83
Ament, R.H., 141, 281
Annoni, A.J., 143
A posteriori probabilities, 274
A priori probabilities, 274
Association between variables, 63, 73
Assumptions of simple linear regression, 60, 249
Autocorrelation in data, 223, 249
Autoregressive models, 224
Axioms of probability theory, 153, 156

Basic forecasting techniques and their characteristics, 36–39
Bayesian analysis in forecasting, 269, 278 likelihoods, 274, 286
Bayes' Law, 154, 270, 274, 277
Bias in forecasting, 88, 163
Bills of material, 5
Box-Jenkins method, 223
Bright, J.R., 214
Bureau of Economic Analysis, 14, 248

Calculations for cross-impact studies, 170
Calculations for serial correlation, 253
Calibrating a forecasting system, 29, 161
Capital expenditures, 134, 244
Causal relationships, 20, 40, 62, 66, 71, 175, 269

Chambers, J.C., 30
Characteristics of forecasts, 2, 33, 41, 122, 137, 173, 217
Choice of a forecasting technique, 7, 19, 30, 41, 84, 90, 108, 121, 135
Coefficient of determination, 71, 78
Coincident economic indicators, 239
Commercial paper, 243
Computer analysis of example problems, 77, 121, 134
Computer program for forecasting, 77, 108, 113
Conditional probability, 271
Confidence intervals, 66, 70, 75, 80
Conflicting objectives, 4
Consistency in forecasting procedures, 163
Constant variance, 61, 249
Consumer price index, 14, 246
Consumer spending, 237
Control chart of forecasting error, 27
Convergence in Delphi studies, 147, 179
Copulsky, William, 5
Corporate profits, 239
Correlation coefficient, 71, 78, 223
Correlation matrix, 73, 78
Cost of preparing forecasts, 32, 34, 36–39, 56, 73, 226, 228
Craven, J.K., 195
Critical regions:
    Durbin-Watson Test, 253
    Von-Neuman Ratio Test, 251
Cross-impact method:
    actual application of, 172
    advantages and disadvantages of, 172, 189
    description, 164
    linkage in, 166, 182

Cross-impact method: *(Contd.)*
  revision of probabilities, 167, 185
  simple illustration of, 165
Cumulative distribution function, 157,
  162
Cumulative error as tracking signal, 28
Cyclical patterns in data, 10, 23, 35, 101,
  248

Data bases for forecasting, 16
Data input card formats, 110, 112
Data patterns, 10, 24, 86, 98, 101
Data requirements for popular techniques,
  36–39
Degrees of freedom in statistical tests, 66,
  262
Delphi method:
  accuracy of, 145, 148
  advantages and disadvantages, 142, 150,
    207
  case study, 143, 176, 206, 212, 278
  convergence, 141, 147
  description of, 140
  feedback, 140, 144, 150, 281
Department of Commerce, 12, 246
Dependent variable, 68, 72, 77, 109
Deseasonalized data, 55
Diffusion index, 232, 247
Disadvantages of exponential smoothing,
  83
Double exponential smoothing, 94, 106,
  109
Double moving averages, 88, 109
Durbin-Watson test, 65, 251

Econometric models, 226, 248
Economic indicators, 64, 232, 243
Endogenous variables, 226
Envelope curves, 196, 211
Enzer, Selwyn, 172
Errors in forecasts, 5, 23, 26, 149, 163,
  224, 249
Event forecasting, example problem, 278
Exogenous variables, 226
Expert judgment in forecasting, 21, 140,
  144, 152, 174, 204, 227, 278
Exploratory forecasts, 193
Exponential smoothing:
  advantages and disadvantages, 83
  bias, 93
  choice of smoothing constant, 91, 94,
    104, 106
  double, 94, 109
  forecasts, 93, 95, 96, 98, 102, 108
  initial estimates, 93, 94, 96
  single, 91, 101, 109
  smoothed statistics in, 92, 94, 97
  triple, 95, 110
  Winter's method, 99, 110, 222

F-distribution, percentage points of, 263
Federal Reserve Board, 233, 240
Feedback in Delphi procedures, 140, 144,
  150, 281
Fiscal policy, 232
Forecasting:
  accuracy, 25, 32, 74, 161
  advanced techniques, 221, 269
  art versus science, 2, 5, 173, 213, 247
  assumptions, 5, 10, 40, 83, 86, 196
  basic techniques, 36–39, 106
  bias, 88, 163
  characteristics, 2, 33, 41, 122, 137, 173,
    217
  costs of, 32, 36–39, 226
  data bases for, 16
  definition, 2, 191
  error, 5, 23, 26, 27, 149, 163, 224, 249
  exploratory, 193
  hypotheses and models, 6, 84, 200
  information sources, 11, 43, 192, 248
  lead times, 3, 161, 174
  pitfalls, 4, 217
  purpose, 2, 10, 31, 121, 173, 189, 203
  selection of techniques, 31, 36–39, 121,
    135, 145
  strategy, 20, 31, 57, 215
  technological, 22, 191
  time horizons, 3, 23, 49, 52, 217
Fortran IV forecasting program, 108, 113
F-test, 71, 262

GNP deflator, 234
Gordon, T.J., 141, 165
Graphical analysis of data, 6, 23, 156, 205
Gross domestic product, 15
Gross national product, 15, 237, 239

Harrisberger, L., 201
Hayward, H., 165
Help-wanted advertising, 241
Historical analogy, 194
Horizontal patterns in time-series data, 24,
  88, 104
Hypotheses in forecasting, 6, 33, 150,
  200, 261
Hypotheses of statistical tests, 71, 259,
  261

Independent demand products, 5
Independent variables, 23, 66, 72, 74, 77,
  109
Industrial production, 240
Inflation, 234, 236, 239, 242, 246
Information sources for forecasting, 11,
  43, 192, 248
Input data format summary, 112
Input-output tables, 227

Interdependence of events, 165, 179, 226, 271
Interquartile ranges, 140, 146, 177, 207
Introduction of a new product, 41, 206
Inventories of distributors, 49, 51
Inventory-sales ratios, 245
Item forecasts, 7, 18

Lagging economic indicators, 243
Leading economic indicators, 64, 232
Lenz, R.D., 199
Level of confidence in statistical tests, 250, 258, 261, 266
Life cycle characteristics in forecasting, 31, 34, 197
Likelihoods in Bayesian analysis, 274, 286
Linear data patterns, 24, 88, 94, 99, 194, 205
Linear projections of data, 194, 204
Linkage in cross-impact studies, 166, 182
Low probability-high consequence events, 154, 269, 278

Mahoney, T.A., 143
Manpower forecasting, 143, 161
Market research studies, 43, 45
Market size forecasting, 204
Market testing and analysis, 41, 44
Martino, J.P., 202, 283
Materials requirements planning, 3
Matrix of correlation coefficients, 73, 78
Matrix of interrelationships in cross-impact studies, 166, 179
Mean absolute deviation (MAD), 25, 163
Mean square error (MSE), 25, 84, 103, 123, 136, 222
Mean square successive differences, 250
Median estimate, 141, 147, 159, 177, 207
Milkovich, G.T., 143
Model development and refinement, 10, 27, 84, 91, 223, 226
Models in time-series analysis, 35, 83, 108, 221, 223
Monetary policy, 233
Monitoring the environment, 214
Morphological analysis, 201
Moving averages:
  bias, 88
  choice of N, 88, 91
  double, 88, 109
  simple, 55, 85, 109, 221
Mullick, S.K., 30
Multiple linear regression, 72, 224
Multiplicative seasonal factors, 100
Mutually exclusive outcomes, 270, 273

National Bureau of Economic Research, 232, 248
Negative serial correlation, 251

Noise in data, 84, 87, 88, 90, 97
Nonlinear regression, 79, 225
Nonrandom residuals in regression, 250, 253
Normally distributed residuals (error terms), 61, 226, 249
Normative forecasts, 193
Null hypotheses in statistical tests, 258, 262, 266

Objective probabilities, 153
Objectives, conflicting, 4
Office of Business Economics, 248
Office of Technology Assessment, 193
Ostwald, P.F., 193
Outliers in data, 6, 84
Output of computer program, 77, 124–133

Parameters, estimation of, 66, 75, 96
Patterns in time-series data, 20, 22, 53, 86, 88, 94, 101, 223
Penetration curves, 47, 48, 51
Periodicity in data, 100, 110
Pitfalls in forecasting, 4, 217
Plant and equipment investment, 134, 244
Population trends, 238
Positive serial correlation, 250
Precursor events, 198, 214
Predictive probabilities, 276
Prime interest rate, 243
Printout of source forecasting program, 113–120
Probabilities:
  a posteriori, 274
  a priori, 274
  conditional, 271
  cumulative distribution function, 157
  in cross-impact studies, 165, 178
  joint, 272
  predictive, 276
  probability mass function, 157
  subjective, 51, 139, 154, 173, 269
Product development and forecasting, 41, 42, 206, 228
Product group forecasts, 5, 7, 11, 16
Product life cycle and forecasting, 3, 31, 34, 41
Product replacement analysis, 208
Production planning and control, 18, 29, 32
Productivity, 149, 236, 241
Purpose of forecasting, 2, 6, 10, 31, 173, 189, 215

Quadratic patterns in data, 24, 88, 95
Qualitative forecasting techniques, 7, 34, 139
Quantitative forecasting techniques, 7, 23

Questionnaire for eliciting subjective
    probabilities, 156

Raiffa, H., 153
Rand Corporation, 140
Random variable, 155, 158, 249
Rapid growth in product demand, 41, 49
Regression:
    assumptions, 60, 249
    confidence intervals, 66, 70, 75
    example problems, 67, 74
    for lagged data, 63, 79
    for time-series analysis, 65, 83
    multiple linear, 72
    nonlinear, 79
    relationships, 62
    residuals, 61, 251
    shortcomings, 65, 83, 149
    simple linear, 59, 65, 75, 109, 146, 194,
        253
Research and development goals, 210
Residential construction, 237
Residuals analysis, 224, 251
Response variable, 23, 59
Retail sales, 149, 245

Sackman, H., 142
Sales forecasting, 44, 50, 52, 64, 154, 206
Savage, L.J., 153
Scenarios, 200
Schlaifer, R., 153
Seasonal index, trends in data, 53, 55, 99
Selection of an appropriate forecasting
    technique, 31, 36–39, 121, 135, 145
Serial correlation, 65, 224, 249
Shortcomings of regression, 65, 83, 149
Signals of change, 214
Simple moving averages, 85, 109, 221
Single exponential smoothing, 92, 106,
    109, 222
Smith, D.D., 30
Smoothed statistics in exponential
    smoothing, 92, 94, 97
Smoothing constant, 92, 94, 104
Smoothing time-series data, 55
Sobek, Robert S., 231
Sources of data, 11, 192, 231
Standard error of the forecast, 28
Statistical Package for the Social Sciences
    (SPSS), 77
Statistical significance tests in regression,
    71, 251
Steady-state sales and forecasting, 41, 51
Step-growth forecasting, 209
Stepwise procedures in multiple linear
    regression, 77

Stine, H., 198
Stock market, 238
Subjective probability, 51, 152, 165, 176,
    270
Substitution curves, 196, 208
Successful forecasting, 4, 173
Summary of basic forecasting techniques,
    36–39, 106
Survey of Current Business, 13, 248
Systematic error, 163

t-distribution, percentage points of, 264
Technological forecasting, 22, 191
Testing and introduction of new products,
    44
Time horizons in forecasting studies, 3,
    145, 175
Time lag in serial correlation, 224, 250
Time required to prepare forecasts, 36–39
Time-series and simple regression, 64, 72,
    79, 194, 249
Time-series data and analysis, 20, 35, 83,
    194, 198, 223
Tracking signal, 50, 227
Tree diagram of conditional probabilities,
    273
Trend extrapolation, 65, 194, 204, 217
Trends in data, 35, 53, 99, 195
Triple exponential smoothing, 95, 106,
    110
t-test, 71, 262, 266
Turning points, 40, 47, 56, 64, 227, 232,
    241

Uncertainty, 43, 70, 175, 200, 207, 216,
    270
Underlying patterns in data, 22, 86, 88,
    101, 223
Unemployment rate, 154, 241
Use of forecasting error, 23, 29, 164, 216

Variables:
    association between; 63, 73
    dependent, 68, 72, 77, 109
    endogenous, 226
    exogenous, 226
    independent, 23, 66, 72, 74, 77, 109
    random, 155, 158, 249
    response, 23, 59
Volk, William, 77
Von-Neuman Ratio Test, 65, 250

Wholesale price index, 15, 240
Winkler, R.L., 154
Winters' method of exponential
    smoothing, 99, 110, 222.